BLOWING
OUR
BRIDGES

BLOWING OUR BRIDGES

*The memories of a young officer
who finds himself on the beaches
at Dunkirk, landing at H-Hour
on D-Day and then in Korea*

by

Major-General A. E. Younger

Pen & Sword
MILITARY

First published in Great Britain in 2004 by
Pen & Sword Military
an imprint of
Pen & Sword Books Ltd
47 Church Street
Barnsley
South Yorkshire
S70 2AS

ISBN 1 84415 051 8

A CIP catalogue record for this book is
available from the British Library

Typeset in 11/13 Sabon by
Phoenix Typesetting, Auldgirth, Dumfriesshire

Printed and bound in England by
CPI UK

CONTENTS

PREFACE

I hope that this military memoir will be of some interest, not only to comrades in arms, but also to civilian readers, young and old. It covers a good deal of ground and offers first-hand impressions of some extraordinary episodes in the history of the British Army, ranging from Dunkirk to Korea. Younger readers may be surprised to find that I say so little about my life before beginning military training, and about my personal life thereafter, although I do refer to my family from time to time! Perhaps this reflects the way in which my generation of officers was brought up: I am now in my mid-eighties, and come from a family for whom soldiering was their calling. My Grandfather was commissioned into the Royal Artillery in 1859 and served in Canada, Ceylon, India and Afghanistan, finishing his career as a full colonel. Both his sons went into the Army, the eldest, my father, being posted to India at the beginning of the twentieth century and returning to fight with the First Indian Division during the Great War. He finished his career as a brigadier. There was no question of my being anything other than a soldier. Nevertheless, the reader might like to know at the outset that I was a pretty normal child, who enjoyed a happy family life, attended boarding school, where I played the usual games, passed the usual exams, and read historical books with particular pleasure, before I became, yes, a soldier.

Twyford, Hampshire
October 2003

FOREWORD

The object of this book is to try to paint a picture of what war is like for a junior officer.

Basically, the junior officer must do what he is told to do. He can show some initiative, such as by looking ahead at what may happen and then making preparations that will make the task easier for his men when the time comes to do it. He may, on occasions, even be able to suggest improvements to the plans that his commander has made, but most of the time he must just do what he is told.

His responsibility for those under his command is great. He must ensure that they are properly trained for what lies ahead and, when they are trained, he must make their tasks as easy and as safe as possible.

During quiet periods he must make their lives as interesting, and if possible, as rewarding, as he can. And when, on the other hand, the going is really tough, he must watch over them most carefully.

All this adds up to a very demanding life, but also one that is most fulfilling. The efforts of the junior officer will never hit the headlines, unless something most unusual happens but, nevertheless, his work is essential and most rewarding.

* * *

I dedicate this book to the many friends I made during my service in the Army, and particularly to those who did not survive.

MEMORIES

A summons to war means a summons to strain
With harsh noises, cruel actions and merciless death.
These leave scars etched deep on the cells of the brain,
Scars that time can decrease but never erase.

Now if we stray from the strident racket of life,
Far from great crowds, from cars driving too fast,
We may stand at peace by a lonely stream
With a wren for companion, a fox slinking past.

Then we recall faces of those who were lost;
They smile in our memory, we smile back at them.
There is sadness that they cannot join in our walk,
Cannot laugh with their children, cannot sing, cannot talk.

But ultimate evil requires ultimate war
And we're glad we took part, though it touches us still;
And that's why our thoughts will wander afar
As we stand in the evening alone on a hill.

Chapter One

PREPARING FOR INEVITABLE WAR

I sat the exam to enter the army some time in late 1936 or early 1937. My only real problem in passing this test was in languages, at which I had always been near the bottom in my form at school. In an attempt to overcome this, my father had the idea of sending me to stay during my Easter holidays from school in 1935 and 1936 with a French family in Paris. Today my only memory of the army entrance exam is of having to sit all day, in great trepidation, waiting my turn to take the French oral exam. Since my name started with Y, I was, of course, the last to be called forward. In a bare and cheerless room sat an obvious Frenchman, with a neat black beard. Beckoning me to a chair on the opposite side of the table, he said, in French, ' Ah, I see you are the last one. You have never visited France, I suppose?'

'Yes, I have stayed in Paris.'

'Oh, whereabouts in Paris?' showing some interest.

'In Neuilly.'

'Really. What street?' showing more interest.

'*Rue Peronnet, numero dix-neuf bis.*'

'Oh, I know the street well.'

He then broke into a long talk about the Bois de Boulogne, which he obviously loved dearly. When he paused for breath, I said '*Oui*', and I believe I even dared to say '*D'accord*' on one occasion. Finally, he stood up and shook me warmly by the hand, saying how nice it was to meet someone who knew Paris. He gave

1

me one of the highest marks, a level I was not able to match in my written French exam, but enough to carry me through in total.

The Royal Military Academy at Woolwich was a fairly harsh place, but one just buckled down to all the drill, riding and lessons in military tactics as best one could. Looking back, I still find it strange that bullying was thought to be a good way to develop the characters of young officers-to-be. All the officer instructors had been through it themselves, and presumably felt that it had done them no harm, although what good it did them has never been explained. Visiting West Point some 30 years later I was sorry to see that bullying continued to be practised there, and when I asked the Commandant about it, he just replied that it was a long-established tradition.

We were introduced to what lay ahead on our very first day at the Shop, as the RMA was always called. The newly arrived term were gathered together and in walked the Senior Under Officer. He shouted at us at the top of his voice, to take our hands out of our pockets and stand to attention when he spoke to us. All he put over to us was that we were 'the lowest form of animal life in the army, and don't any of you ever forget it'.

The Shop contained three terms of cadets, the senior term, from which the Under Officers were appointed, the middle term and the junior term, known as the Snookers.

However, the main feature of life at the Shop was the emphasis on excellence. Only the highest standards sufficed. Our dress had to be perfect at all times, without so much as a speck of dust on our jackets. The quality of our drill could only be matched by the Brigade of Guards, which was not surprising as our drill instructors were all from the Brigade. In our rooms, our clothes and papers had to be immaculate at all times, neatly stacked and spotlessly clean.

The penalty for any failure was an extra drill, which involved three-quarters of an hour before breakfast of strenuous activity obeying the commands of one of the Drill Instructors. This made an extra demand on one's stamina, which was already stretched by a very active regime. Occasionally a bullying attitude came through, such as in the riding school, where some of the instructors would yell out, "Who ordered you to dismount?"

when some unfortunate cadet fell off his horse. Also, inevitably, there is an element of bullying in the very nature of drill instruction.

All this was very demanding but strict discipline, as long as it is fairly administered, is not bad thing for someone who has just left school.

However, luckily there were breaks from the harshness for Snookers. In the gymnasium, where the PT instructors could have given us a really hard time, a calm and sensible attitude was adopted. If a cadet could not, for example, climb a rope using only his arms, the instructor would not force him in any way. Some of the classroom instruction was pathetic, each one of us being made to stand up in turn and read out one sentence from a military manual on tactics. On the other hand, we had a truly excellent civilian instructor, Professor Boswell, who lectured on current affairs in a way that made his topic most interesting and often amusing. Captain Cowley (later to become General Sir John Cowley), who taught me the elements of field survey, showed a calm determination to ensure that his students really understood the subject he was putting over. Last, but not least, we had a really good padre, the Reverend Victor Pike, who was reported to be an ex-Irish rugby international, and who did what he could to make our regime less harsh. Victor had two brothers and all three of them became bishops.

One cloud hung over my head in that one had to pass out within the top 18 cadets to achieve a commission in the Royal Engineers and my father was very anxious that I should do this because it would lead to taking a degree at Cambridge. I managed to squeeze through, so all was well.

Later we all took and passed the entrance exam for Cambridge, but Hitler attacked Poland just before we were due to start there and our lives were changed. Instead, I joined a newly organized Sapper company at Christchurch, on the south coast, and was given 2 Section to command and train. Incidentally, my Section store, in which we gradually accumulated the mass of equipment we would require for war, had earlier been used by a Gunner troop. All along the wall were big hooks for harness, and against each hook was the name of the gunner who had used it before the battery went over for the Waterloo campaign.

3

On most days we marched out into the New Forest to train in the area that is now Hurn airport, always sending out patrols to guard our flanks against surprise attack. This was a tactic insisted on by our Company Commander, Major W.F. Anderson (Andy), whose previous operational experience had been on the North-West Frontier of India. I never did this again when fighting started, but it was quite good training.

Gradually, with the irreplaceable help of my Section Sergeant Barrett, we developed military engineering skills in our men. They were mostly miners from Northumberland and Durham, tough young men, a quarter of whom could only sign their names with a cross at the weekly pay parades, but they proved they were worth their weight in gold when the going became hard. Probably, life in the mines made them more accustomed to danger than most, but, while they took much of my training with a bit of a laugh, when the war really started they showed a superb steadiness and an ability to do the unpleasant things that had to be done without question and well.

The high standard of the regular senior NCOs in the Company was a pleasure to see. For example, after spending a whole day in our miniature rifle range, trying to improve our men's shooting, Sergeant Barrett and our Company Quarter-Master Sergeant challenged me to the best of ten rounds, the loser to pay for pints of beer. Now, I had shot as a member of the Royal Engineers team at Bisley and I well knew that neither of my opponents had been there, so I looked forward to a free beer as I settled down to shoot. When the targets were collected, to my considerable surprise, one of them had beaten me by one point, and the other was only one point behind my score. I cheerfully paid for beer and then the loser, I forget which it was now, insisted on paying for another round, so honour was satisfied.

We were indeed lucky to have a man of the highest calibre as our Commanding Officer, Lieutenant Colonel Robert (Bobs) Maclaren. He had been awarded an MC in WW1 and was a professional in the best sense of the word. There were lessons to be learned for a beginner, like myself, from all that he did. Practical, knowledgeable and highly intelligent, he set an example of sensible leadership that was to be of value to me for the rest of my service. Tragically he was to be killed later in the war, an irreplaceable loss. Of course we saw much more of our company commander, Andy, who also wore an MC from his North-West Frontier days. He came under the heading of strong and silent. He said little, never wasted a word, but expected the highest standards.

The other officers in the company were Captain Mackenzie, Mac, the second-in-command, who was responsible for all our administration. He was a reservist with WW1 service, who liked whisky and girls. He was probably about 40 and we much appreciated his cheerful and helpful nature, although he seemed an old man to us. He was to be taken prisoner at the end of the Dunkirk campaign and, sadly, to die in a POW camp, as I heard many years later. Then there was Lieutenant Cave, who commanded 1 Section, and with whom Hugh and I had little in common, and, lastly, another Second Lieutenant, Hugh Davis, who was my main friend and commanded 3 Section.

Hugh was a couple of years older than me and had volunteered to join the Corps from Oxford. Although we were both young, our different backgrounds provided some complementary experience. For example, I, as Officers' Mess Secretary, was most grateful for his recommendations when we reached France to purchase Vouvray, Chablis and Nuits St George for our little group before the fighting started. At that time I had no knowledge whatsoever about wines. On the other side of the coin, he came to me for help when he was told to carry out some bridge demolitions later on, since I had completed a full demolitions training course which gave me a much better background knowledge than his potted war course at OCTU.

To revert for a moment to Sergeant Barrett, a delightful example of his knowledge of men occurred just before we left for France. Andy told me I would need a cook in my Section, which incidentally was about fifty men strong, because we might be sent off on detachment and be separated from the company cookhouse. I asked Barrett what we should do.

'Call for a volunteer, sir,' he said. I had already thought this would be a waste of time and asked him whether he thought anyone would come forward.

'No sir, it's most unlikely.'

'Then what shall we do?'

'You will have to nominate someone.'

'Yes, but who?'

'Nominate one of our concreters, sir. They are used to mixing stuff.'

Next morning on parade, as he had expected, nobody volunteered, so I nominated one of our two concreters. He proved to be a pretty primitive cook, but the effort and the cheerfulness he put into his work endeared him to us all.

Finally we moved over to France in April. The trip was uncomfortable and dreary in the extreme. Having disembarked at Le Havre, we waited all day for a train which the Movement Staff said they had arranged for us. Finally it arrived, with one third class carriage for the officers and sergeants and big wagons labelled '40 hommes/8 chevaux' for the men. Possibly Andy knew our destination, but I certainly did not. The train crawled along for a whole night and stopped at a deserted country siding where breakfast was served. After the meal, as there were no toilet facilities, the majority of our company could be seen squatting with their trousers down against the hedges surrounding a nearby field. The sordid remains against those hedges indicated that countless other units had done the same thing there before us.

At long last we arrived at Arras, which incidentally housed the British army headquarters, and were driven west a few miles to the little village of Lattre St Quentin, where my Section was allocated a barn with holes in the roof and a floor that was rotten in places. However, Sappers sort out problems like that quickly, and soon the roof was patched with flattened-out petrol tins and the floor shored up.

We were put to work straight away at deepening the ditches on either side of a road to Arras from the south. The exact value of this slow, back-breaking work was difficult to see, but Andy told me when I asked him that the road might become very important if the fighting front neared Arras. The only interest in doing this job lay in what we dug up every day. Old shell cases, grizzly bones and skulls, tin hats, belts from machine guns and endless miles of barbed wire were pulled up. Obviously this had been one of the trench warfare battlefields of WW1, and, from the work we were

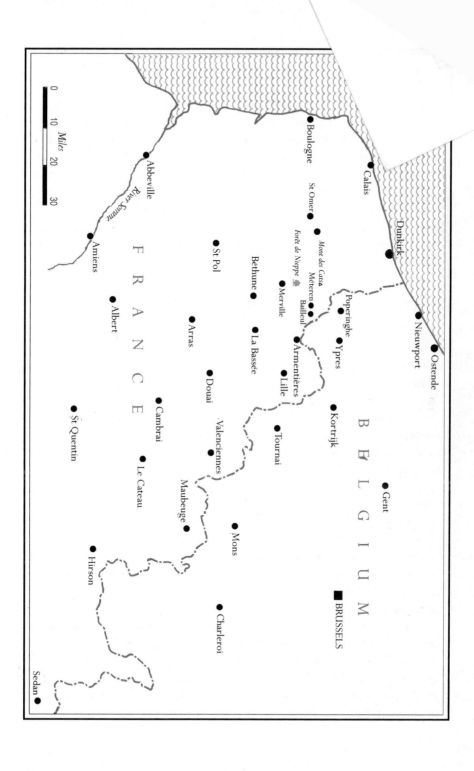

ing, it looked as if the the great General Staff expected WW2 to develop in a similar way.

On 10 May 1940 the inevitable happened; the Germans attacked in the Ardennes and in eastern Belgium and Holland. Suddenly, German aircraft were all over the sky by day, whilst their heavy bombers came over and hit towns at night. We were called out at midnight on 14 May to go to Arras and help in fire-fighting. Large blocks of buildings were on fire. My Section was directed to the Hotel de l'Universe where seven people had been killed, but it was burning so fiercely that there was little we could do. Then we took over some hoses from French firemen and I got one up the stairs of a house and broke a hole in the roof, from where I could really attack the blaze. The heat was intense and the roof I stood on kept catching fire, so I sometimes had to turn the hose onto that. I was there for 3½ hours before we finally got the fire under control.

Before the fighting started I had not realized how much sheer physical strain can build up during operations. A couple of days before the fire-fighting episode, we had been called forward to a wooded and farming area in Belgium, north of Tournai to search for parachutists. After driving slowly along crowded roads, returning friendly waves from the locals, late in the day we reached a wood where we dossed down for the night. Our food arrangements broke down, but luckily I had enough cash on me to buy some bread and some bars of hard black chocolate from a farm, which the Section shared out. Next day we were up at dawn beating across the area in one long line of men. For several hours we plodded forward, alert in case we should be fired at and with our rifles at the ready. We found nothing. In the late afternoon we marched back to our trucks and then returned, very late, to Lattre St Quentin. It was after this long day that we were called out to fight the fires in Arras, resulting in a feeling of complete exhaustion.

On 16 May a Wing Commander Sugden turned up. I think he must have been a friend of Andy's. He informed us that the Germans had broken through the French defences at Sedan and were approaching Reims. Also, Holland had capitulated after the whole of her air force had been destroyed. Hugh and I discussed this surprising news over a glass of wine, but there were no great conclusions that a couple of raw second-lieutenants could come to. Earlier, when we were officially resting from our arduous fire- fighting, Hugh and I had gone off to a local bistro for a change of scene and a drink. I asked him what I should order and he said he did not know but we might try absinthe. I requested two glasses, to be met with a memorable reply that absinthe was '*pas bon pour les jeunes officiers anglais*.' So we settled for a couple of glasses of red wine.

When we stood to at first light next morning Andy came over and told me to go to the main HQ on the edge of Arras and collect a thousand anti-tank mines. The HQ turned out to be a rambling complex of inter-connected huts containing offices. There were abbreviated titles on the doors, such as DAQMG Ops, which meant nothing at all to me, and anyway there was nobody in them. At last I found one that was occupied, labelled French Army Liaison. I realized the incumbent was rather senior, but as he appeared to be the only person available, I saluted smartly and asked him where I could get anti-tank mines. He looked severely at me over his glasses and said, 'Young man, I cannot help you. You must go and find the quartermaster.' The name on his desk was Brigadier General C. de Gaulle.

I had not realized that a large HQ had such a mundane character as a quartermaster, who I related with our company QM sergeant, but the advice was good, and I finally found an officer who told me where to go. There were very few mines left and I took all I could find, which my diary tells me was 167.

On returning to Lattre, Andy told me that we had been placed under command of 1st Battalion, Welsh Guards to defend Arras against an expected German attack. He showed me on a map the sector for which I would be responsible, which was on the eastern outskirts, the direction from which the main attack was expected.

Nothing daunted, I passed the orders on to Sergeant Barrett and the corporals in charge of my sub-sections, and told them to pack up everything and move in two hours' time to our sector. I drove off straight away to reconnoitre the area and to plan exactly where my men should go. My sector was between two main roads to the east, on each of which there was a Welsh Guards detachment. A road ran north and south between these two detachments and three minor roads ran off this towards the east. Obviously I had to put one sub-section to defend each of these three roads, which left my fourth sub-section as a small reserve. I sited my head-quarters in a central, empty house. There was much activity in the area when I arrived, as French families, having heard the latest news, prepared to move out.

I had split my anti-tank mines with the other two sections in Lattre and had about sixty for myself. When my men arrived, I gave the three leading sections twenty mines each, with instructions to put them in their road to the east and then to prepare defensive positions against a possible attack. Sentries, of course, were put out by each sub-section as we retired for the night.

Having done a final check of the sentries, I retired to bed myself, only to be woken at about 1 am by a most shattering explosion, which blew broken glass all over my room. What had happened was that a huge French lorry, wanting to go eastwards, had refused to obey our sentry's order to stop and had driven over a mine. The French driver was miraculously still alive, although suffering from severe shock, but our sentry, who had jumped out of his slit-trench in a last attempt to stop the lorry, was desperately wounded. This was my first experience of the results of war at close quarters, and a most sobering one. I told one of our drivers to take the wounded man to the Welsh Guards medical post at once and two of his friends volunteered to go with him. He never complained as we laid him in the back of the truck, although we could see from his face the pain he was in. His friends returned a couple of hours later with the news, which I had been expecting, that he had died before reaching the doctor. We were all deeply affected.

Next day we dug in more deeply and, to avoid any repetition of the night's disaster, I commandeered a number of civilian cars to block the roads from our side. This caused understandable resentment from the French civilian owners, and all I could do was to give each one a note, signed by me, to say that their car had been commandeered for the defence of Arras and that compensation would be paid by the British government. I have often wondered whether any of these notes were handed in at the end of the war and, looking back now, I feel nothing but sadness for the wretched owners whose property I had seized.

On the lighter side, it turned out that I had the main NAAFI storage depot in my sector. This was a huge building, like three aircraft hangers built together, and it contained tens of millions of cigarettes in large crates, plus tins of food and cases and cases of beer and spirits. I found it rather odd when a staff car drew up and a brigadier stepped out and said he had come to inspect my defences. However, he showed little interest in anything until we passed the entrance to the NAAFI building. He insisted on having a look inside and then said, 'I might as well take one of those cases with me whilst I am here,' pointing at a case of Scotch. His driver was summoned and he drove off. This routine was followed by another senior officer, and then another, after which I ceased to bother to take them round my rather pitiful defences, but took them straight to the NAAFI. When the time finally came to leave, I asked whether I should set fire to this valuable stock, but was told firmly not to. The Germans must have been delighted with it.

The outcome of all this was that two German tanks appeared round the corner of the road on which our sentry had been hit. They must have seen the anti-tank mines, which were just laid on top of the road. They fired a few rounds blindly from their main armament into the houses round about without causing any casualties, and then backed off. We had no way of damaging them.

As often happens during mobile operations, we received sudden orders to abandon our positions and to move at once to near Bailleul to prepare some bridges for demolition. It did not take long to pack up, nobody wanted to hang about, and, with an air-raid in progress, we drove, well spaced out, to the west. Passing the main square in front of the railway station, civilian casualties were everywhere. I led and had to stop where a fallen house largely blocked the road. Our sappers worked fast to open up a way through and, as I climbed back into my truck, I saw a man carrying a young girl along the pavement next to us. The expression of utter horror on his face has stayed with me to this day, and it was only when I looked down and saw that the girl had no head that I realized why.

The harsh reality of what war is all about was being brought home to us young men in no uncertain way.

But I hereby promise to include no further glimpses of the basic

11

horrors of war in this narrative. Enough is enough! The only comment I would make is that, certainly in my case, being exposed close to the horrors of war does not make a person casual about them. Quite the opposite; I was far more casual before I ever went to war about the death and destruction it caused than I was after I had experienced these in earnest.

CHAPTER 2

BLOWING UP BRIDGES

After leaving Arras, with sighs of relief, we were finally redirected from Bailleul to the small town of Merville. Here there was not a single old building, spelling out clearly that the original Merville had been totally destroyed in WW1. Andy stayed on in Arras for a couple of days. He never told us what happened during that time. It would have been against his nature to do so, but, whatever it was, he was awarded a bar to his MC for it.

We were briefed by Colonel Maclaren to prepare bridges over the Béthune-La Bassée canal for demolition. The only difficulty in this was that the Colonel used all the WW1 pronunciations for French towns and villages, and some of these were so grotesque as to be almost incomprehensible to us. However, he was not a man to give out orders that could be misinterpreted, so he also gave accurate grid references of the bridges he wanted each of us to tackle.

I had three bridges, one of reinforced concrete, another a steel girder bridge and lastly a narrow steel footbridge, and all of these were sizeable as they spanned not only the canal but also a railway line that ran alongside it. After I had reconnoitred them, I made a plan for each and despatched a truck to collect the necessary explosive and stores.

I do not want to go into technical details about bridge demolitions. It is sufficient to explain that the steel girder bridge was straightforward but complex, as it was a much larger structure than anything we had ever done training on. Each steel beam had to have its correct quota of gun cotton slabs fixed firmly

13

to it, and all these connected by an electric ring main to the exploder. We also prepared the homeside abutment for demolition. I listed the sizes of all the charges and put Sergeant Barrett in charge of completing the work.

The reinforced concrete bridge was a different matter. Six or eight months before, at the School of Military Engineers at Chatham, our instructor had brushed such structures on one side, saying that if any of us had the misfortune to be ordered to blow one, then that man's luck had run out, as no formula had been found to cope with reinforced concrete. I considered this great arched construction and felt that if I could damage all the beams at the same point across the canal by removing the concrete and exposing the reinforcing bars, then the whole thing would have to collapse under its own great weight. I was highly relieved to find out that this worked in practice a few days later. I put my second senior NCO, Lance Sergeant Smith, a particularly reliable man, in charge of this bridge.

Lastly, the footbridge. The difficulty here was that we only had two electric exploders and these would be required for the two main bridges. This meant that we could not use electric detonators on the footbridge. I decided that the only solution was to overload the bridge with a single bulk charge of ammonal explosive, well tamped round with sandbags. However, this meant that someone would have to run up to the charge and light the fuse with a match when the order to blow was given. This could be a most dangerous errand if the Germans had reached the far bank, but it was the best we could do.

Having started the men on this work, which would take several hours, I moved to the west, by previous arrangement, to seek out Hugh Davis, who wanted help with his bridges. When I found him, he had already started work on his two bridges. I checked his detailed calculations on the main girders and these were good, so I left him to it.

Work on our three bridges proceeded fairly smoothly. There were problems, of course-beams that were difficult to get at or to fix charges on to – but these were successfully overcome. I was amazed at the apparent nonchalance of individual sappers, sitting on a beam high in the sky and leaning over to fix explosive under it without safety harness of any sort. But we all knew that this job must be finished quickly, or we could risk disaster in the shape of machine gun-fire from the far bank.

At last all was complete and the electric leads from the complex ring mains ended in slit trenches, where the exploders were held awaiting the order to blow. Also a great pile of sandbags concealed the charge on the footbridge, with a piece of safety fuse sticking out, waiting to be lit.

What I had not realized before was how much tension builds up when an important bridge must be blown, particularly if it is likely to be in the face of an enemy attack. So many things can go wrong, and these are not just odd chances, such as a stray bullet cutting a wire, but also more fundamental possibilities, such as whether I had really done all my calculations correctly or whether I had left out some additional factor. After all, one never has an opportunity to demolish a major bridge in peacetime training, so it will be a totally new experience.

The longer the time dragged on after the charges had all been connected, the more tense I became. I tried to conceal this from Sergeant Barrett and the others, and I hope I did. Some diversions occurred; for example some French refugees wanted to cross the big iron girder bridge but we had to stop them, as they would just be walking into the fighting. I tried to explain why it was not advisable to go that way, but one of the refugees, an attractive but heavily pregnant woman, became most distraught, as a result, I suppose, of all the argument, and started to have her baby. We carried her into the nearby field with another woman who said we need not worry, as they had been expecting this event. We heard moans from behind the fence and eventually a baby was produced and they left, pushing mother and child on a cart. Even in war, life must go on.

This diversion took up most of one morning, for which I was thankful. On 22 May I went across to see Lance Sergeant Smith, feeling as tense as ever. There was an infantry company dug in near the bridge and I asked their commander if he had any news about how things were going on the far side. All morning we had heard desultory bursts of firing and the unmistakable noise of moving tanks. He said he believed the enemy were quite close but his men had not been fired at yet. After more discussion, we both felt that the time had come to blow the bridge and at 1 o'clock in

15

the afternoon he signed the necessary written order and I told Smith to let it go. The result was even better than I had hoped. The great reinforced concrete structure collapsed completely, twisting itself as it fell to make a really difficult obstacle. I took shelter against the wall of a nearby barn to avoid any flying splinters, and nearly came to grief as heavy tiles were dislodged from the roof by the blast and crashed down. Luckily I was hard against the wall so that they all fell at my feet, but that was a lesson learned and I never made the same mistake again.

With a feeling of great relief at the success of the demolition, I first congratulated Smith on his magnificent work and then walked over to the company commander who had given us the order to blow to say goodbye and to wish him luck. He was talking on a field telephone and when he put it down he said, 'That was Battalion HQ, who had heard the bang and wanted to know what had happened. When I told them, they said that a French armoured brigade had just been routed over this bridge.' This was awful news, but there was nothing we could do to reverse the demolition, so I told him (I think his name was Major Findlater) about Sergeant Barrett's bridge, only a couple of miles further east, and then dashed back there to ensure that that one was not about to be destroyed. Luckily all was quiet there, with Sergeant Barrett calmly in charge.

Later, during the afternoon of 22 May I was summoned back to Merville, where I was told to go at once to reconnoitre some more bridges, this time over another canal on the border of the forest of Nieppe, a short way to the east. Consequently I was not present when Barrett blew his bridges, but I still have the original written order to blow, which says, 'In the face of large enemy forces I order this bridge to be demolished', signed G. Garside, Captain, Royal Irish Fusiliers at 1606 hours, 23rd May at Beuvry. On the back is written in pencil, 'OC 2 Section. Sir, Bridge blown successfully at 1630 hours' and signed C. Barrett, Sgt, RE.

Later, Barrett told me how Lance Corporal Hibbert had run up the steps of the foot bridge and taken shelter from enemy fire behind the sandbags covering the explosive. For a time he fumbled with matches before he successfully lit the safety fuse and then doubled back to safety. The bridge came tumbling down and for this gallant act I put him up for a Military Medal, which he duly received some months later when we were back in England. When the news of this reached us, he modestly said that he had only done what he was told and that all our men there were equally involved. There was much truth in this; the one who really deserved a medal was Barrett, who had been in charge, but I could not pick out a particular act of his that would be likely to result in an award, so Lance Corporal Hibbert wears his medal for all those who carried out this successful operation. I regret to have to say it, but our medal system, as it has evolved over many years, still has some serious faults.

I have described these, our first demolitions, in some detail, so I will pass quickly over our next lot on the western edge of the forest of Nieppe. The main difference on the second occasion was that, whereas before we had just dug positions to prevent an enemy patrol from rushing our bridges, this time I was told to prepare to hold off an attack across the canal in addition to blowing a fairly major bridge. I sited defensive trenches and we dug them and waited, not knowing what to expect. Soon after dawn the next day, it must have been 26 May, an infantry company appeared to take over my positions and we were told to blow the bridge. This was a great relief, as I could not really see how we were going to stop a determined German attack across the canal, probably supported by tanks. The incoming company commander did not seem very enthusiastic about my dispositions and I noticed that he only adopted a few of the trenches we had dug. However, that was his affair; at least we had removed the bridges over the canal for him.

From the forest we moved to a collection of farm buildings near the village of Meteren, just north of Bailleul. It was here, I think two mornings later, that Andy called us together to tell us to abandon our transport and all the kit it contained and march at once to the Mont des Cats, which was about 6 kilometres to the north, and there to take up defensive positions to hold off any attack. All our three sapper companies were to do this together, and Colonel Maclaren would set up his HQ in the monastery on top of the hill.

This quite unexpected order we took in our stride, and I reluctantly left my best uniform, my sleeping bag, spare boots and clothing in the attic in our farm. The farmer said he would gladly keep it for me for no matter how long. He could not have been more friendly and helpful. On my map I put a circle round his farm, so that I would know exactly where my kit was, but, needless to say, I mislaid the map sometime later and I have never been back. I only hope at least some of my kit was of use to him or to his children.

CHAPTER 3

BACK TO DUNKIRK

After marching for a couple of hours, the Mont des Cats came into view. It was a distinct hill in what was otherwise dead flat country for miles around. On top of the hill was a large building with a chapel at one end and this was the monastery that our regimental headquarters moved into. I was given a sector on the south-facing slope between our other two Sections. I suppose that the other two companies in the regiment were on either side of us.

I sited some trenches to give us all-round defence and we spent most of the rest of the day digging these. The main advantage in completing them was that they gave us comparative safety against attack by German dive bombers, which paid us altogether too much attention for comfort.

Early the next day, around 3 am, I was woken by a runner from the OC summoning me to his headquarters. There, together with the other two Section commanders, I was told to abandon my position and march back to Dunkirk, a distance of some 40 miles, for evacuation to England. We all realized that the campaign was not going well for us, but this was a completely unexpected order. We had received no information about what was really happening, except that heard on our Company Quartermaster Sergeant's battery-operated radio. From the BBC we heard that German troops had broken through to the south and attacked Calais, but had been repulsed there. The reality of this report had been brought home to us in no uncertain way the previous evening, when four German tanks emerged from the wood below, about five hundred yards away. We kept very still in our trenches as we observed them, in the hope that we would not be noticed, because we had no means of stopping them if they should advance against us. Luckily for us they seemed more interested in the big old monastery where Colonel Maclaren's staff suffered some casualties, including our adjutant, who was killed there.

I returned to our Section position and briefed my NCOs. There was a glimmer of daylight in the east, so I told them to get their men out of their trenches quickly, whilst they were still invisible to the Germans, and form them up behind the monastery. They all saw the sense of speed and it only took a few minutes before Sergeant Barrett reported to me that the men were ready to move. I had been studying my maps and had worked out what appeared to be a safe route back. Unfortunately Sergeant Barrett, with his usual efficiency, had found that two men were missing. It was getting lighter by the minute, so I ordered the men to proceed and went back to find the missing men. A search of the trenches revealed nothing and only when I returned to England did I hear that they had been offered a lift by the Quartermaster, who had the only company vehicle on the Mont, and they had, of course, jumped at the chance and gone off. I had a good look round and then returned up the hill to the back of the monastery. Who should I meet up there but Hugh Davis. He had been on a similar mission and had also sent his men on under his Section Sergeant. 'Come on, let's get out of here,' he said and I could not agree with him more.

Shells were landing at frequent intervals, but nothing too close to be worrying, until, after about ten minutes we reached the top of the rise and a salvo landed fairly close in front of us. The track we were on dipped down steeply and then rose up again to our level. There was a road junction at the bottom of the dip and, peering over the top of the ridge, I could see several battledress-clad corpses down there. Another batch of shells arrived, so we took cover and considered what to do. There appeared to be no prominent observation post from which the Germans could watch what was going on at the road junction, so they had to be firing blind at it. The fact that the junction was marked clearly on the map rather supported this conclusion.

The shells were coming at regular intervals and I timed this on my watch and calculated that we could reach safety on the far side if we ran really fast. Obviously we could not lie where we were indefinitely, and Hugh agreed to give it a try. So, after the next burst, we took off. I have never run so fast in my life. I kept an eye on the second hand of my watch and, just before the next batch of shells was due to arrive, I shouted to Hugh, 'Down'. We flung ourselves into the ditch and, exactly on time, the next salvo burst behind us. We quickly covered the final few yards to the top of the hill and then left this unpleasant place.

Reaching comparative safety, I heard a moan coming from the ditch and, on investigation, found this had come from an army padre, who had a nasty wound in his right shoulder. He was bleeding quite badly, so we put a field dressing over the wound and then, with an arm over each of our shoulders, helped him down the road. He told me he was attached to the Somerset Light Infantry and he showed great courage.

Methodically, we plodded on and I was wondering just how far we would be able to continue with the padre, when we came upon an abandoned small staff car, half in the ditch. It was obvious that the same thought passed through all our minds. Could we use it? In those days cheap cars did not have an ignition key, just an on-off switch, so, lowering the padre gently onto a bank, Hugh clambered into the driver's seat while I prepared to push. The engine started almost at once and, after a good deal of effort, we got the car onto the road. We lifted the padre into the back seat and started off. This was an unbelievable piece of luck. I pulled out my map to chart a course back to Dunkirk, where I felt sure we would be able to find doctors who could cope with the padre. However, we had only covered about half a mile when, on a long straight stretch of road, we saw ahead what looked like a piece of machinery. As we approached this, two soldiers ran into the middle of the road and I realized, first, that we were looking at a machine gun pointing at us and, second, that the soldiers were German.

Mercifully there was a road off to the right, with a house on the corner that blocked us from view. With a squeal of tyres, Hugh turned down it and accelerated away.

The road took us towards Poperinghe, of World War One fame, and not too far off our direct route to Dunkirk. As we approached the town it was under heavy attack by German dive bombers, but by another piece of luck, there was a sign on the outskirts indicating that a field ambulance was located there. Bombs were dropping all round as we drove in and the unit was packing up to move, but we managed to hand the padre over to the duty doctor, who gave his opinion that the wound would raise no serious problem. Hoping for the best, we left him there and I have often wondered what happened to him. He never once complained and I felt he deserved to survive.

Walking out of the field ambulance's building, we were highly disappointed to see that our beautiful staff car was on fire and burning fiercely. However, it had been a real help for the padre, so we abandoned it and walked into Poperinghe. The bombing was still going on, but one asset when being attacked by dive bombers was that one could see when an attack was dangerous. Needless to say, we watched the sky continuously and whenever a bomber appeared to be coming our way we took cover at once.

Poperinghe proved an unpleasant place to walk through. A Belgium regiment of horse artillery had been caught by the bombing and the streets were full of dead and dying horses, with up-turned guns and spilled ammunition everywhere. Emerging from the north of the town, we passed a building outside which were stacked hundreds of bicycles. The battalion that used these for transport was inside and a bored Belgian sentry sat smoking outside. He appeared to pay little attention to his task, so, reaching the end of the stack, we pinched a couple of bikes and rode off fast. A shout went up behind us, but we took no notice, hoping that the sentry would not use his rifle. All too short a time later there was a roar of rage just behind us, and the sentry, clearly a professional cyclist, had caught us up. We dismounted, apologized and gave up our loot. There was nothing for it; we were going to have to walk back to Dunkirk.

By this time it was midday and we were starting to feel a need for food. We stopped at a few farmhouses and succeeded in buying two hard-boiled eggs at one. Continuing our march, I noticed a tin in the ditch which turned out to be greengage jam from a British ration pack. We ate this complete, and I still feel a touch of nausea when offered greengage jam today.

As we walked on we passed hundreds and hundreds of abandoned British army trucks and the scale of the disaster that was hitting us became more apparent. There was very little on the road, but after some hours we were overtaken by a French army lorry, which stopped in front of us and we were invited to jump in.

Joining the poilus in the back, we found that a bottle of brandy was being passed round. We gratefully accepted this and took good draughts of the fiery liquid. They were all most friendly, and their leader, a sergeant, said, in good English, 'Now you tell us dirty joke to make us laugh, I translate.'

Hugh took up this challenge at once. 'Before this war started,' he said, 'I was up at Oxford.'

'What you study?' said the sergeant.

'Forestry,' said Hugh.

'*Ah oui; les arbres. C'est bon.* Now the joke.'

'I went to the wedding of the man who was captain of the Oxford boat race team. You know, the rowing team.'

'Yes, I know.'

'We made an archway for the bride and bridegroom to pass under when they left the church by holding up oars. Well, I heard a man behind me say, "Cor, look at all them oars." At this his friend replied, "Them's not whores, them's bridesmaids!"'

The only laughter came from me, but Hugh gallantly tried to explain in his schoolboy French why this was meant to be funny,

During this our vehicle had stopped and we heard an argument going on at the front. We were told that no vehicles were permitted to cross the bridge in front and that we must all dismount. Reluctantly, with much handshaking, we said goodbye to our good-natured hosts and set off again on foot.

Immediately across the bridge we realized we were quite close to Dunkirk, as French troops were busy digging trenches along the canal bank. A French officer harangued the line of marching men, telling them to remember Verdun and to come and help him defend this ground against the 'sales Boches.' We walked on towards Dunkirk, which was clearly marked by a huge plume of smoke. Later we were to see that this came from burning oil tanks, but it had a most beneficial advantage for us as the wind carried the cloud directly over the beaches. Any German dive bomber that flew below the cloud was fired at by tens of thousands of rifles, and most were shot down. Quite a lot of bombs exploded on the beach whilst we were there, sometimes causing casualties, but the damage they would have inflicted if the pilots had been able to see their targets would have been infinitely greater.

Soon after leaving the French officer we heard a single rifle shot. A British soldier came running up in some distress and asked us if we had seen the French officer at the bridge.

'Of course,' we said.

'Well, one of those Frenchies has just shot him,' he said.

Clearly not all the French soldiers wished to be reminded of their responsibilities, and were more interested in escaping the threatening net than in volunteering to help the gallant officer.

After a miserably uncomfortable night on the concrete esplanade, we rose at first light to decide what to do next.

A number of pleasure boats and yachts were coming in from the sea. Most did not anchor, but dropped off a rowing boat which made for the shore. There were hundreds of men standing in the shallows, who immediately waded or swam out to these rowing boats, with the result that several were swamped, to the obvious annoyance of both the owners and those who wanted to climb into them.

I felt that this was not an attractive route home for us, so we set off towards the main harbour to see what that had to offer. On the way, who should we run into but Sergeant Barrett with my Section. He reported that they had suffered no casualties, but also like us, had had no food and were wondering just what to do. After trying to obtain advice from various officers, most of whom were just as confused as we were, I discovered that there was a rudimentary organization at the port. Groups of fifty men were assembled, given a number and then, when a fresh destroyer came alongside the mole, numbers were yelled out and the relevant groups moved up to the mole, where a final control directed them to a ship. The need for rapid movement was obvious, as the area was being shelled, and neither the Navy nor those ready to embark wanted to hang around.

This simple organization was run by a major sitting in a slit trench in the sand and the groups of fifty were within earshot of him. I approached, saluted and was told that my group would be number 26. Destroyers came and went, each one taking about half a dozen groups. After about an hour I noticed the major emerge from his trench, join a group, which was presumably his normal command, and double towards a destroyer. Nobody took his place, so, rather than allow this tenuous organization to break down, after a few minutes I stepped into his trench.

I should explain that many of us were wearing our plastic gas capes over our uniform, as an extra slight warmth after the chilly night in the open. One's military rank was therefore not visible, but it did give me some mild amusement when a captain, a senior officer in my eyes, came up and saluted me smartly. I gave him a number for his group and pointed out to him where he should take them.

I sat there for a couple of hours, telling successive commanders what their numbers were and ordering the earliest groups forward methodically when a ship came in. At one point Sergeant Barrett came up with the gloomy news that a Lance Corporal from 1 Section had joined the group and he had seen Major Anderson and the whole of Company HQ being marched away by German troops and carrying some wounded with them. He also reported that 1 Section had stopped in a barn for a rest and a smoke soon after starting the march from the Mont des Cats. He had dived into some bushes to answer a call of nature, only to see the barn being surrounded by Germans, who then fired through the wooden walls. He did not know about casualties, but feared the worst. The only good news was that Colonel Maclaren had been seen safely back.

On a signal from the mole that three more groups should move forward, I shouted to 18, 19 and 20 to go. Strangely, no one answered for 20, so I called out the number again. Still, no response. So, pointing at Hugh, I shouted, 'Go on number 20, get moving.' Without hesitation, he called our men to their feet and moved off. Also, without hesitation, I followed my predecessor's example and left the command slit trench to join my men.

Once on the mole, we saw that it was 'Y'-shaped, with the two arms pointing out to sea. An officer was standing at the centre of the 'Y', directing groups down whichever arm a destroyer had come alongside. We had only been at the base of the mole for a couple of minutes when a salvo of shells arrived and burst on the concrete surface, killing the officer and a number of the members of a group that happened to be passing at the time.

Getting some of our men to help the wounded back, I once more assumed authority and stood in the centre of the 'Y' to order groups forward as requested by the Navy. Another ship arrived, and with it another salvo, but luckily this dropped into the sea and nobody was the worse for it. It seemed a very long time, probably about 20 minutes, before the next one arrived. The Navy yelled at me to tell the men to double up, so I shouted at the groups. It was with not a little pleasure that I saw that Hugh was leading the last group and when it went past I joined the tail, once again, I regret to admit, abandoning my responsibilities to whosoever would take them on.

We were shelled as we left and bombed on several occasions on the way back to Dover. It saddened me greatly to learn later that our wonderful destroyer was sunk on the very next trip it made back to Dunkirk. However, once on board, what a relief! No responsibility! I slept the whole way apart from being woken for a mug of tea and a good chunk of beautiful fresh bread. It had been quite an eventful couple of days.

CHAPTER 4

THE WAR GOES ON

When we were disembarked from our destroyer at Dover we were marched to a train and crammed tightly into carriages. We had no idea where we were going and we did not care much anyway. All we wanted to do was sleep. The train stopped occasionally at wayside stations, where kindly women woke us up with cups of tea and sometimes a sandwich. On one such halt a dear old woman asked us for addresses of our next of kin and I wrote out my mother's name and address. I still have the postcard she sent to my mother, saying that her son was well and safely back from Dunkirk.

At last, after some hours, we stopped at yet another station and this time we were all ordered out. It turned out that this was Tidworth in Hampshire and our whole train-load were marched off to a large tented camp. Hugh Davis and I were put into a bell tent with some others and one of them told us that we were all being given 48 hours' leave, which was exactly what we all wanted. Of course, we had no English money, but an Army Paymaster was on duty and solved this problem for us. We returned to the tent to collect our haversacks, which held the only kit we had, only to be told, 'Oh, haven't you heard? All leave has been cancelled.'

It took about ten seconds for Hugh and I to agree that if Nelson could find it impossible to read an order, we could find it equally impossible to hear one. We wasted no time in returning to the station and in catching trains that would take us home to our parents, mine in London and his in Somerset. A truly blissful couple of days followed, mostly with the girl who was to become my fiancée, but also in buying essential clothing and another sleeping bag.

All too soon this joyful time ended and I took the train back to Tidworth, carrying my new possessions, only to find that all the tents had gone. I never heard what the cause of this sudden change was, but in due course I caught up with the residue of 61 Company, who were being collected together at a camp called Barton Stacey. Here reinforcements arrived to make us up to strength quite quickly. A new Chief Clerk came, which was a relief as I was trying to cope with all the company paper work, and, soon after, a new OC, Major R.M.A. Welchman, 'Taffy'. Taffy was as different as chalk from cheese to his predecessor, Andy. A cheerful extrovert, who had played rugger for the Army, he was disarmingly open and frank. Quite early on, I asked him some question about training and his reply was, 'Tony, you know far more what your men need than I do. You make your mind up about what they want and I will help you get it.'

Soon we were moved down to the village of Bridge, east of Canterbury, to help prepare defences against the expected German invasion. The Battle of Britain was taking place above our heads, as huge armadas of German bombers flew over, protected by banks of fighter aircraft above them in layers. We did not have much time to watch them, but occasionally we were rewarded by the heartening sight of a Spitfire, with its engine screaming, diving out of the sun at great speed and shooting down a bomber. The Germans set up some heavy artillery on the French coast, which occasionally landed a shell in or near Dover, but most of their efforts were directed against shipping which soon ceased to use the Straits.

Our next task was to create a Stop Line in Somerset and Devon, from coast to coast, working with the other companies in our Group. The idea of this was to form a base for defence against a possible German landing further to the west, in Devon or Cornwall. Far from all the noises of war, we worked hard all day and then relaxed in a pub in the evening. Once or twice all talk in the pub fell silent as we all listened to the memorable words of our indomitable Prime Minister, Winston. What a man!

During this time we lived in Ilminster, travelling out each day through delightful small, unspoilt villages to the north-south railway line that was the foundation of our efforts. We found that the people of Ilminster, a local metropolis, spoke of the villagers rather contemptuously, as ignorant farmers. They even claimed that the story of a farmer who, when asked the way by a passing motorist, replied, 'Turn left where the soldiers used to stand' had actually originated in one of their local villages. Be this as it may, they proved very ready to help us when we asked them.

We completed our work in about a month, as far as I remember, and then were ordered down to Lynton, on the North Devon coast, another very pleasant area. I was told to build a road from the Oare River valley up on to Exmoor, which was due to be opened as a training area. Hugh was given a similar task, and we decided that by far the best way to reconnoitre these would be on horseback. We had seen a notice by a farm in the valley advertising ponies for hire and, sure enough, they proved only too pleased to rent us a couple. We left with strict instructions to be very careful of bogs on the moor, although we found that this warning was hardly necessary, as the ponies firmly refused to cross any patch that looked suspicious. However, the extent of the danger was brought home to us when we did a night exercise up there and one of my trucks missed the way and drove into a bog. The driver realized what was happening as his vehicle started to sink and jumped to safety. Next morning we went up to retrieve his truck but there was no sign of it. It had sunk completely.

The road my Section made still stands, but it is much too rough for private cars now. One very sad result of the opening up of Exmoor was that our greatly respected Commanding Officer, Maclaren, by then promoted to Brigadier, was killed on the moor by an experimental rocket that misfired. This was a bitter blow to all who knew him, and a sad loss to the Army. A simple stone memorial to him still stands where he fell, in the middle of nowhere.

'Taffy' Welchman left us at Lynton, on promotion to command a Group, and quite soon after I received a posting order to join his Group as second-in-command of one of the companies. This meant promotion to captain, so, as with several of my contemporaries, I missed the rank of First Lieutenant completely. I found my new job, which made me responsible for all the administration of the 250 or so men in the unit, interesting and very full time, but being tied to an office desk was a change that took some getting used to. I have to admit that I found it most agreeable to escape when an opportunity arose.

One such opportunity did arise and it proved, most unexpectedly, to be one of those rare occasions when one's whole life is changed by a chance meeting. There was to be a major exercise for all units in the south-east of the country. I have an idea that it was the last exercise to be run by General Montgomery before he left to command the 8th Army in North Africa, but my memory may be wrong on this. It was given the code name of Exercise Bumper and it was set up in the usual way for such training, with two opposing forces and a host of umpires to adjudicate and to see fair play. I cannot now imagine how I managed to arrange for my usual responsibilities to be dealt with, but I had my name put in as an umpire. To cut a long story short, I ended up by spending the whole exercise as a personal assistant to the senior Sapper umpire, one Colonel 'Ginger' Watkinson. I liked working for him and the way my life was changed will appear in due course.

For much of this time we were stationed at Shoreham in Kent to the south-east of London. Night after night we heard the throbbing engines of heavy bombers on their way to drop their loads of incendiaries and high-explosive bombs on the capital. Quite often the odd bomb was dropped near us, sometimes sticks of four or five bombs. Presumably these came from crews who decided not to face the heavy anti-aircraft fire over London, but the black-out was most thorough and usually no damage was done.

I spent about nine months as second-in-command of 71 Company and after that I was posted to 142 Officer Cadet Training Unit (OCTU) at Aldershot to teach demolitions. This was a quite a happy choice for me, as I had had some good practical experience. I made a particular point of recommending how to tackle reinforced concrete bridges. Another good aspect of this posting was the quality of the other instructors, among whom I made some lasting friends, one of whom, Tony Hewitt, was to be my best man some months later. Tony had one marvellous contact in the person of Rosa Lewis, ex-girlfriend of King Edward VII, from whom she had received the Cavendish Hotel, just off Jermyn Street in London. If Tony wanted rooms for us at short notice in London, Rosa never failed to oblige. In the bitter lottery of life in wartime, Tony was to join the airborne Sappers and to be killed in North Africa. The grim harvest was to take many of my closest friends, indeed most of them.

After about a couple of months, during which I polished up my instruction, life at the OCTU settled down to a pleasurable routine, punctuated by visits to London and the officer's club in Aldershot. This was not to last long, however, for after six months I was unexpectedly posted to the Chemical Defence Experimental Station (CDES) at Porton, near Salisbury. Only when I arrived there did the penny drop; the Commandant was 'Ginger' Watkinson.

CHAPTER 5

BACTERIOLOGICAL WARFARE

In the spring of 1942 I reported to the CDES and paid my respects to the Commandant. He shook me warmly by the hand and told me he had been expecting me and that he was placing me in the Trials Section. It transpired that this group was run by the awesomely intelligent O.G. Sutton, who was later to be knighted for his work with the Meteorological Service. Retrospect softens the edges of strong personalities, but I still remember with respect the formidable logic of Sutton's comments and the way he could make complex problems appear straightforward.

The methods of work in an experimental establishment were quite different to anything I had experienced before. I was given a desk in an office with two civilian scientists, who gave me excellent practical advice on how to tackle the tasks that were given me. My theoretical scientific knowledge, gained from lessons at school, was not in the same class as theirs, but they did not hesitate to help me in every possible way.

Sometime in the summer of that year Sutton called me into his office. Once in there, he removed from his mouth the pipe that he smoked incessantly and told me I was to take a small convoy of vehicles up to Gruinard Bay in Wester Ross in Scotland. I told him that I was sorry to have to do this, as I was just getting involved in some experimental work with shaped explosive. I should explain that someone had discovered that if a block of explosive was moulded into a conical shape that was hollow inside and if the inside of the cone was lined with metal, when the explosive was detonated a bullet of molten metal would be projected out at a very high velocity. The possible application of this to demolition techniques naturally interested me. However, Sutton said that this trip to Scotland was much more important, and he was not a man to be argued with. He told me that I would be carrying some extremely sensitive and potentially lethal containers in my vehicles.

It was not until I reached Gruinard Bay that he explained what this was all about. The objective was to find out by practical field experiments whether it was possible to disperse anthrax germs, so as to make a reliable military weapon. We were sworn to secrecy, particularly regarding the type of germs and I have always honoured the pledge I gave. However, that was half a century ago and since then the details of what we did have gradually been made public. Indeed, when I visited Gruinard Island about ten years ago it was surrounded with notices saying that its soil was contaminated with anthrax.

The reason for the projected tests was that an intelligence report had indicated that the Japanese had carried out some successful tests and that they might be producing weapons to release bacteria into the air. There were no reports of German work in this field, but the possibility could not be discounted. Our work was directed towards discovering what was feasible, in order that defensive arrangements could be made to protect our civilian population against attack if it was found that such weapons were practicable. Protection would involve mass immunisation, but before this could be planned, we must discover which bacteria could be used, and how.

Of the various dangerous germs known to science, anthrax was always high on the list of probable starters. Not only was the disease extremely lethal, but also anthrax spores appeared to be virtually indestructible in ordinary circumstances. In nature anthrax occurs in the soil in some areas, and when an animal that has picked up the disease dies, the spores can be spread by carrion feeding off the corpse. Also bones of diseased animals contain spores and other animals, such as sheep, like to eat dried bones, again spreading the disease. Even if the bones have been left to weather in the open for many years, the spores lie dormant, only to multiply astronomically when they find themselves at the correct body temperature.

The problem of how to disseminate these amazingly resilient spores still remained. Ordinary chemicals can be released by putting them in a container, such as a bomb or a shell, and then bursting it open with a small explosive charge over the target area. The first question that had to be answered was whether anthrax spores, which, although resilient, are still living organisms, could withstand the force of an explosive bursting charge.

The Microbiological Experimental Establishment at Porton developed a method of growing large cultures of anthrax spores and then collecting them in the form of a thick liquid gruel. This was put into glass containers, which were bedded into crates filled with Fuller's Earth. I then took these crates up by road to the west coast of Scotland, together with various bits of apparatus necessary for completing the experiment.

When I arrived with my valuable cargo, a tented camp had been set up by Captain Dalby of the Royal Artillery and some of his Gunners. The site chosen was a patch of grass separated by low sand dunes from a small beach in the north-eastern corner of Gruinard Bay. Across the bay, uninhabited and unspoilt, lay Gruinard Island, home to countless sea birds and, as we found when we went over there, hundreds of rabbits that took so little notice of us that our Gunners could knock them over with sticks when they felt like augmenting our army rations.

The team that assembled was a mixture of civilian scientists, supported by soldiers, who ran the camp and generally did the donkey work. The head of the Microbiological Establishment, Dr Paul Fildes, arrived, together with two of his assistants, Drs Henderson and Woods, who had been doing the detailed research. Paul Fildes was a short, thick-set man, with a pleasant and rather cynical sense of humour. Already a highly respected member of the Royal Society, he was someone of national, if not international, renown in his field. With his analytical attitude to everything he saw and did, he fitted in well with the formidable Sutton, who was also a member of the Royal Society. Decisions on what should be done were made swiftly by these two and, although joint leadership is generally considered to be dangerous, they found no difficulties in exercising it. Both were to receive well deserved knighthoods in due course.Other members of the team were Lieutenant Colonel Bamford of the Army Veterinary Corps and Dr David Sinclair of the RAMC.

The plan was simply to place a metal canister containing anthrax on a flat area on the island and then to tether sheep down wind of this. We just needed a fine day with an off-shore wind and then the experiment could be carried out. My own particular responsibility was to find a suitable site where any dead sheep could be thrown over the edge of a cliff, and then to bring down the cliff with explosive to bury the dead sheep, hopefully under hundreds of tons of rock. This was my main task and I also helped with any odd jobs that wanted doing.

Although I had by then acquired a fair amount of experience in the use of explosives, no task even remotely like this had come my way before. I therefore arranged a quick trip down to the School of Military Engineering at Ripon, the fount of all demolition knowledge. The instructors there could not have been more friendly, but none could give me any practical advice, nor did thorough research in their library produce any help. I was on my own.

Back on the island, I first studied the strata of my target cliff, but was unable to be sure which way it ran. Hoping for the best, I put my trust in the sheer brute force of explosives. Estimating the height of the cliff, I paced out the same distance inland from the edge. Then, with the help of a couple of Dalby's gunners, I dug a trench a couple of feet deep until we hit solid rock. Then I ordered up a thousand pounds of ammonal, the same explosive I had used on the footbridge over the La Bassée canal, and placed this along the bottom of the trench, tamping it down well with a couple of hundred sandbags.

With my arrangements completed, I gave a hand to Colonel Bamford with the tethering of sheep. These were purchased from local farmers and we ran into a little difficulty regarding times. The government had introduced double Summer Time as an economy measure in wartime, so we had put our clocks back two hours from Greenwich Mean Time. However, many of the Scottish farmers refused to accept this and worked on God's Time, two hours later than us. To make it even more difficult, some farmers belonged to the Wee Free Church, who, in order to show their independence, put their clocks back only one hour. Consequently, we had to question each farmer about his religious beliefs before we could agree a time for the delivery of sheep.

In due course all the arrangements were made and a convenient offshore breeze permitted the bomb to be exploded. During the following days sheep started to die, so the main question had been answered positively: the spores had survived the explosion and the weapon was a practical proposition. To an ignorant non-biologist like myself, it became abundantly obvious that anthrax was a formidable killer. Chemical weapons had been used extensively in the First World War and had inflicted many casualties, but the volume of anthrax spores necessary to institute a lethal dose was minute compared with even the most toxic chemical. The first atomic bomb had yet to be detonated, but the comparative lethality of anthrax compared with chemicals could only be compared with the effects of an atomic explosion compared with TNT. Needless to say, the process of inhaling anthrax spores carried by the wind would be as odourless as inhaling influenza germs from a passer-by in a city street.

To complete the story of the initial test, the results were conclusive and the dead sheep were thrown over my cliff. I was duly told to set off my explosive charge and, as expected, hundreds of tons of rocks and rubble tumbled down on the infected remains.

A couple of months later I took a Sapper sergeant and some men up there to build some Nissen huts, principally as laboratories, but also to improve our standard of living up there. By then any work on the island had to be done in full protective clothing, which was decontaminated after use. Another experiment was carried out, this time with a bomb dropped from an aircraft, with equally positive results. I selected another cliff and, at the end, again brought this down on the dead sheep.

The final demolition of the cliff was the last act for the team. I had to stay to the very end and, for some reason I now forget, David Sinclair, our doctor, stayed on with me. We moved along the loch to the Dundonnell Hotel, to allow the camp to be closed down. Life in the hotel was rather simple, there was nothing fancy like electric light there and chickens were apt to wander into the dining room, but the food was first class. We had steaming bowls of porridge for breakfast and we were not worried by the food rationing under which the rest of the country suffered. Our naval landing craft left us, so we rowed across to the island when we had to, and when this was not necessary we explored the lovely countryside round us. On one memorable outing we climbed An Teallach, the sizeable mountain that over-looked the whole area.

There was an unexpected sequel to this Gruinard expedition. In the winter of 1942/43, after all the trials were finished, a couple of cases of anthrax were diagnosed in sheep that had been browsing on the promontory across the bay to the west of the island and a message came down to say that we were suspected of causing this. It seemed possible that either a variation in the wind had deposited some spores up there, or even that the autumn gales had uncovered one of my buried sheep, which had then been carried over by sea currents. Dr Fildes decided he must go and investigate, and he asked me to accompany him. It was arranged that we should fly to Inverness from Boscombe Down, which was next door to Porton, and then we would be met by a car in which there would be cans of petrol in case we decided to try to reduce the contamination by burning. We set off in a Beaufort, a torpedo bomber, which Boscombe Down had been using for some experimental work. The pilot and co-pilot sat together in the nose and Paul Fildes sat in the wireless operator's seat, whilst I was relegated to a turret in the centre of the plane, from which a couple of machine guns pointed skywards. I asked if they were loaded and received the reply, 'Of course they are, and you jolly well keep a good look out and use them if we are attacked.'

All went well for about an hour, except that the intercom system on the plane obviously did not work. I tried several times to tell the pilot that oil was appearing on the tail of the aircraft and that this seemed to be coming from one of the engines. I could not get this through to him, so I concentrated on my main task of keeping my eyes peeled for enemy aircraft. Suddenly, on looking over my shoulder, I saw a horse galloping away from us. I realized we were about to crash land and gripped the machine-gun supports with all my strength. We landed in a ploughed field and slewed around in a hideous way. One of the supports I was holding buckled and I just managed to move my thumb in time

37

to avoid getting it trapped. Finally the tail of the plane broke at my turret and we came to a halt in a cloud of dust.

Slowly we all emerged. The only minor casualty was Paul Fildes, who had cut his hand trying, so I was told, to save his whisky bottle. Some Land Girls were working in the field and they kindly contacted a local army unit, which provided transport for us. This took us straight to a hospital in York where we were given a check-up. All was well, so we continued our journey by rail, which was a lot slower, but mercifully less sensational.

We rowed out to the island and had a look at the demolitions, which seemed to be perfectly all right. Paul Fildes thought that it could be possible that spores that had fallen on the heather might be blown across to the mainland, but this seemed a very remote possibility. We had had a very dry spell of weather and the wind was blowing out to sea, so, as an extra precaution, we decided to try burning the heather. It caught beautifully and, back at the Dundonnell Hotel that evening, we climbed one of the foothills of An Teallach to see a broad band of fire stretching right across the island, with a great plume of smoke going far out to sea. I felt a great sadness that such a peaceful and beautiful place had been contaminated with such vicious germs, but looking back on all this now, after almost half a century, I firmly believe that the good results far outweigh the bad. As with all wartime secrets, this one was shared with the Americans and it was the British and American governments which were instrumental in drafting the international agreement to ban the use of bacteriological weapons in warfare. Any other countries could equally well have been the leaders in this effort to humanize warfare, but perhaps they did not do so because they could only guess what the effects of bacteriological weapons would be. The British and American authorities did not have to guess; they knew.

One final point: at no time was it ever suggested that this weapon would or should be used against our wartime enemies. The trials were conducted for purely defensive reasons; to see if the use of anthrax was practicable, and, if it was, to work out what defensive measures would be needed in case it was used against us.

CHAPTER 6

BACK TO A REGIMENT

I did some heart-searching in early 1943 and came to a firm decision that the time had come for me to leave Porton. I had had a most interesting time there, but I knew that I was more fitted and would feel more in my element if I was back in a regiment. I therefore put in an application to this effect. I had a talk with Sutton about it and he was his usual helpful self and sent it on to the Commandant with his backing. 'Ginger' Watkinson had left and his successor barely knew me and was quite ready to accept Sutton's recommendation, so I awaited a posting order as I continued with my work.

One disadvantage to this arose because I had been promoted to the rank of major. This was only temporary rank, given because of the job I was doing, and I knew I would have to drop back to captain if and when I was posted away. The other disadvantage was that I had made some good friends at Porton and it would be a sad moment when I had to leave them.. One of these was a Polish major by the name of Weiss, a friend of the first order, whose wedding present to me, in the shape of a pair of silver napkin rings inscribed with good wishes in Polish, I still treasure. I learned a bitter lesson from him one day. A Russian general, with a staff officer, came to visit Porton and these two were in the officers' mess anteroom before going in to lunch. Weiss did not notice them when he came in and I asked him to join me in a drink, which he readily accepted. Suddenly he saw them and his whole demeanour changed instantly. He stood up and said that he could not stay in the same room as them. He walked out and that was the last we saw of him that day. I well knew how badly Poland had been treated by Stalin's Russia and when I thought about this later I fully understood his hatred, but, as he was such a sensible and well-balanced person, the depth of his loathing was an eye-opener to me.

In due course my application took effect and I was first sent on a company commanders' course at Ripon. I did not learn much from the course, but the other members on it were a good bunch and the experience they brought with them was interesting. One thing I did learn about was the use of radio in field formations and units. At Dunkirk, and afterwards in the time of the Battle of Britain, we had no way of communicating with a superior head-quarters other than by sending a dispatch rider or by telephone if we were lucky enough to have had one installed by the previous owner. However, by mid-1943 a big change was coming about and all companies were being issued with radios, not only to enable them to talk to their superiors, but also down to their platoons, as their subordinate sub-units were now called (instead of sections as I had always known them).

In June I was posted to 88 Company as second-in-command, dropping down to the rank of captain as I had expected. I was only to be with them for four months, during which we were kept busy, first in running some trials of new equipment that had recently been evolved in the fighting in North Africa, and which I was going to have to use in earnest in my next job, and, second, in adapting some buildings in the West End of London for use as a planning headquarters for the invasion of Europe. All I remember about this second task is that, in my initial inspection of the buildings, I visited the kitchens of what was to be their officers' mess. I have, thank goodness, never seen anything like it before or since. Every inch of the walls and ceilings were crawling with cockroaches, whilst squashed ones littered the floor. Cooks were working away preparing a meal and, when I asked them about the bugs, they explained that someone came and gassed them every so often, but that they soon returned. Some time later I found a cockroach in a glass of beer I had ordered in a well known hotel in London and it made me wonder just how many hotels in the great capital city had similar populations of bugs in their kitchens!

From the military point of view I found myself in the middle of a most tricky situation. From the moment I arrived I realized that morale was not good in the company. The Officer Commanding seemed to be away a great deal, but it was not up to me to question him, so I just carried on with my job and standing in for him whenever necessary. Soon after I arrived the Company Quartermaster Sergeant said he must talk to me in strict confidence. It turned out that the OC had a habit of taking pieces of company equipment and also food rations away with him when he went on leave and he never brought them back. On this last occasion he had taken a radio set, quite an expensive item and one for which the QM was responsible. It would have been unthinkable for any of my previous OCs to have behaved like this, so I had no experience to look back on. I did the only possible thing and asked for an interview with the Colonel. He listened carefully and then asked me just the questions I had asked our QM. Finally he told me to leave the matter with him. I do not remember what happened to this major. I do not even remember his name, which is probably a good thing. Anyway, he departed and I was left in charge. In many ways this made life easier, although it kept me busy, doing his job and mine.

Just as the paperwork to make me up to major again was completed I received another posting. I was to proceed at once to HQ 1st Assault Brigade, Royal Engineers, in Suffolk, as Intelligence Officer. To say that I was surprised at this unexpected development would be an understatement, but the moment I reported there the reason became clear. The commander of the Brigade was 'Ginger' Watkinson. My brief meeting with him on Exercise Bumper, already more than two years past, was paying another dividend.

I spent an interesting, and at times hectic, month visiting many different places and people for, and sometimes with, 'Ginger'. His Brigade contained three Regiments, each of four squadrons, and it had been specially formed to lead the forthcoming assault on Hitler's Europe. It would be responsible for clearing ways through the mass of obstacles that the Germans were erecting on the beaches in order that the rest of the army could move inland as quickly as possible and attack the enemy. The need for such a force became clear after the disastrous Dieppe raid in August

1942, when the tanks had been unable to leave the beaches and could take little part in the fighting. We must not be caught like that again.

After this month my whole life was changed once again when 'Ginger' called me in and told me that I was to leave at once and to take command of 26 Assault Squadron, a unit with which, almost half a century later, I still keep in contact.

26 Squadron, which Ginger sent me to command, was rather a different sort of unit to the others I had served in before, in that it had a hundred years of continuous history behind it, whilst the others had been started for the war. When I took over, I found in my desk a typewritten history of the unit which included a nice story from WW1. This recorded that King George V, on one of his visits to the trenches in France, had met two Sappers. They saluted him smartly and he said to them, ' I see you are from the Royal Engineers', to which they replied, 'No sir. We are from the 26.' He was delighted with this response and gave instructions that the unit should wear its number on its shoulders. It still did this when I joined; a unique privilege in wartime which was not shared by any other Sapper unit.

My predecessor in command had been promoted and sent out to command the Sappers in 82 (West African) Division, so I never met him until I went out to Burma in 1946. There we sometimes met for lunch and exchanged reminiscences about 'our' Squadron. His predecessor had, by all accounts, been a formidable character. His name was Cloutman and he was one of the very few Sappers to have been awarded the VC.

As I got to know them, the officers and men seemed to be in good heart as they strove to learn the ins and outs of tank warfare. We had been issued with some obsolete, and most unreliable, old Churchill tanks. The new AVRE, as the Assault Vehicle Royal Engineers was always called, would also be a Churchill tank and until these new ones were available, we had to make do with old ones. There were four Troops in the Squadron, each with six tanks, and we had two more tanks for Squadron Headquarters, making a total of twenty-six in all. As we had never used tanks before, we received twenty-six tank-drivers from the Royal Tank Regiment. My sergeant major was most doubtful about these men

42

when they arrived as, he said, this posting was too good an opportunity for the RTR to get rid of all their trouble makers. Certainly the one who arrived to drive my tank told me that he had spent time in prison, but I never enquired what for, and, when the chips were really down and we were under accurate enemy fire, his coolness and common sense made him worth his weight in gold. I would not have changed him for anyone.

Our training was directed at overcoming any obstacle designed to stop a tank. These included anti-tank ditches, minefields, concrete walls and soft ground, such as sand dunes. We made as many of these as we could and then, day after day, we tried to overcome them. Various gadgets had been developed to do this and I will not go into the technical details that would be required to describe them; just to explain one of them, I will describe what was known as a fascine. This was a large cylinder made up from rolls of chestnut paling. It was six to eight feet in diameter and, in length, slightly more that the width of one of our tanks. Mounted on the top of an AVRE, on a wooden cradle, it could be released to roll forward into a ditch, which the AVRE, followed by other tanks, could cross. This was all very well in theory, but in practice we found it took a great deal of experience before this could be done quickly and confidently. We made endless mistakes, but we were learning all the time.

In December 1943 we were ordered up to Fort George, just outside Inverness, where we met for the first time the naval landing craft that would take us at some future date to the Continent. Quite soon after we arrived there we were sent out on a major expedition in our naval flotilla half way to Norway and back. Presumably the object behind this was to make the Germans think we were planning to invade Norway, but the seas were too rough for comfort and when we were finally disembarked in a rather rocky cove just north of Elgin just about everything that could go wrong did.

After Christmas we moved back south again, this time to Barton-on-Sea on the Hampshire coast. Our flotilla took us out to sea again, to land at dawn on the beach at Studland Bay. A number of new problems arose and at least as many new mistakes were made, but we were still learning. Soon after that we embarked for our most successful trip to date. We were told to embark and carry out an assault landing on a narrow beach just below Osborne House on the Isle of Wight. The novelty of this occasion was that we were told to fire our main armament, the Petard, against the sea wall there, to see if we could knock it down and then drive our tanks up over the rubble and move inland against an imaginary enemy. I should explain that the Petard was a short (80 yard) range weapon which carried the formidable amount of 26 lbs of high explosive. A wall of anything greater than 5 feet in height is a complete obstacle to a tank and many such walls existed behind the beaches in France. So the idea was to explode some Petard shots against the wall to smash some part of it to rubble. Then, hopefully, tanks could mount what had been an obstacle and carry the battle farther inland, instead of being stuck on the beach, as they had been on the Dieppe raid. We knew all about this in theory and here at last was a chance to try it out in practice.

The exercise went well; we were landed at the correct place and we succeeded in making ramps which the tanks climbed up. The Petard was very inaccurate, so we had to fire more rounds that we expected, but by the time we left we felt a new confidence in the weapon.

A curious sequel to this training exercise happened several years later when I was serving in Burma. I received a huge bill, addressed to me personally, for the repair of the damage caused by the unit under my command to the sea wall at Osborne during the war. Some civil servant must have spent months in tracking me down. Anyway, I replied that I had been told to carry out this exercise and that I was just obeying orders and I heard nothing more about it. However, a few years after that I had a house on the Isle of Wight and I had a look at the wall, to find that it was just as we had left it, with gaping holes made by our Petards.

As winter turned into spring we trained hard, steadily learning to overcome the many and varied difficulties that faced us. For example, we found that soft sand dunes presented a problem, so Dickie Boase, who commanded 3 Troop, tried using a tank to push a steel pipe filled with explosive into a dune and then detonating it. The result was successful, so the Boase Bangalore became part of our equipment.

Sometime in April '44 I was summoned to the headquarters of

3rd Canadian Division and told that my squadron would be leading their 7th Brigade ashore astride the River Seulles in Normandy. This was very much Top Secret at that time and I was not able to tell even my officers. With various Canadian staff officers, I got down to the detailed planning, using good large-scale maps, aerial photographs and even some direct photos of the beaches taken from midget submarines. I worked out what looked to be the most practicable four routes off the beaches and what equipment we would require to open them up, bearing in mind the obstacles that would face each Troop. Finally, in early May the Canadians produced a huge long landing table, showing the exact order and time at which literally hundreds of assault and reserve units would land on our two beaches. The first unit on this list, landing at H Hour, was, of course, 26 Squadron. I was still the only person in 26 who knew exactly where we were due to land, but I did not know what the planned date was for the landing, nor the exact time we would land. These were still referred to as D Day and H Hour.

The pace quickened and I briefed my commanders, using exact maps on which all the French names had been replaced by British, American and Canadian substitutes, such as Newcastle, Pittsburgh and the St Lawrence River. At the same time our war fighting equipment was pouring in, including brand new tanks, jeeps, which we had never used before, and the masses of ammunition and explosives that we would need.

General Montgomery, one of the most successful British commanders during the War, had been pulled back from the Italian campaign to command the critical operation of launching a new front in Western Europe. In the British sector the initial landings were to be carried out under three Divisional head-quarters, the central one being 3rd Canadian Division. Each of these Divisions had to attack with two Brigades forward, and each of these six Brigades were given an Assault Engineer Squadron to lead them in and clear away whatever obstacles faced them. The two Squadrons nominated to lead the Canadians ashore were 26 and 80, so we worked more and more with 80 Squadron. Unfortunately for them, 80 Squadron developed a serious problem, as the commanders of the Assault Troops in the Squadron gradually lost confidence in their

Squadron Commander's ability to lead them in battle.

The commander of our Regiment, Lieutenant Colonel Denis Cocks' action was quick and decisive. He removed the Squadron Commander and replaced him with a Troop Commander from 77 Squadron named Wiltshire, always known as Wilts. By chance I had served with Wilts before and greatly liked his forthright and cheerful personality, but I fully realized what a monstrous task he had in front of him to lick 80 Squadron in shape in order that they could achieve the task that lay ahead of them so soon. He deserves nothing but the highest credit for the fact that he succeeded.

The arrival of Wilts made a difference for me also, as it meant that there was now someone whose company I enjoyed and with whom I could discuss anything. In May our two squadrons were moved to an open patch of ground in Gosport and all our training ceased. Our whole effort was now directed to waterproofing our new tanks and preparing them for an assault landing on the Continent. Waterproofing was a mammoth task as the tanks had not been designed to be driven into five feet or more of sea water and a great deal had to be done to enable them to do this.

There was one notable break in this intense effort. We were warned on 22 May that HM King George VI would inspect our regiment on 26 May. The Engineer in Chief and Hobo (Major General Sir Percy Hobart), our Divisional Commander, also visited us, but, of course, the King's visit was something special. We creased our trousers and polished our boots to a standard we had never attempted before. The whole Regiment was paraded on both sides of a road and, exactly on time, His Majesty appeared, flanked by Denis Cocks and our adjutant.

Across the road from us in Gosport were the 1st Hussars of Canada. They operated the Sherman tanks that would land with us and, staying safely in sea water, would provide us with essential covering fire. They were a good bunch and I found it very pleasant to drop in on them, particularly in the early evening, when they were most hospitable with their whisky. Towards the end, however, their Colonel, with considerable embarrassment, had to ask one of his officers whether he and I could possibly have a whisky. He later explained that he and his officers played poker every evening, there being little else to do, and that this officer showed a marvellous touch at poker, and had won every cent of money from every other officer. I was to see their regimental sign beside a field in Normandy only a few days later and called in on them, only to find that there was no officer there I knew. All had become casualties.

Finally the day came when we were told to load our tanks onto our landing craft. The yard where we did this was a bustling mass of men and vehicles doing the same thing. Our monstrous tanks, carrying fascines and assault bridges, edged smaller machines out of the way, and slowly met up with our craft. I was kept very busy supervising our movements and, as a result, missed a rare pleasure. It was not until late that evening when one of my officers asked me if I had spoken to Winston Churchill, as he had. I would have given a lot to have met that great man face to face, but I had not even known that he was there. Apparently he had walked among our men, smoking a big cigar and wishing them luck in the task ahead.

At last it was all finished and our landing craft pulled out into Southampton Water and anchored. Accommodation on board was cramped, but we were well experienced in coping with that, and the food was good. We spent rather a long time on board with very little to do, I think it was two days. We did not know about the storm warning that delayed General Eisenhower's final decision and almost forced him to call off the operation. Thank goodness he did not do so. It had been sufficiently exhausting preparing everything and then loading the ships; to have had to do it all over again would have been crippling. On board there was strict radio silence, for obvious reasons, so our ships – we filled ten – could not talk to each other. However, radio silence was routine at the start of any attack operation and I had insisted that each tank commander should be familiar with the semaphore code, so that messages could still be sent. This proved to be most worthwhile, particularly in Southampton Water, where small problems arose and could be sorted out.

Ultimately the order to sail was given and I remember feeling a strong sense of relief. We sailed in the afternoon, went round the Isle of Wight and headed for the open sea. Our convoy consisted of two lines of ships, my own being the leading one in the right-hand line and that of Dickie Boase the leader of the left-hand. In front of us was one Royal Navy frigate, presumably in case of attack by U boats, and behind us were countless landing ships of various sorts stretching to the horizon, and probably beyond. It was extremely rough and our ship, with its horribly top-heavy load of tanks, was heeling a good 30 degrees either side of the vertical, as well as pitching violently fore and aft. Luckily, I had been born a good sailor and had never been seasick, but standing with the skipper on the bridge, I could see that most of the others on board, sailors as well as soldiers, were not so lucky. Finally I went below to get some rest, but the close atmosphere of the cabin proved too much for me and I too succumbed. As this is the only time in my life, at any rate so far, that I have had to surrender to this unpleasant affliction I cannot complain, but I found it deeply disagreeable.

Having disposed of my lunch, I found there was a job for me to do. I had been guarding a sealed roll of maps that was on no account to be opened until we had set sail. There were some for each tank and they would be quite essential for carrying out operations once we landed. I had a young subaltern on board with me, by the name of David Pratt, and I had given him the task, once the time came, of splitting the roll into bundles, one for each of our tanks (I think we had five aboard). David had just been posted to us and was to prove to be a first class officer, but he was very young and the circumstances proved to be just too much for him. He was about 6 feet 5 inches and he lay sprawled across a bunk, out to the world. He had obviously been very sick and he was clearly quite unable to sort out the maps, which by then were all over the cabin, so I settled down to do this. The only difficulty arose once I had sorted them all into bundles and this was to find someone in each tank who had sufficient energy to accept the maps and stow them sensibly away.

When I had completed this, I tried to get some sleep, but this was not easy as it was necessary to hold on to the side of the bunk to avoid being flung about. Eventually I heard the sound of gunfire and realized it was time to move. I got up and shaved and woke David. The noise was becoming louder every minute. A sailor appeared with a cup of hot tea, which was most acceptable. I went up on to the bridge. The flotilla commander had been on the bridge all night and looked exhausted. He explained that we had had engine trouble and that he had been forced to order the

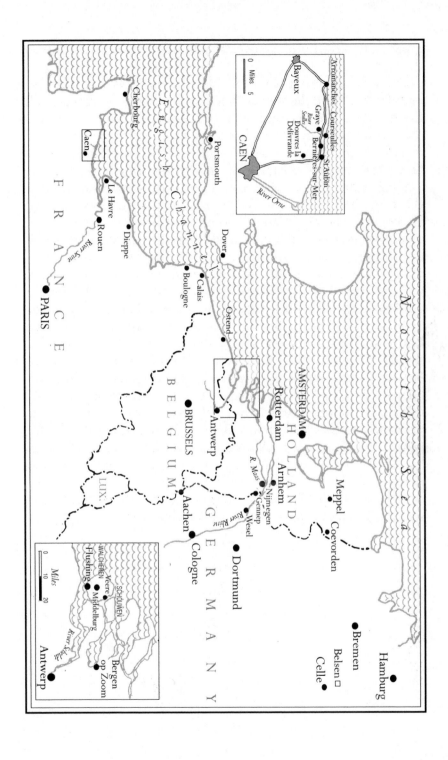

other craft in the flotilla to overtake us, until we were bringing up the rear.

The sight in front was formidable. The shore was still a couple of miles away and the sea was filled with countless naval craft, all firing ashore. We were just passing in front of a large cruiser and the crashing noise it made when it fired a salvo really hurt my ear drums. Farther out was a battleship and the sound made by its huge shells moving through the air was like an express train. A landing craft passed just in front of us and sailed parallel to the shore line firing salvo after salvo of heavy rockets. As we moved closer to the beach another landing craft beside us slowed to a stop, lowered its front ramp and allowed a DD (duplex drive) tank to drive into the sea. At once a wave hit the canvas screen that allowed the tank to float and in a moment it was gone, sunk without trace. I kept an eye on this ship and saw that the skipper sensibly decided that it was better to move in until he grounded.

As we closed to the beach, the time came for me to leave the bridge and move into my tank. I shook hands warmly with the flotilla commander and thanked him for all he had done for us. He was looking much more relaxed than he had been before and he wished me luck with a sincerity that I greatly appreciated. At this stage I suppose I should have felt that this was a momentous occasion and that history was about to be made, but in fact this never crossed my mind. All I wanted to do was to get on shore as quickly as possible so that the complex task we had to do, and that we had been training to do for so many months, should be completed as quickly and as efficiently as possible. I little knew what a difficult problem we would have in front of us.

That was a problem everyone faced: all the training and preparation was focused on getting the army ashore. Nobody had given much thought to the details of what to do after that

CHAPTER 7

H-HOUR ON D-DAY

As I went down to climb into my command AVRE I saw that a number of the crews of the tanks were just sitting around outside their tanks. The fact was that they were feeling so awful as a result of sea sickness that they could not raise enough energy to do anything. With an NCO I went round helping these men into their allotted tanks, hoping they would recover sufficiently to be operational when we touched down. In the event, the impact of the firepower of the German defences soon woke them up.

From the turret of my tank I could see literally hundreds of obstacles on the beach and in the shallow water. We had expected a lot, but not in this quantity, nor that so many of them would have large anti-tank mines wired on top of them, designed to tear open the hull of a landing craft. Some craft had already been damaged and were marooned on the beach, although they were still using their armament to good effect against the huge concrete pill-boxes among the sand dunes. Either by luck or good steering, we avoided trouble and came to rest high on the beach. The bow door splashed down and the first tank crawled gingerly forward into the shallow water.

The other craft of our flotilla had already touched down and I could see a large group of our distinctive tanks centred on the place in the sand dunes where I knew that 2 Troop's gap was due to be created. Some infantry were starting to come ashore and they were taking casualties as they struggled through the shallow water and ran across the beach to the shelter of the dunes. It was lucky that the beach was much narrower than we

51

had expected, presumably due to the strong north wind.

I was taking in the situation from the opening in the turret of my tank as we pulled out of the water when suddenly, to my complete astonishment, I found myself sitting on the floor of the tank. The wireless operator was looking down at me with his headphones on and I said to him, 'What the hell have you done?' At first I did not hear his reply, but when he repeated it more loudly it was, 'Sir, we've been hit.'

I realized then that I was very deaf. Although I could remember hearing nothing, we had indeed been hit, probably by a German mortar bomb. I had seen some bursting in the water and this one had landed a few inches from my head, but mercifully on the other side of the strong steel door of the escape hatch where I had been standing. The only damage done to the tank was the removal of the two wireless aerials, one for the squadron command net and the other the link to Brigade HQ.

I soon recovered enough to tell my driver, Corporal Sorensen, to move up closer to the sand dunes, and as he did this I was pleased to see a DD tank pouring fire into the embrasure of a huge concrete gun emplacement. From the cluster of immobile AVRE, it was clear that something had gone wrong at 2 Troop's exit, so, as I could no longer command anything from my tank, I jumped out of it and ran over to see what was happening. The first thing that was obvious was that 1 Troop, who should have been 300 yards further west making their own exit, were all mixed up with 2 Troop in the latter's exit. I found 1 Troop's commander in his tank and told him to extricate his Troop and tackle his proper task. However, even as I told him to do this, disaster was overtaking his leading tank, One Charlie. This AVRE, carrying a fascine, had led through the sand dunes and had found its way blocked by a huge crater, 65 feet across and full of water. With commendable determination, it edged its way forward, not knowing the depth of the water. As the centre of gravity of the tank crossed the edge of the crater, its nose went down and the whole tank started to slide in deeper. To avoid being drowned, the crew baled out and ran back for the shelter of the sand dunes. Three were killed outright by enemy fire and the remaining three were severely wounded. One of the survivors, Sergeant Ashton, the tank commander, was blinded and suffered multiple wounds. To the great sorrow of the Squadron, he died before the day was out.

I had a Troop of 22nd Dragoons under my command on this beach and two of their flail tanks had also penetrated the sand dunes. Both had come to a halt, one with its flail boom seized up in a great tangle of barbed wire, and the other, having mounted 2 Troop's assault bridge to cross the dunes, had gone up on a mine and lost a track as it tried to make a new route round the crater. This last tank contained the Troop commander, Lieutenant Barraclough, who, although immobilized, lost no time in co-ordinating the fire of the main armament of his tanks against the defences. This was invaluable, as he controlled the only fire power we had south of the dunes. However, at what should have been the main exit from the beach everything was at a standstill.

The first thing I did was to find the Squadron commander of the 1st Hussars and the company commander of the Canadian infantry and persuade them to get as much firepower as possible to the top of the dunes to give cover to our men working south of the dunes. To cut a long story short, we ordered up another AVRE to push One Charlie deep into the crater and then launched an assault bridge so that the far end rested on its turret, which was just showing above the water level. One Charlie's fascine was then cut loose and dropped beyond the bridge, and another fascine was dropped beyond that. Driving with the greatest care, an AVRE succeeded in getting over this makeshift crossing. As many men as possible from 26 then went over to the far side to collect rubble from a demolished house nearby to improve the crossing. A line of infantry then went over and we called forward some of 1 Hussars to have a go. Unfortunately, the driver of their second tank lost his nerve and toppled his vehicle over the side of the bridge. I had stationed the AVRE on the far side with a winch ready just in case this happened and it succeeded in dragging him over, but it wasted a lot of time.

All the while work continued to improve the crossing, later much helped by a willing farmer, with his horse and cart, who had somehow survived the bombardment. The water in the crater was held there by some sluice gates and Jimmy Hendry, the 2 Troop commander, succeeded in opening these gates, thereby lowering the level of water in the crater. In doing this he had to pass the back entrance of one of the large concrete pill-boxes, from which a couple of dozen highly demoralized enemy soldiers emerged and surrendered.

My right ear had become increasingly painful by this time, so I went back to the beach where I felt sure a medical dressing station must have been set up. I soon found one and a business-like naval doctor filled my ear with sulphanilamide powder, telling me that I should be evacuated and that the powder must not be touched for at least a week. This piece of first aid undoubtedly saved me from the possibility of infection.

1 Troop had still not completed their route off the beach, partly due to enemy fire but also because all the flail tanks had been immobilized. Flails had been used in North Africa and we had been warned that the Germans had developed a new mine fuse to defeat them. This fuse would accept a blow from the flailing chain and only detonate the mine after a second pressure coming from the track itself. Clearly there were a number of such fuses in the large minefield that faced us. The only course left for 1 Troop was the slow one of hand-clearance of mines. 2 Troop were outnumbered at their huge crater by the men of 85 Field Company, from the Beach Group, and work there was proceeding steadily, although inevitably rather slowly, due to the difficulty of the site. It was probably just after midday and I felt that the main crisis on this beach had passed. A steady procession of Canadian units were crossing the bridge and moving southwards, and it seemed that the time had come for me to try to visit my other half squadron on the east side of the River Seulles.

I walked into Courseulles but found that there was no way over the river there. A swing bridge existed and this had been swung into the open position, but looked otherwise intact. However, as I looked closer to see if it had been prepared for demolition, and found that it had, a shot rang out and hit the bridge close to me. I jumped into the doorway of a house and was joined there by a Frenchman and a Canadian soldier, who had heard the noise. The Frenchman knew exactly where the shot had come from. He directed the Canadian as the latter fired about five shots from his rifle rapidly into a window down the street. We had no more trouble, so I went out and cut the electric leads to the explosive charges and then crawled under

54

the bridge and pulled the explosives off and dropped them into the water below. With the Frenchman lending a hand, we turned a large wheel and slowly swung the bridge round until it spanned the river. I then crossed the bridge and made my way through the badly damaged and apparently deserted town towards the shore. I saw someone dart behind a house, only to find that it was Dickie Boase, bound on the same errand as myself, to make contact. His report was excellent, all had gone as planned. Both he, commanding 3 Troop, and Ray Mare, commanding 4 Troop, had laid their assault bridges against the esplanade wall and tanks, vehicles and men were now streaming inland across them.

To complete the story of One Charlie, next day, when things had calmed down a bit, 85 Company dragged our assault bridge off the turret and built a much more respectable Bailey Bridge across the gap. This was named Pont AVRE and it happened that King George VI, General Eisenhower, Field Marshal Montgomery and General de Gaulle all crossed over it when they first landed in Normandy. In due course a civilian bridge replaced the Bailey, but One Charlie remained under this, undisturbed for thirty-two years until 26 Armoured Engineer Squadron, direct descendants of the original builders, decided to extricate it as an exercise. After a lot of hard work this was successfully accomplished in 1976 and One Charlie now stands as a memorial to all those who fell on the beach, men of the 7th Canadian Brigade, of the Beach Group, of the Royal Navy and of the Royal Engineers themselves. For those of us who crossed over to Normandy to witness the tank being extracted from the mud in which it had lain for so many years, it was a particular delight to see the only two survivors of the original crew there, Bill Hawkins and Bill Dunn. Both had been badly wounded, but they had survived and their cheerfulness, in spite of all their artificial limbs, was a tonic to us all.

However, the really outstanding factor that emerged from the whole exercise that was launched to extricate One Charlie was the hospitality shown to all the British visitors by their French hosts. I should explain that on the east side of the River Seulles, where 3 and 4 Troops had successfully made their beach exits, lay the town of Courseulles. This is a medium-sized coastal resort, with hotels, shops and seaside villas. On the western side of the river is the small, unspoilt village of Graye-sur-Mer, and it was this little village that looked after us all. There is no hotel in the village, so the local people provided food and lodging for us all. The mayor, who had been a nine-year-old boy on D Day, but who remembered it well, and his wife were towers of strength and endlessly watched over the needs of their mass of guests. Later they invited me to unveil a plaque in the main square in the centre of the village, renaming it 'Place des Royal Engineers'. The mayor made a welcoming speech and the only thing I could think of to mark the day for him was to take off the Sapper tie I was wearing, luckily a new one, and present it to him.

But to return to 1944, reconnaissance revealed a reasonable field in the southern outskirts of Courseulles where we could give ourselves all-round defence in case of a counter-attack. By early evening we were all tired, but we set up our defences against any surprises and tank crews started to prepare a much-needed meal. However, there was one more task I had to do, which was to visit 7 Canadian Brigade HQ and obtain the release of 26 Squadron from under their command.

I had always realized I would have to do this and, as we had left all our jeeps and trucks in England, I had arranged for a motorcycle to be put on the back of one of the reserve tanks. This proved to be undamaged, so I had it unloaded and set off to find the HQ. I was not a very proficient motorcycle driver, but there was no traffic at all on the road so I was able to follow the signs without trouble. I had gone two or three miles and was passing through a wood when I saw ahead of me a man standing in front of a cottage and waving a bottle at me. The meaning was quite clear, and if there was one thing I could really use at that moment it was a good drink. I pulled up beside him on the left of the road and he produced two glasses, which he filled to the brim. I shook him firmly by the hand and wished him well in my best French, and his happiness was obvious. We raised our glasses, clinked them together and I took a good pull at the contents of mine. I realized that this was strong stuff and my new friend explained that it was Calvados, which, at that stage in my life I had not heard of. He explained that he had kept this bottle, which was from an old vintage, specially hidden away and not to be opened until the day of liberation. After my first surprise at its strength, I found that it slipped down the throat very nicely. When I had finished it, I explained that I must move on and we parted the best of friends. Only a couple of hundred yards beyond my new friend's house was a sharp bend in the road to the right. I was going round this bend, luckily slowly, when, going in the opposite direction, came the first vehicle I had encountered, a Canadian despatch rider on a motorcycle, going fast. He was, correctly, on the right of the road, whilse I had not yet adjusted to being on the Continent and was driving on the left. We hit and both sailed through the air, landing in the ditch which was full of water. Our two motorcycles were crumpled write-offs and I realized that the fault was entirely mine. Luckily, neither of us was hurt in any way and, fortuitously, the entrance to Brigade HQ was just in front of us. Sopping wet, I explained to the Brigade Major what had happened and that the other driver had been in no way at fault. Mercifully, he laughed and told me he would look after the despatch rider and would fix a Jeep to run me back.

I reported to the Brigade commander, Brigadier Forster, who was in very good heart, as his men had moved well inland, obtained his agreement to our release from his command, and was driven back to Courseulles as promised in a Canadian Jeep, moving on the right of the road. A meal was waiting for me and, after I had checked our sentries, I lay down to a dreamless sleep. D Day was finished.

CHAPTER 8

HOME AND THEN BACK TO WAR

We stood to before dawn on 7 June and I realized what a poor place I had chosen for defence. We were overlooked by houses, which would also restrict our ability to manoeuvre if we came under attack. I therefore studied the map and then drove out early in the morning to find a better place.

Several areas of woodland looked promising and, quite soon, I was lucky enough to find one that seemed almost ideal. It was about three acres of woodland, which would give us cover from the air, and running through the middle was a sunken road containing several concrete shelters. On further inspection, I found some hundreds of large rockets in a field nearby, aimed exactly at the beach on which we had landed. Electric wires leading from one of the shelters to these rockets had been cut by a bomb, which was just as well for us, as, if they had burst on our beach, none of us could have survived. The warhead of each rocket contained about thirty pounds of explosive. One rocket was different to all the others and, from the German markings on the outside, it looked to me as though it contained a gas. I reported this, but never had any confirmation, so I may have been mistaken.

I returned to the squadron and we all moved out and settled in to our new location. Later I drove along the coast road to Bernières-sur-Mer to make contact with our sister unit, 80 Squadron, and to check that all was well with them. There was quite a lot of shooting going on when I entered the village and a Canadian officer warned me to avoid the area near the church, as there were still some Germans there who were giving trouble. I soon found 80 Squadron, near the beach, with Wilts very much in charge. He had done splendidly in the early landings and had established four routes off the beach, which were in constant use. I left him with a considerable feeling of confidence, generated by his cheerfulness and his obvious control of the situation.

On the way back I made a diversion to have a look at the German radar station in a defended location near Douvres la Delivrande. This had been by-passed by our advancing units and the Canadian brigade commander had told me that it would have to be attacked soon and that he would call upon us to assist. A marine commando was keeping an eye on it and I met their commanding officer. His plans for attacking the place were in an early stage and merely involved a frontal assault from the north. However, on going right round the area, which was quite large, it was clear that all the main defences, particularly the anti-tank guns, were sited in concrete emplacements facing north. It would be much more difficult for the defence to repel an attack from the south.

I passed this thought on to Dickie Boase and, later, to Frank Simpson, the second-in-command of our Regiment, who had now taken over command as the outstanding Denis Cocks had been killed. Frank had landed behind Wilts' squadron, but had not been involved in any of the fighting yet, although his intelligence officer had been killed trying to open up a German bar mine for him. This was a large anti-tank mine that we had not seen before and it contained a built-in booby trap to prevent opening once it had been armed.

Shortly after, as my ear was still painful and my hearing was bad, I went back to our landing beach to try to find the doctor who had first treated me. There was a medical unit established there and I was shown in to a different doctor, who surprised me by becoming quite cross. He told me that it was quite wrong that I should still be in the beachhead, that I should have been sent back to a hospital on D Day and that I must leave at once.

I returned to the Squadron, told Dickie Boase to act as

59

commander and told Frank Simpson what had happened. I then went back to the beach, passing yet again over our sunken AVRE, where I was ordered on to a landing craft full of casualties. We were all disembarked at Gosport and driven to a naval hospital just outside Portsmouth.

Only one incident remains in my mind concerning my time in hospital and this occurred on the morning after our arrival. A very senior naval doctor came slowly down the ward inspecting each patient. When he reached my bed, he told his attendant nurse to clean out my bad ear so that he could look down it. I immediately told him what the doctor on the beach had told me, namely that it must not be touched for at least a week. An angry look crossed the doctor's face. 'Who do you think you are talking to?' he said. I replied that I was only repeating what I had been told. He turned away abruptly and left me.

I believe that this incident was merciful for me. In the bed next to mine was a naval officer, who, like me, had a ruptured ear drum. The great doctor ordered his ear to be cleaned out, and then peered into it. This naval casualty had appeared to me to be having much less trouble with his ears than I was, but I was to leave the hospital ten days later, by which time the discharge from one of his ears badly stained his pillow each morning. Whether the sulphanilamide powder in my ear was permitted to heal me, whilse his ear became infected after the doctor had peered into it, I shall never know. It certainly looked as though this was the case.

After leaving the hospital I was sent to a convalescent home at Harewood House, near Leeds. This was the home of the crusty old Earl of Harewood and his most charming wife, the Princess Royal. She spent much of her time with us patients and she could not have been more friendly and considerate. I spent another fortnight there. I received some long letters from Dickie Boase telling me how they were getting on. One of these described the final attack on the radar station at Douvres, in which 26 Squadron played a major role. I was glad to read that they had put in the main attack from the south. Ray Mare, commanding 3 Troop, received a very well earned Military Cross for the part he played in this. Unfortunately my tank was one of the casualties. It was hit by an anti-tank round which caused some of the explosive inside to catch fire. The crew just had a few seconds to get out before the whole lot detonated, and they succeeded in doing this, except for Lance Corporal Catling, the co-driver. There was a terrific explosion and the tank was blown to bits. This was a bitter blow to me, as Catling was a fine young man, with much potential. I wrote to his parents to express my sorrow, always a difficult task.

When I was allowed to leave Harewood House I reported to Brigadier Ginger Watkinson, whose headquarters had moved to Eastbourne. He had sent his Brigade Major, Chris Waters, to command 26 Squadron. Casualties had forced him to reduce our squadrons from four Troops each to three and he wanted me to run a training squadron to provide reinforcements in case of further losses. A supporting regiment for the Brigade was being set up in the grounds of Parham House, near Storrington. This was the historic and beautiful home of the Pearson family, who welcomed us with a delightful, open hospitality. I was left very much to myself to organize this training and it proved to be a busy but rewarding period.

I continued at Parham, training mostly in a valley on the edge of the South Downs where it was safe to fire live ammunition, until the end of October. Then I heard from Ginger that his new Brigade Major had been killed and that he was recalling Chris Waters to his headquarters and he wanted me to return to 26.

This was like returning home for me and I flew out to Brussels in a Dakota aircraft to rejoin 26 in a place called Terneuzen on the south bank of the Scheldt estuary. Bob Butterworth, my second in command, was there and greeted me warmly. It was very good to see him again. The operational Troops of the Squadron had just landed on the island of Walcheren, a few miles to the north. They had been completely re-equipped and the heavy Churchill AVRE replaced by the much lighter amphibious LVT or Landing Vehicle, Tracked, known by the code name Buffalo.

I had been away for about five busy months and, of course, the Squadron had taken casualties during that time. Among the officers, Dickie Boase had been killed and Jimmy Hewitt replaced. Their successors were Pat Lythe and Jimmy Lees, both of whom quickly proved their worth. It was great to see the others again,

61

all in very good heart, with Ray Mare now wearing his well-earned MC. It was apparent that Chris Waters had been an admirable commander.

The operational Troops returned back across the Scheldt a couple of days later, cold and wet, but having completed a most successful operation. The Buffalos of the other three squadrons in 5 Assault Regiment also returned and the first memorable event at Terneuzen was a party given by Ken Fergusson, who commanded 77 Squadron. After the attack on Walcheren some of his men had found an abandoned naval landing craft with a cargo of rum. Alcohol is usually in short supply in war, but this was one of the rare occasions when there was no shortage, and everyone was in a mood to relax. Among those present was Wilts, who had led his squadron straight into the heavily defended harbour of Flushing and whose determination and leadership had been a major factor in the fall of this vital port. He had also done very well in Normandy and I felt certain he would now receive an award, which he richly deserved, but, alas, he never did, a clear indication of the inherent shortcomings of the honours system.

From Terneuzen we moved to Bergen-op-Zoom, a long and bitterly cold trip to make in LVTs in mid-winter. We spent Christmas there and then moved back to Middelburg, the capital of Walcheren. The town was entirely surrounded by flood water and this meant that our LVTs were completely in their element, able to move across dry land, mud or water or any combination of these, whilst all other transport had to stick to a few roads. In a sense Walcheren was still in the front line against the Germans, as they occupied the island of Schouwen, just to the north. German patrols would cross over to Walcheren to inflict whatever damage they could. Our job was to patrol the northern shores of the island to guard against such incursions, and we took marine commandos, who were stationed nearby, on these trips. I sent Jimmy Lees, who now commanded 1 Troop, out on the first patrol and went along with him, both to see what the problems were and to see how able Jimmy was to deal with them. The winter of 1944/45 was particularly cold and conditions were really arctic when we set off. We went up to the deserted and flooded village of Veere and then to the northern tip of the island. After some alarms, but no actual sight of our enemy, we returned to Middelburg and I had seen enough of Jimmy to feel confident in him for the rest of the war.

One night there was a heavy storm with gale-force winds. This resulted in a dyke on the edge of Middelburg being breached and about a third of the town was swamped with sea water. Soon after first light next morning, I sent some of the Buffalos out to see if we could help in rescuing families cut off by the flood. I went out with the first Troop in order to see what the problem was. It was a really pathetic sight. Depending on the height of the ground on which they had been built, houses had between four and about twelve feet of water in them. In the first case, we could see through the ground floor windows chairs and tables floating in the rooms, and the families were at their upstairs windows, waiting to be rescued. In the second case, the families had climbed into their attics and pushed a hole through the tiles of their roof so that they could clamber out when we reached them.

The Dutch authorities opened up schools and churches for these people, and we spent a busy day ferrying these wretched families, often with no personal possessions at all, since the flood had hit them so quickly. Next morning the Mayor came round to thank us for all we had done, which was nice of him. Our lads certainly did well, but we could hardly have done less.

Early in 1945 we moved back to Bergen-op-Zoom, on the Dutch mainland, to rest and sort ourselves out. Casualties had caused each Regiment in our Brigade to disband one squadron. In our case the junior squadron, 80, had to go. This meant that we had to say good-bye to Wilts, who had consistently done so well but needless to say, the three remaining squadrons were all pleased that they had not been selected to go. Another change was necessitated because our regimental commander fell down a steep bank and broke his leg. Ken Fergusson was told to take on the job on a temporary basis, but when a new commander was posted in to his Squadron, 77, we all hoped that his promotion would become permanent.

In the middle of all this reorganization, our Divisional Commander, General Hobart, announced that he would come and inspect us. He visited my Squadron first and asked to be taken down to the tank park. He went round, continuously asking penetrating questions about the men and their machines. Ken joined us, but took little part in the inspection, as most of the questions were fired at me. He seemed to be in a good humour when his party left to inspect the next unit, 77 Squadron. However, things went wrong there. He fired questions at the new Squadron Commander, who had not yet found his feet enough to give complete answers.

Hobo became more and more aggressive and Ken Fergusson, who was not a man to be cowed by senior rank, stepped in to support the young Squadron Commander. The end result of this engagement was that Hobo said he had seen enough of both Ken and the new Squadron commander, and he ordered them both to leave his Division within 48 hours.

On previous visits there is no doubt that Hobo had done well, indeed very well, in sacking commanders who were not up to the job. On this occasion, however, he made a mistake. Ken was a brave and competent commander, with whom we were all very happy to serve. It was a bitter blow when he was suddenly removed from us. If Ken had been a lesser man prepared to see Hobo demolish the new commander of his Squadron, he would have stayed with us, but this was not in his character, so we lost a really fine commander.

Quite soon after this sad loss, and the equally sad loss of Wilts, our Squadron was ordered to move to the east to the southern outskirts of Nijmegen. Bitter fighting was going on in the Reichswald, some miles to the south of us, as our troops attempted to clear the ground up to the River Rhine. The Rhine flood plain, to the immediate south and east of us, was flooded to the depth of several feet. It had been cleared of the enemy, but they were in strength on the far bank and could send fighting patrols over to our side. In addition, they had good observation over our side and could bring down heavy and accurate artillery fire on any sign of movement by us. Our infantry defence posts along the river bank had to be relieved or reinforced when in trouble by Buffalos swimming through the floods. Most of this work had to be done at night, but the Buffalo's ability to move through all depths of water stood it in good stead.

Sometime in early March we were told to hand in our Buffalos and we were re-equipped with Churchill AVRE tanks. Clearly our high command was looking ahead to leaving the flooded Rhineland, crossing the great river and fighting battles further east. Although we were well pleased with our ability to handle our Buffalos, we accepted this change without comment, realizing its inevitability if this war was ever going to be brought to an end.

CHAPTER 9

CROSSING THE RHINE

It must have been on or about Thursday, 15 March 1945 that our new Commanding Officer, Lieutenant Colonel Ernest Hall, told me that he was putting me in command of 77 Assault Squadron for the Rhine crossing operation that was to take place in three or four weeks' time. He said that I would still retain responsibility for 26 Assault Squadron, my normal command, but that, as the officer commanding 77 Squadron was in England and would not be back in time, I was to take charge of them for the battle. 26 Squadron had a reserve role in the Crossing, one that my second-in-command, Bob Butterworth, could well handle in my absence. 77 Squadron was still equipped with LVTs and by then I had had plenty of experience with Buffalos.

Having tied up loose ends in 26, I left next day and in the evening reached 77, who were located, if my memory is correct, in the village of Gennep on the banks of the River Maas. I was met by the second-in-command, Bill Carruthers. I knew Bill quite well from odd meetings over the previous year. He was a cheerful, likeable character, who had won a good MC in Normandy, but his opening remark as I arrived was worrying. 'Thank God you've come,' he said, 'this is all getting too much for us.' Bill's outstanding quality was his complete honesty. If he found that he had a problem, he would never attempt to cover it up. He would bring it out into the open, ask for advice or for whatever help he felt he needed. When I arrived, he was still doing all the administrative tasks of the Squadron second-in-command, a full-time job in itself, and in addition was trying to command the Squadron in the run up to a major operation.

The moment I arrived there I arranged for a night exercise for the Squadron involving a simulated assault across the Maas. Disappointingly, the exercise was a failure. Everything went wrong. Buffalos turned up in the wrong order, got tangled up with each other, missed the designated exits from the river or just got lost. It was after 2 am before the dispirited troops returned to our camp. So we did it again next night and the night after, introducing all kinds of route marking measures to make our moves, which of course were without lights and in radio silence, as fool-proof as possible.

After the third night, feeling a bit tired but more confident, I was summoned to the headquarters of 1st Special Services Brigade. Here I met for the first time the man who was to be my commander for the coming operation, a slight, dapper ex-Guardsman who commanded two Army and two Marine Commandos. He gave out his orders for the crossing, and it was a surprise to hear that the planned date was 23 March, much earlier than I had been expecting. In outline, the plan was for 77 to carry the Commandos over as quickly as possible, starting at 2200 hours after an artillery bombardment of the far bank. The artillery would lift to targets farther inland when the first wave of Buffalos were safely in the water, and I agreed to signal this moment by passing back the codeword 'Splash' over the Brigade radio net. After landing, the Commandos would move as quickly as possible through the German defences, wheel to the east and attack the town of Wesel from the rear to form a bridgehead there. 77 Squadron would lie low after the crossing and next morning would move upstream to a point opposite this bridgehead to ferry over the rest of the Brigade. 17 (US) and 6 (BR) Airborne Divisions would drop that morning on the high ground further inland and we would also ferry over their non-airportable elements. After the orders, I contacted the CO of the leading Commando to arrange details of the numbers we would take over in each wave and where we should meet up. I should explain that 77 had four Troops, each with six Buffalos, plus two Buffalos in Squadron HQ. There were two types of Buffalo, the Mark II and the Mark IV, the difference being that the Mark IV had a ramp at the rear which could be lowered to take on board a jeep or a small piece of artillery. Each would hold about twenty men for an attack or thirty for follow-up trips. I decided to cross my command craft on the right flank of the leading Troop, the Troop commander going on the left flank.

Later that day I reconnoitred a small village, Ginderich, which we had been allocated as our assembly area and ordered the Squadron to move up there.

It all seemed fairly straightforward. We would wait till dark and then move up to the Forming Up Position (FUP) just behind the main bund on the south bank of the Rhine, load up there, cross the bund, cross the flat flood plain beyond it and then into the river to make our best time to the enemy shore, unload and come back for more. However, nobody had been over the bund to see what the flood plain was really like. The Germans had registered the top of the bund very accurately with machine guns and mortars, and a number of casualties had been sustained by our infantry when they attempted to look over the top. I arranged for an infantry patrol to escort me that night down to the water's edge to ensure that no hazards awaited us over there.

I carried out a preliminary reconnaissance up to the bund with our officers and the HQ sergeant, who would be responsible for marking the route from the assembly area to the FUP, where the Commandos would meet us. Since we had to do this in daylight and would be under observation from some high buildings on the German side, we dressed ourselves up as a relief party of infantry, carrying rifles and packs, with me as the corporal in charge. We looked a pretty motley crew in our ill-fitting uniforms as we slouched up to the front line and the Germans left us alone. The CO of the forward battalion was not so lucky when he chose to visit his positions at that time. The Germans mortared each section as he approached it, causing casualties to each. He was lucky not to be hit himself. He soon abandoned his tour of inspection, to the great relief of the remaining platoons.

We completed our trip and the HQ sergeant finished up with a neat sketch of the exact route we had decided on, which he was to mark most clearly with torches screened from enemy view when we moved out for the actual operation.

That night I did my recce in front of the bund with a fighting patrol led by a young officer of the Seaforth Highlanders. It was just as well I did this as, having rolled quickly over the top of the bund without incident, we found a deep rivulet about five yards across on the far side, and with impossibly steep banks. This would have caused nothing less than a disaster to our plan, so we recced a new route to avoid it. We took this new route right down to the water's edge. The patrol rested about twenty yards from the water, whilst I went to the bank and watched that enormous river gliding past in the eerie silence that can occur on a battlefield. For many months the Rhine had seemed to be an objective infinitely far away and now here it was at my feet. I am not prone to making dramatic gestures, but suddenly I felt an urge to pee into it; I thought it would be fun to tell the boys back at the Squadron that I had done this. When I started, it seemed to make an awful noise, but I could not believe it could be heard on the far bank. Suddenly a German machine gun opened up, its bullets passing quite close to us. I flung myself down and edged my way back to the rest of the patrol, whilst our machine guns opened up in reply, followed by mortars from both sides and then artillery. We all lay there, glued to the ground, for what seemed ages, but was probably only a few minutes. Gradually it all quietened down and, when it did, we did not waste any time in returning to the safety of our own lines. I did not mention this incident when I got back to 77.

Next morning I went to Brigade to obtain agreement to the change to where we would enter the river, resulting from the knowledge gained from the night patrol. This done, I became involved in a rather heated discussion with the staff on whether or not explosive charges should be used to blow gaps in the bund for our Buffalos to pass through. I had looked at the bund carefully. It was about fifteen feet high, with slopes of 45 degrees on each side. It was a formidable looking obstacle for any vehicle to cross, but I knew that a loaded LVT could manage it as long as the driver knew what he was about, and our drivers were very experienced by then. I also knew how accurate the German artillery fire was, and the last thing I wanted was that our exact crossing places should be advertised by gaps blown in the bund. So I refused to agree to the idea, in spite of the fact that the staff said that all the Buffalo Regiments further downstream were insisting that it should be done.

One other piece of experience had come out of the previous night's patrol, the possibility of sound being heard over calm water. I therefore asked that an aircraft should patrol over the enemy lines during the period of our approach march to the river. This was agreed, and I am eternally grateful to the pilot, whoever he was, who could be heard all through that tense time, passing up and down the enemy lines. I am certain he saved us endless trouble.

The Brigadier summoned all his commanders and gave out his final orders for the assault, incorporating the new crossing place. At the end he asked for any questions and, on receiving none, turned to me in front of all the others and said, 'I hope you realize that the entire success of this operation depends on you.' I was a little taken aback and wondered if I had somehow given the impression that I was a bit casual, which I felt to be unfair, as I was, in fact, being stretched to the limit. I replied, 'I'll get you over there if it's the last thing I do,' which was a pretty meaningless response, but all I could think of. Looking back now, I think that perhaps this Brigadier was a rather unfeeling character. We were to deliver him and his men across the great obstacle that lay in front of us, on time and as promised, but when it was all finished he never even said thank you to me.

Back at the Squadron, I, in my turn, gave out final orders. I included in these a special job for the Sergeant Major. He was to take under his wing all those not in LVTs, cooks, drivers, storemen, etc, march them up to an area just south of the bund and dig there slit trenches for all the LVT crews to rest in. I also arranged for two bulldozers from 84 Company, Royal Engineers, to report to him up there to scoop out pits so that the Buffalos themselves would have some protection against shellfire.

I do not remember much about the day before the attack. It would have been a period of intense activity making the hundred and one final preparations. Some time in the later afternoon we received the single codeword that confirmed that the operation would go on as planned that night.

Night of 23/24 March

There was a final glimmer of light in the sky as I took my Buffalo out of Ginderich at the head of the rest of the Squadron and followed the track marked by the HQ Sergeant across the fields towards the river. By the time we reached the vicinity of Perrich, behind the bund, we could hear the friendly drone of our aircraft flying above the far bank. Thanks to him, I feel sure, we were not shot at.

We had about half an hour to spend in the FUP near Perrich. During this time the leading Commando arrived and sorted itself into LVT loads. We did not have to be particularly quiet as the artillery barrage opened up. We could use no lights, but this was no problem as searchlights were reflecting light from clouds overhead. We had mugs of hot tea with a shot of rum in for those that wanted it. I certainly did. Time passes dreadfully slowly when waiting to start an attack, so, more to pass the time than anything else, I set out to have a last chat with the other crews who would be in the first wave.

I was doing just this when the Troop commander came up to tell me that 'Hobo' had arrived and was talking to some of his men. My heart sank because Major General Sir Percy Hobart, our Divisional Commander, was a very strong personality, who could reduce strong men to tears with his persistent, probing questions. I saw his black beret in the middle of a group of our men. I walked over quickly, determined to persuade him to leave, even if this involved a stand-up confrontation with him. I could not afford to have men going into enemy fire with their morale at rock bottom after 'Hobo' had given them the rough edge of his tongue. I need not have worried. He knew far too much about war to do what I had feared. As I approached there was a burst of laughter from the group. He saw me and beckoned me over. 'Have you had your rum, Tony?' he asked. 'Yes, General, I have,' I replied. 'Good lad,' he said, and, turning to a Sapper, who he had discovered had refused his rum ration, said, 'Your commander has had his, and I can tell you that the only thing that got me over the top in the last war was a good shot of rum!'

In high good humour, he moved down the line of LVTs, transmitting his enthusiasm to all those he met. When I finally had to leave him as H Hour approached, he shook my hand warmly, wishing us well and saying how pleased he was with all he had seen. I thanked him for coming with real sincerity.

Back in the Buffalo, now filled with Commandos, I held up my hand to give the pre-arranged signal to move. The second hand of my watch took an age in crawling to the exact time of 9.57 pm, but finally it did so. I brought my hand down smartly, and we were off.

A quick check showed that the other six Buffalos had all moved off with us and slowly we all climbed the steep bank of the bund, teetered a bit on the top, then dropped down the other side. Bursting artillery shells lit up the far bank.

In no time we had crossed the couple of hundred yards of grass leading down to the river, then in we went, turning up-stream at once to counter the current. I opened up my radio and sent the agreed code-word 'Splash' back to Brigade. There was no acknowledgement of my signal, only some hideous interference. I repeated my message, 'Splash; I say again, Splash. Over.' Still no acknowledgement. Only after that did I realize that we were being deliberately jammed, something I had heard about but never experienced in operations. With a heavy heart I faced up to the probability that we would run into our own barrage, which was now making a spectacular mess of the far bank.

Another difficulty occurred. A new infra-red vision apparatus, which looked like a pair of heavy binoculars, had been mounted on my LVT. The Corporal was peering through this instrument and giving instructions to the driver through the intercom. He kept saying, 'Driver, right; driver, right,' and consequently we steered more and more upstream, till we were not moving towards the far bank at all. I realized that something was wrong, switched my own microphone to intercom and overrode the corporal's orders. I guided the driver to the far bank, still bubbling with shellfire.

The Commandos were all crouching low in the craft. Their officer was near my feet and I doubt if he realized what dramas were going on. It only took us about four minutes to cross the water and soon we nudged into the far bank. The Corporal and I jumped up onto the roof of the driving compartment to help the commandos up. The noise of bursting shells was unbelievable, but mercifully the barrage suddenly lifted a bit farther inland and I felt a welcomed relaxation of tension. One after the other the commandos clambered up and jumped down onto dry land. We backed away and the other LVTs could be seen doing the same. Two did not move; one was on fire and the other had been abandoned.

Luckily we had an excellent young gunner captain in the forward observation post (OP) in a farmhouse near the bund. He had been waiting to hear the codeword 'Splash' over the radio to tell his guns to lift. When he did not hear it, he realized that something was wrong and, quite soon, he ordered the guns to fire further inland on his own initiative, thus undoubtedly saving us and the leading Commando from many casualties. His name was Denis O'Flaherty. The fact that the barrage continued for so long on the forward defences at least meant that the Germans kept their heads down and did not meet us with the murderous machine-gun fire, which we knew they possessed.

Back on the home bank, with the three other waves of LVTs still crossing, I left the Corporal in charge of my command Buffalo to continue ferrying Commandos across. I moved to my scout car to control the rest of the operation from its radio. Crossing the FUP area, I saw that Bill Carruthers was well in charge. He had organized the Commandos into groups of thirty, and these were lying down to avoid the shellfire that was starting to come in and waiting for him to tell them to double into each Buffalo as it became available. I was kept busy by a host of messages coming over the radio net, but where there were problems they were not insurmountable. One good thing was that the second LVT from the first wave, that had not returned, had now came back safely. I thought it to be abandoned, but its crew had been attending to some wounded from the one that was on fire.

46 Royal Marine Commando had crossed first, and they were followed by 6 Commando and then 45 Commando and lastly 3 Commando. Apart from those in the Buffalo hit by our own fire in the first wave, there were no other casualties. There was a spectacular bombing raid on Wesel whilst our crossings were taking place. The whole area was lit up by bursting bombs and by the fires they caused. Some unpleasantly large waves came rushing down the river, but these caused us no serious difficulty.

Finally, the last group was safely delivered and I told the commanders to take their Buffalos to the pits that had now been dug for them. I closed down the radio net and set out for a check round the Troops to see if there were any final problems and to congratulate them on a magnificent performance. As luck would have it, a shell burst uncomfortably close as I started off and I rapidly decided to postpone any congratulations till the morning and made a quick dash to the farmhouse in the centre of our area, where I knew a hot cup of tea awaited me. In the cellar there, I settled onto a large pile of potatoes to try and get some rest in what was left of the night. Incidentally, I do not recommend potatoes as a comfortable bed. They are like sleeping on a heap of cannon balls.

By dawn the shelling ceased. Our men emerged from their trenches looking tired and dirty, but it was clear that morale was high. There was only one casualty from the shelling overnight, one unfortunate man received a splinter in his behind while out of his trench answering a call of nature. Our sentries on the bund started to receive some attention from German machine guns, but we silenced these with LVT Bofors guns. After a quick breakfast, I drove off to reconnoitre a fresh crossing site opposite the town of Wesel, which, hopefully, was in the hands of the Commandos by then. The area we had agreed on was next to the huge demolished railway bridge. This was at the end of a salient pointing into enemy lines, which had been impossible even for night patrols to visit before the attack started. We had arranged for 84 Field Company to check the area for mines and when I reached it they were already on the job and told me that no mines had been found. On this trip I had a grandstand view of 17 (US) and 6 (BR) Airborne Divisions dropping on the hills a mile or so further east. It was a spectacular sight, although German anti-aircraft fire looked persistent, but I heard later that casualties had been comparatively light.

Down at the bridge, I could see a concrete ramp on the far bank which looked to be just what we wanted for Buffalos. This site suited Brigade HQ, so I ordered the Squadron up and soon after midday sent two Buffalos over to test the route. They came under fire and the Troop commander's craft was badly holed and started to sink. It just succeeded in reaching the ramp, where it had to be abandoned, half in and half out of the water, but effectively blocking the ramp. We succeeded in silencing the enemy machine gun and had no more trouble from it.

A new exit was found only just downstream from the ramp, and for the rest of the day we ferried over all manner of groups who arrived at our assembly area. First came 1 Cheshire Battalion, who were attached to the Commando Brigade, then quite a number of airborne troops, who had been dropped on the wrong side of the river, and groups such as Sapper mine-clearing parties, Gunner OPs and medical units. A total of 207 loads were taken safely over, while some wounded and about 400 German prisoners-of-war were brought back.

By the end of the day I felt that my task of seeing 77 Squadron through the assault crossing was done, and I knew that 26 Squadron would be on the move. The last incident of this memorable period for me occurred that evening. Back at Ginderich I found an invitation from 'Hobo' to have dinner with him at his advanced HQ that evening. After a shave and a rudimentary bath I went to obey this royal command, to find that the great man was as good a host as he had proved to be an operational commander on the banks of the River Rhine.

CHAPTER 10

OVER THE RHINE

Back with 26 Squadron, we were ordered to go north into what had been German – occupied Holland throughout the winter months. After their defeat on the Rhine, the main German defences were protecting the Ruhr industrial centre, while their forces further north were more thinly spread. They abandoned Holland, in an understandable effort to concentrate the maximum effort in defending their homeland. When we entered northern Holland there were still quite a large number of enemy units making their way eastwards, and these were experienced troops who were quite capable of defending themselves when we caught up with them. However, when we found a village that was being held, our forces would outflank it on both sides and then put in an attack from the best direction. Often the Germans would pull out during the night, before they were completely surrounded.

We moved further north every day, spending nights in fields and woods. It was a busy time and I do not remember our exact route. One memory does stand out, however, and I think this occurred at an attractive border town called Coevorden. We were the leading troops and we approached the town along a wide thoroughfare lined with trees on both sides. Jimmy Lees happened to be commanding the leading Troop, I followed him, with Jimmy Hendry just behind me, and Pat Lythe and Ray Mare spread out after him. Jimmy L. kept me informed of his progress over the squadron radio net. When we entered the outskirts, moving slowly and very much on the alert, I saw him stop. He reported that he thought he could see the gun of a large tank pointed towards him. I could see nothing, but then I was a couple of hundred yards behind him and my view was obscured by his tanks. He said he would have to open fire. As he said this, I saw an orange flag come out of an upstairs window of one of the houses which lined the road. I ordered him to hold his fire and moved my tank up to join him. The last thing we wanted to do was to start smashing up houses, particularly as Coevorden looked comparatively undamaged.

Events overtook us quickly. Even as I approached Jimmy's leading tank, more flags came out of other windows. I never did see what it was that he had suspected to be an enemy tank as people started to pour out of the houses and we were literally swamped. Girls clambered onto our tanks and kissed the soldiers and we were completely engulfed by cheering, laughing people.

There were not many men in the crowd, but one oldish man spoke quite good English and I asked him if there were any Germans in the town. He said that there had been plenty there the previous day, but that they had moved out that morning. He could not say for certain, but he doubted if any had remained. With more than a little difficulty I managed to get the squadron on the move once more and, thankfully, we found no enemy. We spent a couple of nights in Coevorden, being received everywhere with the greatest friendliness.

A more sobering incident occurred shortly after. We moved into a wood for the night outside a small village just on the Dutch-German border and still in Holland. We were settling in when one of our sergeants came up to me, I believe it was Sergeant Trimble, to say there was something nearby that I ought to go and see. He took me to a lovely moated castle on the outskirts of the village. It looked like an undamaged and unspoilt relic from the past. However, inside was a different picture. The owners, an oldish woman and her daughter, were providing accommodation for about a couple of hundred, maybe more, very sick and weak men. They were packed tightly across the floor of every room and they looked desperately ill. The owner explained that these were Dutchmen taken from their homes by the Germans to work in factories and at building defences. Many were shopkeepers, doctors and others quite unused to hard manual work, which they had been forced to do until they literally dropped. They were then sent home, without food or transport. They had made a great effort to reach the border, where they had collapsed. Many had died *en route* and the survivors were pitifully emaciated and obviously near to death themselves. Their wonderfully kindly hostess had taken them in, but the problem was obviously too much for her to cope with. She said that several died each day.

There was a desperate shortage of food and Sergeant Trimble said that the men in his Troop had volunteered to go without food and to give their rations to the suffering Dutch. Returning to the Squadron, I called the officers and sergeants together, with the end result that we all decided to give up our rations for the next day. Our quartermaster took all the food down to the castle where it was very gratefully received. As luck would have it, we found in the wood we had selected a dump of German Army rations, abandoned by their retreating troops. We loaded all this into trucks and took it to the castle, where again it was received with deep gratitude.

I had not had direct experience of the results of Hitler's rule over neighbouring countries before, but I shall never forget the skeletal appearance of these pathetic men. When I entered a room some would smile and attempt to sit up, usually dropping back after making the effort, but most just lay there without movement. I began to realize something of what they had been through.

Passing into Germany after this traumatic experience, we halted just north of Meppen. In the woods nearby we found what had obviously been an experimental establishment for armoured vehicles. There were a couple of enormous tanks, with equally enormous guns, and the devastating results of firing these guns at sheets of armour plate were all too obvious. General Hobart, always interested in the development of armoured vehicles, visited us next day and spent the morning making a critical inspection of everything there.

Pressing on eastwards, we supported various divisions, including for a time the Polish armoured division. The atmosphere there was efficient to a degree, even ruthless, as they worked out how to gain their next objective. Some divisions were becoming loth to put in attacks against German positions. They realized that the war was, at long last, coming to an end and they were reluctant, at this late stage, to risk the death of any of their men.

The Poles had no such inhibitions. If the objective they had been ordered to take turned out to be firmly held, they would arrange a fierce artillery bombardment and then attack with great vigour, accepting casualties. The cause of their determination was very understandable.

If there had been any strong defensive fortifications, perhaps with anti-tank ditches and other tank obstacles, round the towns and villages of the North German Plain, our special skills would have been in great demand, but, perhaps luckily for us, the Germans had not had time to build anything substantial, so we were not called on – and stayed in support of the leading troops. We spent our days on the move and our nights mostly in woods and, as the climate was getting warmer, it was a busy, but not too stressful, time. The country, of course, was new to us and often interesting. For example, we passed through the town of Celle one evening and then camped out in the extensive woodland to the south of the town. Before this, most of the towns and villages we had passed through had suffered considerable damage, so it was a delightful change to see this lovely medieval town, which appeared to be untouched by war.

It must have been during the morning of the day we reached Celle, that I happened to pass through the village of Belsen. At the time the name meant nothing to any of us. At a road junction in the village I met the commander of one of our cavalry regiments, travelling, as I was, in an open armoured scout car. I drew up beside him to exchange any useful information and he asked me if I had visited the large camp nearby. I had not heard of this and said that I had not. He said, 'I'm afraid it's a dreadful place, but you really ought to visit it.' He told me where it was and, as I had a bit of time in hand, I drove there. We came to a high wire fence, with barbed wire at the top, and then a large gate, which was open. I told my driver to go in and, as we approached some wooden huts, quite a large number of people, probably about sixty, came out and surrounded the scout car. They were all dressed in what looked to me like pyjamas, presumably the only clothing they possessed, and they were so thin as to be almost walking skeletons. There were some men, but most were women and children, and obviously they were all in the last stages of starvation. One of them said to me, 'Cigarette, cigarette,' and

79

several of them took up this cry. I smoked in those days and took out several packets to hand round; I felt this was the least I could do. They pleaded with me and I dished out my entire stock. My main feeling, which was perhaps a bit selfish, was that I must not spend much time among them as they were clearly diseased and might be infectious. My driver gave me some cigarettes of his and, when I had handed out the last of these, I told him to press on through the crowd. We drove further into the camp and I told him to turn left behind a large hut, with the idea of making a circuit and getting out of this sickening place. However, even worse was to come, as our circuit took us beside a huge pit filled with hundreds of naked corpses. I have heard it said that soldiers in wartime become casual about seeing dead bodies and about suffering. In my experience nothing could be further from the truth. Certainly I think I felt then, and still do feel, more deeply about this hideous place than most of my contemporaries, all of whom must have read about it.

My life has contained one or two most strange, and therefore most memorable, coincidences, and this quite unplanned visit to the Belsen concentration camp was to be the cause of one of these. More than thirty years later, in September 1976, I was invited to Toulouse in southern France to watch an exercise conducted by the French airborne forces. After the exercise a large dinner was arranged for the many spectators and at this I found myself placed between two French generals. One surprised me by insisting that we had met before, although, when we discussed our two Army careers, we had never been anywhere near each other. Suddenly he said, 'I know. You visited Belsen.' I admitted that I had done so and he then said, 'Yes, I remember you. You handed out cigarettes.' I was astounded by this, after all the time that had elapsed, but he also accurately described the vehicle I had been in. He went on to say that he had been aged 13 at the time and that he had been put in the camp with his mother. I supposed that their liberation had been such a traumatic experience, that I, who happened to be one of the first to visit the camp, was indelibly etched on his memory. His name was General d'Astorg and he explained that he was now commanding in Paris, I believe at their main Staff College, the Ecole Superieur de Guerre.

After this amazing revelation, I asked him a question, which I told him had been worrying me for years. 'Why,' I asked, 'did you not ask for food?'

'You just don't understand, do you?'

'No, I don't.'

'Food: we just could not care less about food. But a cigarette; that would be heaven.'

I realized the fundamental truth of this remark, and my admiration for the sheer stamina of this man was intense, remembering what the inmates had all looked like in 1945. I could only guess at what he had been through, but I knew it was something tougher than that of anyone else I had ever met.

A recently read remark that the holocaust never really happened obliges me to mention another death camp that I have visited, Auschwitz, in southern Poland, where three million people were killed. The gas chamber still exists there, as does the hundred-odd acre field containing scores of brick-built ovens for cremating the dead.

With their usual efficiency, the Germans initially kept accurate records of those who were disposed of there, mostly Jews but also a large number of Poles. However, towards the end, the SS guards merely ordered prisoners off each train as it arrived, made them strip naked and walk straight into the gas chamber. Their bodies were then taken directly to the cremating ovens, whilst their clothing and their few possessions were searched for hidden money and valuables. For some reason all pairs of spectacles were kept and there is one room in the camp almost completely filled with tens of thousands of pairs, a truly pathetic sight.

There were many other camps dotted all over Germany and Poland, most with special branch lines connected to the main railway system. Obviously this was a massive programme, planned at the top and requiring a large and expensive organization to run it.

To complete the story of Belsen in 1945, a couple of weeks later, when I was attached to Divisional Headquarters for a week for staff experience, I became involved in a suggestion that we should send some flame-throwing tanks to burn the place down. What had happened was that our divisional doctors had taken over the handling of the medical problems there and they felt that the huts that the inmates had slept in must be so impregnated with germs

81

that the only safe course was to burn them down. From what I had seen, I could not agree more. General Hobart gave his agreement and the next day the flame-throwers moved in and the awful place was burned to the ground.

After Celle we were ordered north, and as the month of May started we approached Hamburg from the west. I was becoming a bit tense, as the date for my wife to produce our second child was very close and our mail was taking several days to catch up with us. However, there was nothing I could do about this, so I just tried to appear normal and get on with the jobs we were given. On 4 May, which happened to be my birthday, we were told to halt where we were. Soon a signal arrived, which had been copied to all units in our army, an enormous distribution list, saying than an armistice had been signed and that all shooting must cease.

We were in a village about a dozen miles west of Hamburg and I was told to settle down there and that I, personally, would have administrative responsibility for the civilian population. Regretfully, I have forgotten the name of this village. On the evening of our first day there, Bob Butterworth, the second-in-command, told me that two youths had passed him in the street and that one of them had spat at him deliberately. I summoned the Burgomeister and told him that such behaviour was unacceptable and that if it ever occurred again I would carry out training exercises in the village. To rub home the point, I explained that our tanks were very large and cumbersome and that damage to property would be inevitable, as some of his streets were very narrow. He seemed to take my point immediately. He appeared to be a reasonable man and I told him that my intention was to help him with any problems he might have, but not if his people behaved rudely towards us.

From then on we had no difficulties and, in fact, were able to help each other significantly. He sent round some eggs and ready-plucked chickens, welcomed additions to our dull tinned rations, and he also arranged for a piano to be put in the men's dining room. For our part, we cleared many tons of rubble from his streets and put transport at his disposal for urgent requirements.

It was a considerable relief to be able to sleep under a roof once more. Since crossing the Rhine, we had slept in the open, except for our luxurious couple of nights in newly liberated Coevorden.

We each had a bedding roll, which, in my case, consisted of a canvas valise that I had bought after Dunkirk, where I had lost everything. This valise held a sleeping bag, made of blanket material, and an extra blanket for warmth. I had a lightweight, metal-framed camp bed, and the whole lot, when firmly strapped up with the bed in the middle of the valise, did not take up too much room when we were on the move.

I had a batman, who became very skilled at pitching a low canvas bivouac and setting up my bedding in it, often in complete darkness. It was not particularly comfortable, but luckily the weather was not too cold or too wet, so, after the usual busy day, I slept well, provided no alarm occurred in the night. Every third or fourth night I would force myself to get up during the small hours to check on our sentries, as our safety depended on them entirely. It is good to remember that I never once found one asleep at his post, in spite of the very long hours we spent working or on the move.

But now, with the fighting and movement at an end, we occupied, with the agreement of the Burgomeister, empty houses and school buildings. We even indulged in the pleasure of a hot bath.

A deep feeling of relaxation pervaded us all. We had sing-songs in the evenings and Bob organized a couple of quiz evenings, when the men could question me, Bob and the sergeant-major about anything. These turned out to be most rewarding and I certainly learned a lot about the main worries our men had.

On a visit to our Brigade Headquarters a couple of days later, the Intelligence Officer, an old friend, said, as I was leaving, 'Oh, by the way; many congratulations.' I asked what he was talking about, and he said it was my new daughter. He had noticed the announcement in *The Times*, whilst no newspapers had reached us for several days. My cup was full.

CHAPTER 11

THE STAFF COLLEGE

Some time in July or early August 1945 I received a posting order to attend the next course at the Staff College in Camberley. The army in Germany was running down in size at a rapid rate, with units being disbanded or amalgamated. We had been told that 26 Squadron would remain as the only Assault Engineer unit, and so we were kept well up to strength with men from other Squadrons. We were still at war with Japan, but we did not anticipate being involved with that, as our skills were not designed for jungle warfare.

I was only given a few days warning to leave 26 and, although my successor, Peter Pellereau, was nominated, he had not arrived before I had to go. I therefore left the Squadron in the able hands of Bob Butterworth, who had been my second-in-command throughout the whole period of almost two years during which I had been connected with 26.

It was sad to leave so many firm friends and I was forced to dash round to say goodbye to everyone. My orders were to report to the School of Military Engineering at Ripon for a two week pre-Staff College course, so I packed up my few belongings and caught a boat back to England and took the train to Ripon.

The short course at Ripon was very worthwhile. There were about twenty students on it, all due to go to the Staff College. I had met most of them before, but some not since before the war, so it was most interesting to hear something of their experiences. In addition, I was able to learn much about areas of the Corps in which I had not served, a good and necessary preparation for the Staff College.

Then, after meeting my sparkling little three-month-daughter for the first time, we did some hectic house hunting in Camberley. Accommodation was hard to find anywhere in England then, due to bomb damage and lack of building in wartime, but finally we found some digs and I moved my little family to Camberley. This was the first time we had lived together and it meant a new life, and a most rewarding one, for us all.

The method of instruction at the Staff College, the syndicate system, was one I had not experienced before. Each syndicate contained about a dozen students, drawn from all parts of the Army, plus a sailor or airman and a member from the Commonwealth or the United States. Syndicates were changed three times during the six-month course, but during each of these spells of six weeks or so one got to know the other members well. A wealth of practical experience was grouped in each syndicate, culled from active service all over the world. We would be issued with a list of questions each evening, often with some reading to be done. We all prepared our answers and brought them to the meeting next morning. The leader, a member of the Directing Staff, a bit older than most of us and who had completed the course a few years before, would pick one of us to answer the first question. Other students would then be invited to discuss or criticize the answer given; many interesting points would emerge, and I found my knowledge of the Army, which had previously been narrowly confined to commanding a small unit in an Armoured Division, broadening rapidly. The other members of our syndicate all had war experience and many wore a gallantry medal, some had two medals and a few had three.

On the day I left Germany, the first atomic bomb had been dropped on the Japanese mainland and this was followed quickly by the news that they had surrendered. The development of this awesome weapon had been a closely guarded secret and so it came as a surprise to us. Indeed most of us had fought the war in Europe and North Africa and fully expected that we would have to join the forces that were fighting Japan when our staff course finished. Suddenly all this was changed. As I remember, we did not discuss these developments among ourselves very much, although we read the reports that appeared in the newspapers fully. The

Commandant of the College, a thoughtful and highly experienced soldier, did make a statement about the new bomb, concluding that it was just another weapon and that it would not alter our military arrangements. The syllabus of our course had been written well before, and was already very full, so we had no syndicate discussion on this new factor, but I could not help feeling that the Commandant was wrong. Here was something that was not like, say, a new and better gun. It was something that was many orders of magnitude more dangerous than anything that had previously been invented or used and I felt that it must have a profound impact on warfare. In saying this I do not wish to imply that I was cleverer, or more far-sighted, than my contemporaries. I am sure that many had exactly my feelings but, perhaps because of the Commandant's remarks, we kept our thoughts to ourselves.

As a side issue, some ten years later the British Army carried out atom bomb explosions at Maralinga in Australia, so that as many officers as possible could witness exactly what happened when one was set off. I was desperately disappointed when my boss said he could not spare me to attend one of these trials. I still felt that this was such an important development that I simply must observe it. Looking back now, I am very pleased that I did not go, as three great friends did and all three died of cancer some twenty years later.

Looking back on the course now, about half a century later, I can remember that I greatly enjoyed it, but I cannot remember much of the detail that I learned. One exception to this is the lecture we received from Arthur Bryant on the writing of English. In my ignorance, I had not heard of him before he came and spoke to us, but I enjoyed his lecture so much that I started to read his books immediately after it, and I now must possess a copy of just about every book he ever wrote. His use of the English language was nothing less that superb.

Also, he had a lovely sense of humour. 'Do try to stop your soldiers,' he said, 'from using that meaningless four-letter word beginning with F. Or at least try to decrease their use of it.' He told how he had heard a soldier in the First World War say, 'The f***ing f***er's f***ed!' He had turned on the man and berated him for making such a puerile and meaningless remark and then, to drive home his point, he had asked the man whether he had been explaining that the colonel's horse was lame or was it that the liner *Titanic* had sunk? The man had sheepishly replied, 'I meant my rifle. It's jammed.'

He went on to say that he had hardly ever heard the word used correctly, although once he had come across a man up a ladder who was hammering something into a wall. Suddenly, he let out a cry of pain and dropped his hammer. His mate on the ground, who was holding the bottom of the ladder, shouted up to him, 'Did you hit your f***ing finger?' 'No,' came the reply, 'but I sure hit the one next to it!'

Arthur Bryant was a man with such a brilliant intellect that he was unforgettable.

One sad occasion at the Staff College occurred when I met an RAF Wing Commander. He had known Hugh Davis (see Chapter 3) well and served with him in North Africa and Italy. I knew that Hugh was dead as his letters had stopped in 1944. He had joined the RAF in 1942 and I last saw him on the night before my wedding, when my best man, Tony Hewitt, had organized a small bachelor party for me in London. Hugh arrived and was in very good form, having passed all his training tests and been posted to Egypt. We exchanged letters continuously and his were full of interest, one of them describing how he had been forced to land behind the enemy lines and been captured, but had managed to escape that night and get back to his squadron.

The Wing Commander told me that Hugh's flight of Spitfires flew into a thick cloud behind the German lines in Italy. When they came out into sunshine Hugh was not with them, but they saw his plane diving towards the ground at great speed. Seconds later it hit. No one knew what had caused this.

It is all too obvious that those of us who were in the fighting age bracket would lose friends during a major war, but the sadness of each incident is deep and lasting. Most of my best friends went, including Tony Hewitt, who I have just mentioned, but the sense of loss that I felt each time has not left me. I still remember them as they were.

The Camberley course lasted for six months and in the new year of 1946 we all received our next postings. We had been invited to give our preferences for where we should be sent, but these made no discernible impact on the Military Secretary, who was responsible for our futures. One highly experienced and amusing Gunner, Peter Hilton, put down 'Anywhere except GHQ India.' His posting was to GHQ India.

In company with some forty others, I was ordered to India and told that I would hear what my new job would be when I arrived there. Therefore, in March 1946 we all assembled in Liverpool to board a troopship for Bombay.

With such an uncertain future, none of us could bring our families out with us. My wife teamed up with another wife from our course, Betty Willison, who also had two tiny children, and together they rented a house in Camberley. Betty's husband, David, was on the same troopship as me. Betty proved to be a delightful companion and a firm friendship was built up between our two wives that was to last for 40 years, until Betty's untimely death.

The three-week voyage in the troopship SS *Britannic* to Bombay was a pleasant holiday. The food was far better than the normal military fare that we had been used to in Britain, where rationing was still severe. Duty-free drink was cheap and plentiful and, above all, we had no responsibilities. We stopped at Port Said, where we dropped off a good number of passengers. We were not allowed ashore there, which was a disappointment, but the one disadvantage of the voyage so far, gross overcrowding, was noticeably lessened.

Our next call was Aden, where we were allowed ashore. Glen Kelway-Bamber, of the Argyll and Sutherland Highlanders, who had become a firm friend, and I hired a taxi and drove round the town, finishing up at the Officers' Club where we had an excellent lunch. On our way back to the harbour, our driver, a talkative Somali, drove us past the Jewish Ghetto, which had a most impressive facade with a heavy gate in a central archway, behind which could be seen elaborate and well-built housing. It was a walled city within the main town and a hive of activity.

Our life on board was dominated only by mealtimes, when we all met. Otherwise we were left to ourselves to read and play games. We played poker dice before lunch, the loser buying a round of drinks for the others, and bridge in the evenings. I had not often played bridge before, but I found that my mathematical background made it all come rather easily to me. The stakes were low, a penny for a hundred, but each evening I made enough to cover occasional losses at poker dice and to pay for other drinks.

My father had spent much of his life in India and had a habit of including Urdu words in many of the everyday remarks he made. As a result of this, to my great surprise, I found I could understand most of what servants and taxi drivers said when we finally arrived at Bombay on 12 May.

We spent a couple of very hot nights on board before being taken to Kalyan Transit Camp, which was an hour and a half by train north of the town. Here we were given our posting orders; mine was to proceed to Rangoon and report to GHQ Burma. Three others had similar orders and one of these was Glen. Most of the rest were destined for the main Far East headquarters at Singapore.

Glen and I had a week based on Kalyan, during which we travelled into the centre of Bombay on most days and spent our time in the Yacht Club, a very clean and very British place. Bombay was different from anything we had experienced before, with street after street filled with sleeping people at night and terrible poverty everywhere. We were swindled in many different ways whenever we bought anything outside the Yacht Club, but we learned quickly and, anyway, our needs were few.

A military Transit Camp is never a particularly interesting place. Most of the residents are just passing through and do not know each other, so there is none of the camaraderie that builds up in ordinary units. Kalyan was typical in this respect, with characterless wooden huts filled with a mixture of British and Indian army officers waiting to return to England.

Our group from the Staff College was an exception, since we knew each other well by then. Perhaps this made those who were waiting to go home a bit jealous of us. I spoke to several of them to try to find out something about Burma, as I was due to go there, but none of them had been there: all had been involved in administration in India. They seemed unfriendly and were most unlike the battle-hardened members of the Indian Army that I was to work with in Burma.

Of course they knew India well, having served there for years, but they tended to be unhelpful and ready to laugh at us when we, ignorant newcomers, asked for information or advice.

However, after one such encounter, Glen told me one day that one of them had asked him if he had visited a club at some address in Bombay, which was totally new to us. This man had recommended it as the best club in town, so that evening we decided to visit it. Our taxi driver knew all about it and delivered us there. We walked in and asked the doorman where the bar was, but we were shown into a room where a middle-aged woman was sitting. She smiled in a friendly way and asked if we wanted a drink, so we ordered a couple of Scotches. I began to suspect there was something odd about the 'club' we had been sent to, and my suspicions were confirmed when the door opened and a particularly tall white girl came in. She sat down next to me and said, 'You nice tall man; me tall girl and me like tall men. Me White Russian, you understand?' I said that I did understand, after which she said, 'Me free now. You come to bed with me!'

It was only then that the penny finally dropped and we realized that we were in a brothel. To the obvious disappointment of the White Russian girl, we finished our drinks and left.

After a week, those of us due for Burma were moved to another Transit Camp in the middle of Bombay called Calabar. Conditions were pretty primitive there, so again we spent our time in the Yacht Club and in the Taj Mahal Hotel. We were only there for five days and then embarked on another Troopship, the *Ormonde*, which was making the trip to Rangoon to repatriate West African troops who had fought in the Burma campaign.

The trip took a week and, at last, on 1 June, we sailed up the Rangoon River to the capital of Burma. The ship was practically empty, so the four of us sat at the Captain's table for our meals. We got to know him quite well. He had, needless to say, visited many ports in many countries and had a host of interesting anecdotes about his trips. One remark he made was that we must be careful when we reached Rangoon as nobody had ever fallen into the river there and survived. When we sailed up it, we could see that it was a mass of whirlpools from the enormous volume of water that came down it and that it seemed to be literally alive with sea snakes, which we were told were very poisonous.

CHAPTER 12

BURMA

After disembarkation I was told that I was to fill one of the posts of Deputy Assistant Adjutant General (DAAG) in Headquarters Burma Command. This HQ was established in the university buildings on the northern edge of the town. Glen was posted as DAAG, South Burma Area, on the other side of Rangoon, but, since quite a number of problems affected us both, it was a considerable help for me to have a friendly and helpful contact there.

I took my job over from Major Roger Wassner, who rather depressed me by saying that he was particularly pleased to be leaving as the work load was killing him. When I took over there was a good pile of files waiting to be dealt with in his 'In' tray, but he also opened up a large crate behind his desk, containing at least a hundred more files, explaining that these were all part of his 'In' tray.

The telephone rang incessantly and a stream of visitors called. However, I was keen to tackle the problems, and arrived at the office every day at 7 am, an hour before work normally started, and stayed on till 6.30 pm, an hour and a half after the close of the rest of the HQ, taking a minimal lunch break in between. This went on from Monday through Saturday and also on Sunday mornings, so I just had Sunday afternoons off.

With this regime, I gradually reduced the heap of problems down to a more manageable load, but the pressure of work was intense. One happy event occurred in my first fortnight out there when I was told to escort a Brigadier Buchanan-Dunlop from Singapore round the Army units in Burma. He proved to be a pleasantly relaxed travelling companion and we took a jeep and a pile of maps and spent ten days visiting Meiktila, Mandalay, Maymyo, Kalaw and other centres. Burma was most interesting and, of course, quite different to anywhere I had previously visited. It was huge, about 1200 miles from north to south, and a good 500 miles across the middle. Its history had been of a series of invasions from China. Each time, the invaders would attack the inhabitants of the fertile Irrawaddy Plain and take this over for themselves, driving their predecessors into the barren hills on either side. The British, of course, came by sea and left the previous owners of the Plain alone. However, when we met them, the hill people seemed invariably friendly and helpful, much more so than those on the Plain. There were several hill tribes, Shans, Karens, Chins, Kachins, etc, and all had hard lives striving to survive in the hills and forests. They were cheerful people, who looked you straight in the eye with a friendly smile. Kipling expressed this well with:

"I've a neater, sweeter maiden in a cleaner, greener land,
"On the road to Mandalay . . . "

Two factors made my daily grind of work tolerable. One was the general atmosphere in the Headquarters. Our commander-in-chief, Lieutenant General Sir Harold Briggs, was a seasoned and professional Indian Army veteran of war and its problems. He set an example of quiet efficiency which permeated throughout the staff. Coupled with this, the more junior members, which included five others from our Camberley course, who had all been through the War, still felt the wartime urge to shoulder responsibility and to act quickly.

The other factor was that a particularly happy atmosphere existed in the various officers' messes. This meant that each evening one really could relax and rebuild one's energy for the next day.

I was given a room in the Gunner officers' mess, which was in one of the outbuildings of Rangoon University, in which we worked. I was allocated a batman, who was a Gurkha called Sherafudin. This was my first introduction to those wonderful people from the high Himalayas. He was absolutely trustworthy and nothing was too much trouble for him. However, it was his friendliness and loyalty that really endeared him to me. He was to stay with me until I left Burma almost two years later and I only wish he had been able to read or write, as I would have liked to keep in touch with him.

In the officers' mess the only entertainment we enjoyed was that which we provided ourselves. There was no television or radio in front of which we could relax, but this was no new experience for us. Sometimes we sang songs, and it gradually emerged that each had their own favourite. Mine was 'There is a tavern in the town'.

There were still some 35,000 Japanese troops held in prisoner-of-war camps in the Rangoon area and I had responsibility for some aspects of their administration. The senior Japanese general came to see me once a week to explain, through an interpreter, his difficulties. One of these was that the Indian Army rations that were issued to the camps did not contain the kind of food they were used to. They could, and did of course, eat them, but many of the extras they would have liked were available in the civilian market. However, they had no currency with which to buy these; could anything be done?

I pondered on this for a week and thought it would do no harm if they could find some soldiers who were sufficiently artistic to produce paintings that could then be sold for rupees. The General said he liked the idea and it might well provide an answer. Only about three weeks later he invited me down to the camp to see an art exhibition where items would be for sale. Many were of Mount Fujiyama or of geisha, which was only to be expected, but there was some very competent work on view and I still have a couple of attractive landscapes I bought that day. An appreciable sum of money was raised. The Japanese were being repatriated as quickly as possible, and the day soon came when the last of them had left Burma.

The whole of this part of the world – India, Pakistan, Burma, and later Malaya and Vietnam – was stirring politically. Rangoon had been recaptured from the Japanese on 3 May 1945 and the last fighting in Burma was on 4 August 1945. By mid-September 70,000 Japanese troops had surrendered. The Twelfth Army was re-designated Burma Command on 1 January 1946 and contained just over 200,000 men from Britain, India and West Africa, plus a few from the United States. So there were about a quarter of a million men who needed to be repatriated to various parts of the world and this was being carried out at the rate of several thousand each month, as shipping was made available. There were literally hundreds of units involved, some large and some containing only a handful of men. We tried to send those who had been away from their homes the longest first, subject always to the need to keep a balance of administrative units in every remaining station to feed, provide medical care and transport for all who remained.

Burma had first been occupied by British troops in 1852 and now, nearly a century later, freedom was in the air. A leader emerged, Aung San, who negotiated with Admiral Mountbatten and later, in October and November 1945, with the new civil administration formed by the Governor, Sir Reginald Dorman-Smith.

Soon after I arrived there were riots, mostly in the Rangoon area. These were probably sparked off by the troubles at that time in India, where, for instance, 4,000 were killed and 16,000 injured in Calcutta in August 1946. We were warned that an attempt would be made to take over the University buildings where we lived and worked. I was told to prepare one sector of our area for defence and that I would be given some Gurkha infantry to do this.

Almost at once, we were ordered out to defend ourselves. This was at the end of September, after a General Strike had been called. I met my Gurkhas for the first time and was relieved to find that their NCO could talk quite good English, as my Urdu was useless for anything at all complicated or technical. I asked if I was really expected to order my Gurkhas to shoot civilians and was told that I must do so if lives were in danger.

The Gurkhas were superb and showed the greatest discipline. I ordered them to fix bayonets and then posted them behind trees, so that they could cover each other and keep intruders away from the building behind us. My hope was to make them lie low and then, if a crowd approached, suddenly to order them to show themselves, in the hope that all their shining bayonets would stop anyone from coming near. Hour followed hour and, mercifully, my plan was not put to the test. No Gurkha moved from the position I had given him, only their eyes moved occasionally to glance at me, in case I made any signal. As it started to get dark, we were told to stand down and, luckily, that was the end of what could have been a very demanding episode.

A new Governor, Sir Hubert Rance, had just been sworn in at this time and he set up a new Executive Council for Burma, containing Aung San and a majority from his political party, the AFPFL (Anti Fascist Peoples Freedom League).

The main HQ, in which I worked, controlled two subordinate HQ, North and South Burma Areas. Glen Kelway-Bamber, as mentioned above, had been posted to South Burma Area, which was in Rangoon. We were not too far apart and so still saw quite a lot of each other. Glen had an amusingly unpredictable streak in his character. For example, one evening, when we had been out to dinner together and were driving back to his officers' mess for a nightcap, he suddenly told our driver to stop and announced that he was going to gatecrash a party that was obviously going on in a nearby house.

'You can't do that,' I said, 'It's the American ambassador's house.'

'So what?' he replied, 'It will be a good party.'

We were both respectably dressed in dinner jackets and I, feeling most irresolute, followed him in. Putting on his richest Etonian accent, he shook hands with the Ambassador saying, 'Frightfully sorry we are so late. We were held up, you know.'

I had to give the Ambassador full marks. He did not look at all friendly when we first walked in, but after Glen's introduction he laughed and ordered up drinks for us. We chatted to some of the guests and then left.

A big change in my life came shortly after all this political upheaval, when I was allotted a married quarter. The house was at Mingaladon, about a dozen miles north of Rangoon, and where a large number of wooden huts were being erected for the Headquarters to move into in May 1947. Our house was a pre-war officer's quarter, with two stories and verandahs all round. Outside were two small blocks, each of four rooms, for servants. The old Indian Army system operated and we employed what seemed a massive number of six servants, each of whom had a strict area of responsibilities. The absurdity of this came to a head early on, when my wife wanted the children's supper taken up to their bedroom. It seemed that such a task was not within the responsibility of any of the servants and could not therefore be done. When I arrived back and heard about this, I had to threaten to sack the whole lot of them unless it was done, and this proved effective.

On 25 October we heard that the SS *Monarch of Bermuda,* in which my family were travelling from England, had arrived in Rangoon, but that disembarkation would not be till the next day. So David McQueen, from South Burma Area, and I managed to obtain a motor boat, in which to visit the trooper. Apart from the fact that we could not wait to see our lovely little families again, our intention was to find if they had any problems that we could fix for them. We were not allowed on board when we reached the ship, but it was marvellous to see our wives on the deck, with tiny children in their arms, waving to us.

Next day, Saturday 26 October, we were allowed on board and, amidst great excitement, collected all their bits and pieces and carried them down the companion way onto a raft, against which was moored the launch that would take us ashore. Our eldest daughter, April, was three years old and she energetically scrambled down first, clutching her teddy bear. She crossed the raft and started to climb into the launch, slipped and fell. It was a godsend that a large sailor was standing close by. He grabbed her and hauled her back, so that she only suffered a bit of a wetting. Laden with suitcases, I watched this incident with horror, remembering the story that nobody had ever fallen into the Rangoon River and survived. If she had been swept away, I would have jumped in to try and save her, so the legend would have been given a good test.

Avoiding any more unpleasantness, we drove out to our quarter in Mingaladon and met the servants. They turned out to be a mixed bunch, but, of course, I had no idea what they would be like when I took them on, so I had to trust to luck. The best one by far, thankfully, was the nanny. She was a Karen and had a sweet and kind nature. She took our two children, then aged 1½ and 3½ years, under her wing the moment we arrived at the house, and they accepted her quiet authority immediately. When we finally left the country a couple of years later, it was with great sadness that we said goodbye to her. She could not read or write

English, so we could not keep in touch with her and we have often wondered what became of her.

On that first night we had all had rather a long day and retired to bed early, after our cook had proved his worth with a good dinner. Sometime around midnight we were woken by loud shouting, which included cries of 'Sahib, Sahib!' Not getting any coherent reply, I went out and started to question our head boy, Joseph, who appeared to be in some distress. It took some time to piece the whole story together. It emerged that our two blocks, each of four rooms for servants, had been taken so that our servants had one room each in one block, and the chowkidar, or night watchman, had the other four. The chowkidar had installed three attractive young girls in three of his rooms, occupying the fourth himself, with his wife. He hired out the girls to anyone who came along, and troops in a nearby RAF station had heard about this and had dropped into the habit of visiting these girls at night. What had caused the rumpus was that two RAF men had opened the door of Joseph's room, found him in bed with his wife, thrown him out and started to make advances on his wife. When Joseph and his wife shouted for help, my Gurkha orderly, Sherafudin, came out of his room and attacked the airmen. He was a tough little man and, with help from Joseph and our sweeper and our cook, they succeeded in driving off the intruders. After a lot of talking, everything gradually quietened down and we were all able to go back to bed. Next day I interviewed the chowkidar who could not see that he had done anything wrong. He was Burmese, while the rest of the servants, except Nanny of course, were Indian, and I had great difficulty in communicating with him, but he finally understood that the girls must go. Actually he turned out to be good at his job of looking after our safety at night, as during the eighteen months we lived in that quarter we were never once burgled, unlike every other house in our road. Perhaps he was in league with the local robbers. We shall never know.

By the end of the year, the strength of Burma Command was down to about 80,000. I think all the West Africans had gone and most of the remainder were Indian Army, including some Gurkha battalions. I was on top of my job by then, although the volume of work was still prodigious. I was much helped in all this by my Staff Captain, a young Gunner called John McEnery. I confess that I did not fully appreciate how much he did until he left on an extended leave trip to Kashmir. During his absence, I had to work even longer hours and had my first taste of the unpleasantness of overwork.

In January 1947 Aung San went to London for independence talks with Prime Minister Attlee. They agreed on a programme of elections to be held in April for a Constitutional Assembly, which would then draft a framework for an independent administration. Some demonstrations and marches took place in Rangoon, but nothing to worry us.

At the end of April, after a year of grinding hard work, I was granted three weeks at the hill station of Maymyo, near Mandalay. I had paid a short visit there during my first trip round the country and been delighted at the coolness of the evenings and nights, as the town was some 4,500 feet above the Irrawaddy plain. David McQueen somehow managed to get leave at the same time, so we teamed up with him, his wife Elizabeth, and their children and spent two days on the train going there. The trip fully lived up to our expectations and it was a particularly good time to be out of Rangoon, as this was the hottest time of the year there, before the monsoon broke and brought welcome clouds overhead.

At this time there were dangers in travelling by road because of the dacoits. These gangs of robbers would come out of the jungle, stop a bus, shoot all male passengers, take any females that attracted them, loot the baggage and then turn the remaining women and children loose and disappear back into the jungle. Dacoits had existed in Burma long before we had come in from India, and they had never been properly controlled. General Briggs had launched a big operation against them, codenamed Operation Flush, in an effort to reduce this menace and, while it did not eliminate them, it was a success. Fifty-four dacoits were killed, two hundred and fifty-five captured and another eight hundred and seventy-one arrested on suspicion. Scottie (Logan Scott-Bowden), an old friend and also from our Staff College course, had a narrow escape when he drove up that month to Maymyo in a jeep. He came round a corner to see a dacoit attack taking place. He drove fast through it, taking several bullets through his jeep, but luckily without any damage other than a shattered windscreen.

It was after this incident that I asked a Burmese officer whether the dacoits were Buddhists. He said he was sure they would all be devout followers of Buddha. I then asked him how it was that they could shoot innocent travellers so often, when, as I understood it, a Buddhist must never kill anything, not even a mosquito. His reply, in all seriousness, was that it was quite wrong to kill a fly or a mosquito, but if a bullet killed someone then that naughty bullet would to go hell. The person who happened to pull the trigger had not technically done the killing. Man's ability to turn religion to his own ends seems unbounded.

When Scottie reached Maymyo he invited me to join him in a trip northwards to the Chinese border and I grabbed at the chance to see more of this unspoilt and little-known part of the country. Travelling in Burma was always interesting as one never knew what would appear round the next corner, perhaps a beautiful temple, or a larger-than-life-sized statue of Buddha, while the birds and flowering shrubs were exotic. We went north through Hsipaw, Lashio and Kutkai and spent a night with the District Commissioner at Lashio. The new District Commissioner for the Wa States spent the night there with us. He was a cheerful character, who had been to that remote area before and he was much looking forward to his trip. He said he would be warmly greeted and that the local girls would be lined up for him to take his choice. He left the next day and, as he had forecast, the arrival of the monsoon cut off the Wa States from the rest of the world shortly after. However, sadly, he was never seen again.

On our return to Rangoon, I found that a new major, just out from England, had taken over my job and I had been switched to be in charge of Operations and Planning in HQ Burma Army. As an assistant I was given a young Burmese captain by the name of Hla Aung. He was totally inexperienced in staff work, but had a sharp mind and was keen to learn. We became firm friends and he took over my job when I left. Later he received rapid promotion and the last I heard was that he had been made Commandant of the new Burma Army Staff College at Kalaw.

My new Headquarters was steadily taking over responsibility for the country from HQ Burma Command and the latter was run down as the inevitable date for independence approached.

On 19 July 1947 our ordered lives received a violent shock. Aung San and six other members of the Executive Council were shot and killed in their Council Chamber. My wife, Diana, happened to be shopping in Rangoon when this happened and she was surprised to find that, quite suddenly, everyone disappeared from the streets. She had no idea why, but felt that it was something unpleasant and drove straight home, mercifully without running into any trouble.

General Briggs acted quickly. He ordered the two battalions in the Rangoon/Mingaladon area to stand to at once and be ready to keep the peace in the city, then ordered three more battalions down from the north to help. However, it seemed that the death of Aung San, whose personality had won over the support and affection of the majority of his countrymen, was such a shattering event that nobody knew what to do. U Saw, an ex-Prime Minister, who had worked for the Japanese, was found guilty of organizing these assassinations and was duly executed.

As far as the British and Indian troops were concerned, we felt nothing but disgust at these killings. None of us had met Aung San, but he had the reputation of being a courageous and far-sighted leader, who was likely to guide his country into a sensible future. We received some unpleasant publicity when it was found that, three weeks before the killings, a good quantity of arms and ammunition had been issued from our Base Ammunition Depot in Mingaladon, to a Burmese officer with a party of what turned out to be bogus policemen. These were not the weapons used in the assassinations, which were all of a different calibre, but it seemed probable that U Saw had organized this.

The Governor, Sir Hubert Rance, was quick to swear in Thakin Nu, later U Nu, to replace Aung San in the Executive Council, but nobody could replace him in the hearts of the majority of the people of Burma. It is not too much to say that Burma is still suffering from the after-effects of this ruthless crime, as power was soon taken over by Ne Win, at that time a major in our HQ, and he has remained as the dictator ever since. He has dealt severely with all opposition to his regime, particularly that of Aung San Sun Kyi, the personable daughter of Aung San.

All our troops were prepared to meet trouble, but, as none occurred, tension gradually relaxed and life in the Headquarters returned to normal. Hla Aung and I were left very much to ourselves to plan the future of the Burma Army, based on the directive I had received from our General. We went about the task methodically. I think it was in September that the lieutenant colonel who was my immediate boss left and a successor moved in, called Ian Robertson. He was a Gunner of wide experience and I had just met him when he had lectured to our Staff College course in 1945. He took a close interest in our work and was most helpful in giving us constructive advice when we had a problem.

The question of what should be done about the Shan States arose. These were far from Rangoon and culminated in the state of Kentung, the easternmost of them, bordering China, French Indo-China (as it was then; it is now Laos) and Thailand. None of us had ever seen the ground, not even Hla Aung, so Ian decided we must visit it and see it for ourselves.

On 2 December 1947 we left Rangoon in a couple of Jeeps and drove up to Kalaw. It took another six days across mountainous tracks to reach Kentung. It turned out that Ian was a most skilled mountain driver, who consistently took less time to cover the distances between outposts than we had been warned to expect. Every fifteen or twenty miles there would be a rest house and a cleared area where, in earlier days, battalions on foot had completed their day's march and stopped for the night. Even with Ian's skilful driving we only covered an average of fifteen to twenty miles in each hour, but the rest houses that we selected to spend the nights in were invariably clean and comfortable.

Finally, on 8 December, we dropped down from the last mountain ridge on to a flat plain and there in front of us was our objective, the walled city of Kentung. We had warned the Sawbwa, or ruler, of our arrival and found ourselves well accommodated in a spacious residence close to the palace.

The Sawbwa, who was known, behind his back, as Shortie, was hardly more than a boy. He had been at school at Canterbury and consequently spoke excellent English; he could not have been more friendly and hospitable. Later he was to be imprisoned for years by the Ne Win government, without any charge being proven against him. Immediately after our arrival he took us to the town baths, which consisted of two indoor pools into which there flowed a continuous stream of natural hot water, presumably from some volcanic fault. The water went first into a room containing the smaller of the two pools, in which we then immersed ourselves, a most welcome experience after the long days of dusty driving. This smaller pool was for the Sawbwa's own use and the water flowed out of that into a much larger pool, which the other citizens of Kentung could use.

Back at the palace we laid out our maps and discussed the possible routes the Chinese might use if they chose to invade Kentung State. Next morning, before we left to have a look at the border country, the Sawbwa asked if we would be interested to see the valuables in his Treasury. Expecting lovely, and probably quite old, pieces of jewellery, we jumped at the chance and were taken down to a well-locked vault. A servant with a huge key opened this to reveal three elaborate metal boxes, each about the size of a large travelling trunk. He was then told to unlock the first of these and we craned forward to see inside. To our amazement it was full to the brim with a thick dark brown liquid. 'Opium', said the Sawbwa. He then explained that opium was the main crop grown in his state. The poppies would be picked by the women, who always worked backwards so that they only saw the plants they had already picked clean, and not the count-less thousands of unpicked flowers that were waiting for attention. Each farmer had to produce a quota of opium, depending on his acreage, and we were looking at the results of this. It would be sold at a fixed price to the government in Rangoon, who then re-sold it for use in hospitals across the whole of southern Asia.

Shortie suspected that there was an extensive black market for the drug, but he could not prove this and had no means of controlling it. I do not know how firm a grip his police had. We never saw a uniformed constable but, while the people looked peaceable and friendly by day, desultory firing could be heard in the town throughout the night.

Shortie asked the servant who had let us in whether he smoked opium, which he admitted he did. I asked him how it was used and he explained that one drop of the brown fluid would be rolled up in dust until it made a small ball. This was then put into an opium pipe where it would smoulder and the smoke could be inhaled.

Next day we drove south to the Thai border to take a look at the country there, which proved rough and forested. On the way we passed through the village of Loilem, which had been a pre-war station for a British battalion. It was a delight to see a typical army barrack square, surrounded by low wooden buildings that had obviously held offices, storerooms and accommodation. It would have been a memorable, but perhaps not too pleasant, experience to have marched all the way out here from the Irrawaddy Plain and then lived here in complete isolation for probably a couple of years, perhaps even more. The barracks were still being maintained, presumably in case of possible use to deter any aggressive neighbour.

It again took us seven days of hard driving to return to Rangoon.

The rundown of British and Indian troops was coming to its finish by the time we returned. Burmese independence had been agreed to occur at 4.20 am on Sunday, 4 January 1948, a time selected by the priesthood as being the most auspicious. Headquarters Burma Command was down to a small rearguard, which would be finally disbanded on 4 January.

Most of my friends among the British officers had been posted home. However, in those days an overseas tour of duty was three years and I had only done about two, so I was ordered to proceed to Singapore for a further posting. I had no great problem in handing over my job, since Hla Aung was to take it on and I had kept him in the picture with all that I had done. However, I completed as much work as I possibly could before I left, so as to ease his work load. He touchingly expressed his gratitude to me by presenting me with a captured Japanese officer's sword and a Japanese military flag, which I later gave to the Royal Engineers Museum in Chatham.

Finally, on 28 January 1948, we left Rangoon in the SS *Dunera*, bound for Penang and Singapore. Also on board were 1/6th Gurkhas, the last of our battalions to serve in Burma. It had been an eventful and very busy couple of years, but I have to admit I was not sorry to leave. Looking back now, I would hate to have missed it, but at the time I felt a sense of relief that the tremendous work load that had fallen to my lot had really come to an end.

CHAPTER 13

MALAYA

The trip southwards in SS *Dunera* proved, as usual in troopships, pleasant and restful. On 31 January we reached Penang and 1/6 Gurkhas disembarked. They had been great company during the voyage and we were sorry to see them go. Penang looked delightful, a steep sunny island, but comparatively cool due to the surrounding sea water.

Two days later we arrived at Singapore. I had flown down to this great metropolis from Burma on two or three occasions for conferences and had a number of friends in the main HQ. On arrival I reported to the Engineer Branch there and was told that I had been appointed to raise and command a new Engineer Training Centre at a place called Kluang in Johore. I drove up straight away to Kluang, but there was not much to see other than an empty ex-Japanese army barracks. I would have to occupy this and then set up a headquarters to supervise and administer instructional courses on all aspects of military engineering. I had to start from scratch, so it would be quite an undertaking.

So life started again, and a very different life from the one we had grown accustomed to in Burma. I returned quickly to Singapore, where Diana had taken on a Chinese nanny, who was to prove almost as careful and loving as her dear Karen predecessor, and then drove the family back up to Kluang. Luckily a small bungalow was available for us there, a poor exchange for our house in Burma, but not too bad. We also took on a Chinese cook from Kluang, who turned out to be good.

On the military side, every few days brought some NCOs and

men sent up from Singapore. We had an excellent Regimental Sergeant Major, RSM Aminudin, a Malay, and a host of more junior ranks from all over South-East Asia.

Some Royal Engineer officers arrived, including a Major Martin, who proved to be a well-balanced character, and some Captains and Subalterns. On the whole the Malays and Chinese we received, who were known as LEPs (Locally Enlisted Personnel) proved to be hard working and loyal, whereas the British Other Ranks were sometimes very good but sometimes more trouble than they were worth, having been posted out of their previous units for some misdemeanour.

However, there was a lot of work to be done and everyone was kept very busy preparing for the arrival of our first batch of trainees. Our barracks, such as it was, was a collection of 'bashas', or wooden huts, built by order of the Japanese when they occupied Malaya, in a wooded area beside a concrete airstrip. After they had been thoroughly cleaned, and after some usually quite simple modifications, they proved to be fully serviceable as offices, storerooms and sleeping accommodation. Once again I found that the job I had been given was a demanding one, but it was full of interest and certainly not as exacting as my first job in Burma, for in Malaya I was at least my own boss and could arrange my own life.

Kluang was surrounded by dense jungle and consequently we were often visited by exotic birds and butterflies. Small monkeys would appear and once, but only once, we saw a huge orang-utan, sitting calmly high in a tree: a lovely and unforgettable sight. Late one night I decided to pay a surprise visit to our guard to check that they were properly alert. When I reached them I found that they were all Malays and they were certainly fully alert as the sentry said he had just seen a tiger cross the road near him. I was never sure how much to believe this, as men on their own on the edge of jungle might well imagine such a thing, but I kept a very sharp lookout as I walked back.

One small aspect of our life always amused me. I held a parade every morning, as military units normally do. This had two main purposes; first to check that all were present, and, secondly, on the insistence of our doctor, to ensure that all ranks took a mepacrin pill every day. The danger of malaria had been very high in Malaya and this had been considerably reduced by the systematic drainage of wet areas where the malaria mosquito could breed. However, malaria was still a significant danger, so all soldiers had to take one mepacrin pill every day to protect themselves against the dread disease. Unfortunately the word had been passed round that mepacrin decreased the sexual abilities of a man and, consequently, it became most unpopular with the troops. However, the doctors' orders were that we must make certain that every man took one pill every day.

To achieve this, I ordered officers to go along the ranks on parade each morning, give each man a pill, ensure that he put the pill in his mouth and then inspect the inside of his mouth to make sure he had swallowed it. This was done methodically, and the pills all disappeared. However, mepacrin was bright yellow in colour and gradually our parade ground became a brighter and brighter shade of yellow!

Another rather unusual side of life were the Rongings. These were dances arranged by the Malays. A raised platform would be erected and, on the selected evening, a party of eight or ten women would arrive and stand in a row along one edge of the platform. Music would then strike up and our soldiers would go up in turn onto the platform, stand in front of a girl and dance with her. There was no physical contact between the sexes, the men just imitated the rhythm that their partners adopted.

My wife and I were invited to attend these functions and the friendly atmosphere made them most pleasant occasions. At the first one we attended we happened to have invited a sapper, Major Frederickson, to dinner and he came along with us. He was in charge of all the building work in Kluang and had much more experience of Malaya than I had. After a few dances had taken place, he lent over to me and said that he felt sure I would be invited to take part in a dance soon. 'When it happens,' he added, 'choose the ugliest girl; they are always the best.'

He had hardly finished speaking when RSM Aminudin, our senior Malay, came and invited me to step up on to the platform for a dance. As I went up there, amidst cheers and much clapping, I took a good look at the girls. About a dozen were young and attractive, with rather tight-fitting garments that showed off their good figures. I avoided all these and took my place opposite an older girl. I could not have called her ugly, but she was certainly not particularly attractive.

Frederickson's advice proved excellent. The girl cavorted around in a most amusing way, which I had to try to imitate. When I made a nonsense, she would repeat her antics until I had succeeded in copying her properly. This was all done with a great grin on her face and with much applause from the onlookers. The attractive, slinky piece on my left, who never smiled and paid little regard to her partner, would have been a poor substitute.

Kluang was a medium-sized town, which contained a mixed population of Malays, Chinese and Indians. On the way into the town from our bungalow, there was a large and spotlessly clean mosque and from its minaret the faithful were regularly called to prayer. Beyond that were a number of food shops, again agreeably clean, from which we could vary our army rations with local products, such as tropical fruit. There were rubber plantations dotted round outside the town and a large, comfortable planter's club on the southern outskirts. I made a point of getting to know some of the planters, and my wife and I were invited to one of the monthly dinners they held there. Liquor was cheap and a large amount was consumed. By about two in the morning there seemed to be no reason why the party should ever end, so, as I had a busy day in front of me, we left. These were always enjoyable functions, but, on future occasions, I always had an excuse for leaving around midnight. However, the planters were a good bunch. Highly individual and self-confident, they ran their large domains efficiently and their hospitality was delightful.

One other strong character we came to know well was the head of the town police force. He was a tough little Scot and had a beautiful Malay wife and his knowledge of Kluang and all its different communities was most impressive.

Our first instructional course came and went successfully, and was quickly followed by more. Most of the students were LEPs, the plan being to develop an up-to-date Engineer arm in the Malayan forces (Malaya included Singapore in those days). Then, one day, I was summoned down to the Main Headquarters in Singapore and told that the decision had been taken to form a Gurkha Division, which would have to contain a Gurkha engineer regiment. The Gurkha soldiers were all infantry up till that time and I was a bit doubtful about how they would take to becoming Sappers, as I knew that the Indian caste system operated quite strongly in Nepal, and this ordained that anyone who handled tools or metal was of low caste. However, I need not have worried. Volunteers were called for immediately and plenty of them came forward. When they arrived they turned out to be keen, smart and very well behaved, and they set about picking up their new skills with a will. Some of them brought wives and families with them and this raised a problem, as we had no family accommodation for them. We had to get bell tents up from Singapore, and we pitched these on part of the airfield that was next to our camp. Diana used to visit this community to try to help with their difficulties and she found them to be an attractively cheerful group. Life was a bit primitive for them, with nothing but a tent for each family and, to make matters worse, a severe epidemic of measles swept through them. Our doctor, who was an Indian, explained that measles was not known in the outlying villages in Nepal, so Gurkhas were particularly susceptible to it when one of their number picked up the germ from somewhere. However, in spite of these hardships, they remained indomitably cheerful.

But this busy, happy atmosphere was about to be shattered. It must have been in May 1948 that the first incident in what came to be known as the Malayan Emergency occurred in the district round Kluang. A rubber planter's home was attacked and the result was a truly revolting sight of dead men, women and children of several different races, and some dogs, all with their throats cut. It seemed that every person who worked on the plantation, and their wives, families and dogs, had been brutally butchered. It was difficult to work out the purpose of this. There had been some stealing, particularly of food, and probably also of money and valuables, although there was nobody left to give a reliable list. The whole thing seemed to be a pointless, but most unpleasant, crime. Our efficient police superintendent called us in to help, but it was difficult to see what we could do. Where had the attackers come from? Where had they gone to? We had no idea.

When this atrocity was repeated, a pattern gradually emerged. A gang, or possibly more than one gang, was clearly living somewhere in the jungle and descending on quite unpredictable targets, which they would then devastate. The planters were quick to build defences to protect themselves and some of the more isolated plantations sensibly closed down. Most of them already possessed firearms and they augmented these rapidly until their living quarters became small fortresses. The heap of weapons that could be seen at the monthly party at the Planters' Club was really formidable.

It must have been in June that we received an urgent call one evening from our Police Superintendent asking if we could produce some men immediately because he thought he had located a base in the jungle being used by terrorists. Under his guidance, our party trekked through dense jungle that night. Just before dawn it arrived at a small village and posted men on every track leading out of it. Then, as dawn broke, the police led into the village, with our men backing them up and ready to shoot at the slightest sign from them. All remained quiet. After a thorough search they found that there was not a single man in the village, only women and children.

We were in no way skilled jungle fighters, and the terrorists, and there may well have been some in the village, had probably been warned of our approach by their own sentries hours before we arrived, and had made themselves scarce. Back at our camp next day, I was sent for by the commander of 1/10 Gurkhas, Lieutenant Colonel Vickers, who had recently moved into Kluang. He had heard about our expedition and he ticked me off. 'I am the senior officer in this garrison,' he said, 'and if you receive any call for military action you must inform me at once. I will decide who shall take it on.'

Undoubtedly he was right, and I am sure the Gurkhas would have done better than us. However, looking back, it never crossed our minds that we should not respond at once to a cry for help from the Police Superintendent, particularly as he was a firm personal friend. Anyway, I rang him up to ask him to contact Colonel Vickers on future occasions, which he agreed to do, although, very sadly, he was to be killed soon after.

My greatly respected late boss from Burma, General Sir Harold Briggs, was then sent to command our forces in Malaya. This was an excellent choice. However, at this stage nobody knew who the real enemy was, or even what he was trying to achieve, so, to answer these questions, General Briggs sent for someone he knew he could rely on implicitly, Brigadier Calvert.

'Mad Mike' Calvert had commanded a brigade in the Chindit operations behind the Japanese lines in Burma in 1944. One of his officers once described to me how they were attacked every single day by the Japanese, and that Mad Mike would go out in front of his foremost battalion positions to gauge exactly where the attack was coming from and to organize a counter-attack on the flank of the Japanese. He said that it was entirely due to Mike that the brigade survived for approximately 139 (I forget his exact figure) days. Mike received a bar to his DSO for this operation, but this officer insisted that he deserved 139 bars for all the risks he took. Clearly he was a fine soldier and a very brave man. General Briggs told Mad Mike to go and find out what the terrorists were trying to achieve, how they planned to do it and then to devise a plan to thwart them.

To cut a long story short, Mike found that the terrorist organization hoped to place the country under Chinese Communist leadership and that they had plenty of arms and ammunition left over from the war years. They had set up a series of camps in the jungle, but they relied for food from civilian villages located in the outskirts of the jungle. The occupants of those villages obtained a living from working on plantations and were in no position to refuse to give food when it was demanded by a well-armed gang. Mike's solution was to build new villages outside the jungle and for these to be surrounded with a heavy fence of barbed wire and armed guards at the entrances. The guards were provided with radio communications, so that help could be summoned at once if trouble occurred. A systematic surveillance of jungle areas, where gangs were suspected to be hiding out, by light aircraft was instituted.

This became known as the Briggs Plan, although Briggs himself did not live long enough to see it to its victorious conclusion. When the High Commissioner was shot, General Sir Gerald Templer replaced him, taking on Briggs' responsibilities as head of the Armed Forces as well. General Templer's dynamic and constructive leadership has become a byword and, implementing the Briggs Plan, the terrorist menace was gradually eliminated, so that Malaysia could proceed towards independence without having to inherit a deadly dispute within its own borders.

However, that victory was all in the future. As far as my family and I were concerned, we found our activities considerably curtailed by the fact that, in those early days, northern Johore was one of the worst areas of terrorist action, and we were in the middle of it. In our military compound outside Kluang town our own guards were supplemented by roving Gurkha patrols and the terrorist never risked a showdown with these, but they kept themselves busy on softer targets in the neighbourhood. We were able to continue to develop our military engineering courses and it was gratifying to see how well the Gurkha volunteers performed.

After about six months in Kluang, I began to feel rather lethargic and listless. Living, as we did, almost on the equator, and with a high monthly figure for rainfall, the average humidity was very high. At first I put my feeling of lethargy down to the climate, but gradually I came to realize it was more than that. I saw our doctor who said I had some complaint of the same nature as jaundice, but he did not know what it was. When I finally returned to England, I was to be sent to the Tropical Diseases Hospital in London, where I was told that I was suffering from a previously undiagnosed disease, for which they gave me various medicines and it slowly died away.

I continued with my responsibilities in Kluang until, one day, out of the blue, I received a letter from England to say that, as I had passed all the entrance exams to Cambridge before the war, but had not taken a degree then, a vacancy was still being kept there for me. If I wished to take it up, I could do so. This seemed a veritable gift from the Gods. I accepted at once and the paper work was quickly completed. GHQ in Singapore told me that they had been planning to upgrade my job as Commander of the Engineer Training Centre to the rank of lieutenant colonel and that they had a replacement for me. This turned out to be Herbie Carrington-Smith, an excellent choice. He soon arrived in Kluang and I spent a rewarding couple of weeks explaining to him our plans for the future and taking him round all we had done so far, whilst, back in our bungalow, we packed up and prepared to leave.

111

Herbie was very complementary about the Training Centre we had built up and, when we finally departed to catch the troopship from Singapore, I felt happy that I was leaving the new school, on which I had spent so much thought and effort, in really good hands.

CHAPTER 14

TRAVELLING HOME

As I have said before, a journey on a troopship involved a rather monotonous, but not unpleasant, routine. However, this particular trip on the SS *Dilwara*, was to contain three unusual incidents during the period of exactly one month that it took to reach home.

There were some other families on board, but the bulk of the passengers were troops, who had completed a three-year tour in the Far East and were returning home, mostly for demobilization. These men were housed in three large troop decks, which were filled to capacity with hammocks, below which was stacked each man's personal kit. Overall control of all the passengers rested with a rather elderly, and very thirsty, lieutenant colonel, who had the title of OC Troops. On the first day out from Singapore he sent for me and told me that he had selected me to be in charge of the largest troop deck. This was an honour I could have done without, but I had no choice.

I used to visit my troop deck each morning to make sure it had been tidied up after the night and to sort our any suggestions or complaints made by the men with the ship's administrative staff. In addition, there were some military police on board, who patrolled in groups, particularly in the evenings. They sometimes arrested one or two of the men, usually for being drunk and disorderly. These culprits would be marched up in front of me next morning, having spent the night in the cells, which were small metal cages at the bottom of the hull, unventilated and highly uncomfortable.

The OC Troops told me that the only punishment available on board was to lock men up in these cages, but when I found a man to be undoubtedly guilty I ordered him to scrub out the latrines or the wash room, necessary tasks, with the warning that he would be sent down to the cells if he came up in front of me again. None of them ever did.

After we had been at sea about a week the Military Police Sergeant came to me to report that there had been a great deal of trouble during the previous night. One of the men in my troopdeck had brought a live python on board, tied up in a sack, and this had escaped and caused near panic. Finally the police managed to corner the animal, swamp it with blankets and throw it overboard. The owner of the snake was to be brought up in front of me on a charge. He was marched in and he turned out to be a man from some obscure unit which held some wild animals, so that troops would know something of what to expect when they went into jungle areas. He claimed that he had captured this python himself, that therefore it was his own property, and he was taking it back to England to sell to a zoo. He had given it a good meal before the boat sailed and he knew that it would sleep for several days after that. Now, a week out, he thought he had better take a look at it, opened the sack and found it to be very much awake. It escaped into the troop deck and the rest of the story we knew.

On questioning, he said that the snake might survive, as it could swim for a long time and we were in sight of Ceylon when the incident happened, although, personally, I doubted whether the wretched animal could have known in the middle of the night in which direction to swim. I feared it must have drowned somewhere in the Indian Ocean. Certainly his action had been most stupid, but, in the event, nobody was hurt, and the man had no more snakes to let loose, so I ordered him to do some good spells of scrubbing and closed the matter. The OC Troops called me in later, having received a report on the incident from the MPs and he told me that I had dealt too leniently with the offender. However, the case had been held and the verdict given, so he could not be charged with the same offence again and that was the end of the matter.

The second unexpected event occurred when we were allowed

ashore at Aden. Glen and I had had such a pleasant day there that I planned to repeat it with my family now that we were on our way home. The main thing was to hire a taxi to go to the Officers' Club for a swim and lunch. This went well, as I had expected. On our way back to the ship I asked our driver to take us past the Jewish ghetto, which had impressed me before as an unusually handsome and massive walled city. Our driver shrugged his shoulders when I asked this, in what I felt was a sign of contempt for a non-Muslim who wanted to waste time on such a pointless visit. However, he agreed to take us there. When we reached what had been the formidable entrance towers, we saw the reason for his reluctance. The whole place had been gutted by explosives and fire. Nothing was left. As Robbie Burns put it, 'man's inhumanity to man makes countless thousands mourn'.

As will be seen, these three unusual events were not related to each other in any way, but the third was perhaps the most dramatic of all. We had passed through the Straits of Gibraltar and entered the Bay of Biscay on the last leg of our long journey home. One morning Diana had the children up on the deck, as it was a fine day, with the ship ploughing steadily through the long Atlantic rollers on her way northwards. Suddenly a strident bell rang out. I happened to be in our cabin and I stepped out into the corridor, where one of the ship's stewards said, 'That means a man overboard.' I quickly climbed up the companion way, praying that it was not one of our family. I passed someone I had come to know on board and he confirmed my fear. 'A child has fallen overboard,' he said.

Seconds later I saw our family and heaved a sigh of relief as they were all present. What had happened was that a corporal's wife, who was returning home for some compassionate reason without her husband, had sat her daughter, who could not have been more that three years old, on the ship's rail, whilst she stood behind, with her arms loosely round the child's waist, knitting. Some dolphins suddenly appeared, swimming alongside the troopship, the child leant forward, pointing at them, and fell in.

The Captain was on the bridge and he cut the engines at once, whilst turning the ship back in a tight circle. One of the lifeboats was quickly manned by sailors and this was swung out over the side and held there until they could be told in which direction to row. With nothing to be seen but frisky dolphins, there was complete silence on board until someone pointed at something white floating in the water. The boat's crew were told and away they went, rowing energetically. When they reached their objective, it turned out to be a sailor's cap, and not from our ship; it just happened to be there. However, when they pulled out the cap, there, only a few feet away, was the tiny child, with nothing but her nose out of the water. She had been knocked unconscious by her fall and, as they reached her, she gave a bubbly cry and turned over into the sea. A big sailor's hand grabbed some clothing and hauled out the child, which then showed she was very much alive, kicking out wildly and yelling for her Mummy.

The ship's doctor examined the child carefully and pronounced that she had suffered no damage, although she had been in the water for over half an hour. A padre, who happened to be on board, appropriately held a thanksgiving service next morning for this quite miraculous escape.

Our first experience of the Far East came to an end on 30 July 1948 when SS *Dilwara* docked at Southampton. I felt a sense of relaxation as I finished all responsibility for other people except for my own family. Diana's parents took us into their comfortable house on the Isle of Wight, where we basked in their affectionate hospitality.

I had to go on a short refresher course at the School of Military Engineering at Chatham to prepare myself for the degree course at Cambridge. It was just as well for me that this had been arranged, as I had not realized quite how much of my academic schooling I had forgotten in the intervening ten years. When I started this refresher course, I was given an old Cambridge entrance exam to take as a test. By chance, this was the very same exam that I had taken before the war to pass into Cambridge. I was surprised, and disappointed, to find that I could hardly answer a single question, whereas, in 1939, I had had no problems and passed in easily.

One seems to be able to retain what one has learned, but if the information is not used, it slips further and further to the back of one's mind and becomes more and more difficult to extract. However, it is still there, somewhere, and I worked hard to re-learn my academic knowledge before reporting to Christ's

1. The AVRE, lost on D-Day and then used as a pier for a bridge to open a route off the beach, uncovered in 1976.

2. The AVRE as it stands today as a memorial to all those killed on the Graye-sur-Mer beach. Standing in front are the author with the two survivors, both badly wounded on D-Day, Bill Dunn and Bill Hawkins.

3. D-Day, 6 June 1944. No photographers landed with us at H-Hour but this air photo must have been taken around midday. Dozens of vehicles wait for a chance to leave the beach. Exit A has been temporarily blocked by an armoured car which drove over a mine and caught fire. Tanks are moving out through Exit B slowly across the AVRE which is sunk in the large crater. Some large concrete pill-boxes are marked C. D are landing craft damaged mostly by mines and abandoned. E, at the top, shows some tanks knocked out by fire from pill-boxes in the early stages. Some of our vehicles can be seen on the main lateral road. The village of Graye-sur-Mer is just off the photo to the right.

4. Crossing the Rhine. The town of Wesel the day after the crossing.

5. Wesel railway bridge; note Buffalo tracks entering river in foreground.

7. A temporary passenger.

6. The author in Korea, January 1951.

8. A temporary bridge for refugees in Seoul. Demolished 4 January 1951.

9. How the city of Seoul, capital of South Korea and one of the major cities of the world, looked in 1951. With not a soul on the streets, it awaited the Chinese attack.

10. The same scene in 1981.

11. The Shoofly bridge over the River Han at Seoul on Christmas Day, 1950.

12. The bridge after demolition on 4 January 1951.

13. The pre-war railway bridge at Seoul. Demolished on 4 January 1951.

14. Korean refugees flee southwards to escape the attacking Chinese in bitter winter weather.

15. 8th Hussar tank after the Imjin battle.

16. The Imijin River seen from the Belgian positions. The river is 100 yards wide in the foreground.

17. Typical Korean countryside.

18. The never-ending Sapper work in Korea, improving communications. Widening a dangerous bend in winter; note the Anti Aircraft gun for local protection.

19. Making a jeep track to a forward position in summer.

College, Cambridge, for the start of the two-year course on 8 October 1948.

I do not intend to write much about life at Cambridge University, as I have really only one point to make. But first I must fill in some of the background to our life there.

The post-war Mechanical Sciences Tripos, which I went up to take, was a concentrated course of two years' duration, instead of the usual three. This was because so many potential under-graduates had joined the Forces between 1939 and 1945. Now, in 1948, they were being released from their military service and so the pressure for vacancies was very great.

Back in September 1939, when we were due to go up to Cambridge, Hubert Woodhouse and I had agreed to put our names down for Christ's College, as it would take two sapper undergraduates. Therefore we could go there together instead of going separately to other Colleges that would only take one sapper each. Hubert had been killed early in the war, which was a great loss to me, but the consequences of our agreement made in 1939 remained in 1948, so to Christ's I went.

By 1948 I was married, with two children, and therefore I needed to find accommodation for our family in Cambridge. However, Christ's had a rule, which ordained that all under-graduates must spend their first term as residents in the College, and only after that could they move out. Consequently, when I arrived for the start of the Autumn Term, I found that I had been allocated a bed in a room to be shared with another new under-graduate. He was a cheerful character, who had done three years as an officer in the Royal Corps of Signals, and who was reading economics.

It turned out that his life was quite different to mine. He would attend one or two lectures each week and was given a good deal of reading to do by his tutor. Each week he would have to write an essay on a subject given him by the tutor. Quite often we would discuss his subject before he wrote his essay, and since I was half a dozen years older than him, and therefore had read newspapers for that much longer than him, I had opinions on the subjects he had to write about. We had some lively and interesting discussions from which I learned a lot.

In the same vein, we quite often went out together to one of the

117

local pubs for a pint of beer after dinner in the evenings. There we would, more often than not, become involved in some lively debate on a subject that had to be written about by some other undergraduate. These discussions were not necessarily about economics, they might be theological or historical, but interesting and, again, subjects on which I had opinions that I could contribute.

The work that was required of me was quite different. I had to attend four one-hour lectures every morning and, on some afternoons, had electrical experiments or mechanical drawing to undertake. The practical nature of our afternoon's work made it quite interesting and worthwhile, but the morning lectures were nothing less than awful. The lecturer would enter the auditorium in which we all sat and, usually without a word, would pick up a piece of chalk and start writing on one of three blackboards. We, the students, soon learned that we could copy his words into our notebooks faster than he could write on the blackboards, so we could come in well after he had started. He would only rub the first blackboard clean when he came to the end of the third one, so we had plenty of time to catch up with him.

If I had gone up to Cambridge straight from school, aged nineteen or twenty, I would doubtless have accepted this procedure without any objections. But I had matured greatly in the intervening years, and had seen quite a lot of life, and of death. I had been through the Staff College course, where I had learned a great deal from the syndicate method of instruction, and also attended several excellent lectures there. I had been a lecturer myself for about nine months, admittedly only on the humble subject of practical demolitions, but even then I had tried to liven up my presentations with anecdotes and slides. Furthermore, the colonel in charge of the Officer Cadet Training Unit in which I was teaching would come and sit at the back for one of my lectures every so often. At the end he would call me over when he would usually say, 'That was quite good, but it would have been better if . . .' He would then make some constructive comment, from which I learned quickly to polish up my deliveries.

No colonel came to sit at the back of those lectures at Cambridge. Sometimes the lecturer would not even complete his sentence on the blackboard. The bell would ring at five minutes to the hour to indicate the time to finish and he would just put down his chalk and walk out, leaving his last sentence incomplete. I found, as did others of my age group, that the standard of instruction was not just bad, it was appalling.

I had one amusing confirmation of this opinion. At the end of our two years our group of sapper officers decided to give a farewell drink party. To this we invited all our instructors and other guests who were involved with us in one way or another. One of the latter was Brigadier Basil Davey, the Commandant of the School of Military Engineering, who was our military boss. I had met him before and liked him, and I spent some time at the party talking to him. He asked how I had enjoyed the course and I told him it had been fine except for the method of instruction, as I have just described. He listened with interest, and when I had made my point, he commented that he had done an exactly similar course in 1923, after the First World War. He finished by saying, 'You cannot have had to endure in 1948-50 lectures that were as awful as those we had to sit through almost thirty years ago.' He finished by saying, 'I can even remember the name of one of the very worst of the dons who lectured us,' and he named the man and his subject.

'Sir,' I was able to reply, 'would you just turn round and have a look at the man who is just behind you. Do you recognize him?'

'How ghastly,' he said, 'that's the same man.'

We had a good laugh about this, but we both realized how pathetic it was that a man who had been really bad in 1923 should still be lecturing, and still very badly, in 1950.

More than fifty years have passed since this happened and I feel certain that the instruction has all changed for the better now.

The thing that made my whole course at Cambridge tolerable, and indeed pleasant, was our home life. Admittedly the first term was a setback, as I had to live a bachelor existence in College. Diana came up to Cambridge for some weekends, which we spent house-hunting. She had to stay in a hotel and I was not even allowed to spend the night with her, having to be back in College by 10 pm, with a fine of one penny if I was up to one hour late, but more severe penalties after that. We tried hard to rent accommodation in Cambridge, but failed completely. There was a shortage of all forms of housing, due to the fact that there had been no rebuilding of bomb damage throughout the war, and what little accommodation there was had been snapped up long before we entered the market. There was no other solution than to buy something, and we found a small thatched cottage in the village of Linton, about a dozen miles to the east of Cambridge. This cost £1,000 and I was able to obtain a good mortgage to pay for most of it. My grandmother had been killed towards the end of the war by one of the so-called buzz bombs that the Germans directed on London, and she left me some money in her will. With this we put down our deposit for the cottage and purchased the furniture we needed, mostly from second-hand sales in Cambridge.

So, for the first time in our lives, we had a little home in England. We had about a quarter of an acre of garden, with some fruit trees and shrubs, two small bedrooms for us and our children and a spare room for a guest. For the best part of two years we lived in this peaceful agricultural backwater. Petrol was still rationed, but my allocation was sufficient for the journey to Cambridge and back on the working days, whilst at the weekends we could take the children for long and varied walks along the tracks and through the woods nearby. Our third daughter was born during this time and we always look back with great happiness to the time we spent in Linton.

CHAPTER 15

PREPARING FOR WAR AGAIN

It was a real relief when the final examinations were finished and I did not have to attend any more boring lectures at Cambridge. I was posted to Perham Down, near Tidworth, on Salisbury Plain, where my old wartime unit, 26 Squadron, was stationed as part of a Regiment. However, I was not to command 26 again, although I would have been delighted to do that. When I reported to Lieutenant Colonel Phil Hatch, he said that I was a surplus major and that he wanted me to supervise the training done by the Regiment. As this was all the Regiment was doing, training, I had a full-time job.

First we had to extricate ourselves from Cambridge, or, to be more accurate, from the village of Linton. We managed to sell our house, inevitably at a slight loss, and we put our furniture into store. Our little baby, Liz, was only a few weeks old, although she already showed a friendly alertness that delighted us all.

At Perham Down there was no quarter available for us, so Phil Hatch most kindly invited us to live with him, a generous gesture, as an extra couple, plus three children, represented a major invasion into an army quarter. It happened that one of his officers, who had been in charge of the Officers' Mess accounts, was found to have been removing sizeable amounts of money into his own pocket. He was warned that he would face a court martial and, presumably knowing that he would be found guilty, he hanged himself. This was a sad tragedy but it did mean that a quarter would become available for us. I told the Quartermaster, who was in charge of housing, not to rush the wretched widow out. In the event she was, perhaps understandably, keen to leave the area quickly, and we duly moved into a rather dreary and characterless quarter, where at least we did not have to impose ourselves on Phil Hatch's hospitality. Phil was to be posted out to Cyprus, with his delightful wife, a couple of years later, to help in coping with the Eoka uprising, which had been brought to a head by Anthony Eden's incautious comment that Cyprus would not proceed to independence in the foreseeable future. Regretfully, the stresses out there killed him, a grave loss to the army of a most capable and likeable commander.

55 Field Squadron was one of the units in Phil Hatch's Regiment and, soon after we arrived at Perham Down, it was due to spend a week at Wyke Regis, a bridging camp on the south coast. I had a word with the Squadron Commander about the type of training he would undertake and arranged that his Squadron should do a major bridging exercise at first light on the final day before they were due to finish at Wyke. I stipulated that this exercise should be as realistic as possible, with precautions to be taken in case of attack from land or air.

I travelled down to see how they performed and on the way I called in at an RAF station to ask if they could stage a simulated attack on the bridge as it was being built. It turned out that the RAF thought this would be an excellent training exercise for their pilots and they readily agreed to do it.

However, the result was a shambles. The first aircraft came screaming out of the early morning sun and caught the whole Squadron by surprise. As other aircraft stormed in, I yelled out 'Air attack! Take cover and return fire at the aircraft.' The aircraft circled round and came in again from a different direction, but the Squadron seemed at a loss to know what to do.

Meeting the officers afterwards, I found that the three Troop commanders were inexperienced Second Lieutenants, recently commissioned and doing their National Service. They were good young lads, but they needed a great deal more leadership to make them into effective commanders. The only officer in the Squadron who impressed me was Patrick Pengelly, the Second-in-Command, who coped with its administration admirably.

I learned that 55 Squadron had two roles, one to train as a Squadron in Phil Hatch's Regiment, and, secondly, as the engineer unit in 29 Infantry Brigade, which was known as the fire brigade, a formation that was theoretically ready to 'put out a fire' anywhere in the world at short notice.

Unfortunately for 55 Squadron, a fire had indeed started in what was otherwise a fairly peaceful world. Communist North Korea, supported by Communist China and Soviet Russia, had attacked South Korea. All this was so far away that it did not seem to affect us at all. However, when I returned to Perham Down from Wyke Regis, Phil Hatch called me in and told me that 29 Brigade would being going to Korea and that he was putting me in to command 55 Squadron.

I moved into the Squadron next day and started the complex task of reorganizing it. The whole establishment had to be changed, from that of a 'normal' squadron in a regiment to that of an 'independent' squadron. This meant a larger headquarters, more transport, two officers in each Troop and an extra Park Troop to hold engineer equipment, such as cranes and bulldozers. Many of the NCOs and men, and all the Troop officers, had to leave, as they were coming to the end of their National Service period and were not eligible to undertake a long expedition. Luckily some of the senior NCOs stayed on, including Squadron Sergeant-Major Brown, who turned out to be a tower of strength. Even Patrick Pengelly had to go, as he was to join the next course at the Staff College, an important step in an officer's career. At least I had him for the first month, when he was able to deal with the huge intake of stores, vehicles and men.

It is not necessarily true that campaigns are won by good administration, but they can certainly be lost by bad administration and this danger is ever-present when war starts after a period of peace. In 1950, when North Korea suddenly invaded South Korea, the British people, and their Army, were more concerned with recovering from the Second World War than with preparing to fight again.

The Army in England was not in a particularly healthy state, in spite of the high quality of its leaders. NATO had just been forced into existence by the autocratic policies of Stalin's government in

123

Moscow, and priority had to be given to British units in Germany both for equipment and manpower. At the same time the Malayan Emergency, which had started when we were out there in the summer of 1948, was demanding a steady stream of units, and garrisons had to be maintained in other colonies where arrangements for self-government were being worked out.

A decree was issued from Whitehall recalling Class A reservists to the colours for the duration of the Korean crisis. In common with most of the units that formed 29 Brigade, 55 Squadron was grossly under-strength in this post-war rundown period. It held about one hundred and fifty men all told and it had to be made up to a little over three hundred and fifty, so we looked forward to the arrival of reservists as the answer to our problem.

Reservists were men who had completed their National Service and those listed as Class A had accepted an honorarium to be available at short notice to return to the colours. Thus, they were men of experience, although the Corps of Royal Engineers embraced so many types of units that their hard-won knowledge might not be particularly appropriate for our needs. However, I felt a keen sense of anticipation when I heard that a truck had been sent down to the local railway station to collect the first batch of these stalwarts.

I walked down to the Sergeant-Major's office to meet our new arrivals. A large three-ton truck arrived and, when the tail-board was dropped, out jumped a policeman, who then helped another man to lift down a third, who had only one leg. Apart from three suitcases and a pair of crutches, the truck was then empty. I went over to talk to the policeman, who was a good-looking man with a tidy row of medals on his chest, but he handed me a letter from his station commander requesting that he be returned as soon as possible, when the undoubted error of his recall had been sorted out. The second man was already pouring out a stream of troubles to our chief clerk. He explained that his wife had just given birth to twins and had nowhere to live and that he was a refrigeration mechanic, which he felt was not a skill we would need. The third man, with only one leg, was relaxed and seemed quite content. He had doubtless accepted payments that one hand of bureaucracy had handed out to him for his war wounds and the other hand in order that he should be recalled to fight again. He knew very well that he would not be going to Korea or anywhere else.

The prospects for producing a really competent unit that could cope with whatever lay ahead in Korea looked gloomy, to put it mildly. More reservists would arrive, but it was clear that a sorting-out period would be necessary before they could be expected to settle down to the strenuous training programme that I was sketching out for them.

Luckily things soon started to improve. All the young Troop Commanders that I had inherited had to leave as they were coming to the end of their National Service periods. The larger organization that we adopted as an independent squadron required two officers per Troop, a captain and a subaltern, and these soon started to arrive. The first to come was Desmond Holmes, a Canadian who had seen service in North Africa, Italy and Western Europe. He was a cheerful extrovert and I put him in charge of 1 Troop. The next captain to arrive was Bertie Beyton-Evans, who I had met occasionally in 79 Armoured Division. He had won an MC in the later stages of the campaign in Germany and was a strong personality with a streak of genuine originality and a good grasp of engineering problems under war conditions. The third Troop Commander was John Page, who I had also met briefly before and liked. He was to prove to be admirably relaxed when under fire and was the sort of leader who completes his task, however difficult or dangerous, without comment or complaint.

Last of all, Patrick Pengelly's replacement as my Second-in-Command arrived at Tidworth railway station. His name was Keith Bean and I went down to meet him.

'Do you know where we are going ?' I asked.

'I heard it was Tidworth,' replied Keith

'We are due to board a troopship for Korea quite soon.'

'Oh, really,' said Keith, and that was all.

What turned out to be so good about these four captains was that each one had a nice sense of humour. They were experienced and professional men and the light touch of humour that each, in his own different way, brought to bear on our problems made them a delight to work with.

New young subalterns also arrived; Keith Eastgate, who had

the build and stamina of the heavyweight boxing enthusiast that he was, and who had to be called Big Keith to avoid confusion with Little Keith Bean; Danny Cadoux-Hudson, Larry Lamble, Peter Chitty and Brian Swinbanks. The last of these was the eldest and most experienced, so I put him to lead the new Park Troop that we had to form. Lastly, a very young Second Lieutenant Robinson was posted in as our First Reinforcement officer, scheduled to wait in Japan with a dozen men until such time as we would need them to replace casualties. Regretfully, they would all be needed.

The situation among the senior non-commissioned officers was better. We needed to double the number we had and some really good volunteers joined us, particularly from Phil Hatch's Regiment.

A feeling started to spread through the unit that there was a real job to be done in Korea. Every day the newspapers and the radio were full of the exploits of the Americans as they withdrew before greatly superior forces and the British government's support for the United Nation's condemnation of aggression was thought to be morally correct.

As the unit's training programme moved into top gear I first concentrated on our own internal administration, taking the Squadron out on exercises that involved sleeping out in the open. In this we were helped by Eric Phillips, a friend of Diana's family, who allowed us to bivouac for the night in his unspoilt woodlands near Royston, as long as we left no mess behind, which we were careful not to do. All this gradually developed a sense of purpose, which had naturally been lacking in the unit before.

The one advantage I had at this time was experience. I had been to war and had had the task of preparing a squadron for war. I knew more or less what would be expected of us, although I have to admit that I did not visualize quite how tough the Korean campaign would be. However, I planned out a comprehensive training programme to cover as many aspects as possible of our likely tasks.

The screening process for reservists developed into a smooth routine. Each man was interviewed as he arrived to discover whether he had any physical disability or compassionate or other reason which would debar him from going abroad. Altogether some four hundred and fifty passed through our hands, from which we were able to retain one hundred and fifty.

The main difficulty for these reservists was concerned with pay. Many were good tradesmen who had been earning up to three times what the Army would give them. Nearly all were married, with young children, and many were faced with rents or Mortgage payments attuned to their civilian pay scale, so their problems were real.

In spite of the fact that those reservists that we eventually took with us had already spent most of their adult working lives serving their country in a war, and probably because of this, when things became really tough in Korea they proved their worth unmistakably. They were hard-drinking and were quick to womanize when they had the chance, but the more awful the conditions, the more unshakeably reliable they became.

The final one hundred men required to complete the Squadron came as volunteers from other units in England, but mostly from Phil Hatch's Regiment.

It turned out that we had six weeks in which to re-equip the Squadron and to train it. The hard working second-in-command, Patrick Pengelly, and his Quartermaster Sergeant, had to complete hundreds of forms requesting a new issue of vehicles, tools, stores, arms and equipment for us to take, and when these arrived, to issue the items out to the Troops so that all could be correctly packed for the long sea voyage that lay ahead.

After about three weeks I was suddenly ordered to send an advance party officer to Korea by air. Desmond Holmes seemed the most experienced, so I sent him. He quickly made his mark out there when, only about ten days after he had left, banner headlines in our newspapers announced 'The bravest man I ever met'. This was the comment made by an American colonel about Desmond, who had been attached to his unit. The hill they were on had come under heavy fire and all their radios had been smashed and their telephone lines cut. Desmond had volunteered to take a message down through the bombardment to explain the situation and to ask for help. This gallant act was to benefit us later.

Another man with a most demanding task during this reorganization period was the Squadron Sergeant-Major, since a big responsibility for discipline fell on his shoulders. If he had been too strong, or a bit of a bully, or too weak, or insufficiently thorough, we would have been in real trouble. But fate was kind in providing just the right man at the right time. The moment I first met Sergeant-Major Brown I sensed that he was a man with even greater depths of character than is usual in those that fill that demanding post. His practical and unflappable good sense was to show itself time and time again. He could spare the time to listen to anyone with a genuine problem and could be relied upon to find an appropriate solution.

As can be imagined, the six weeks allotted to us passed all too quickly. When our vehicles had left and we finally marched out of the barracks at Tidworth past the rest of the Regiment, who, headed by Phil Hatch, lined the route to the railway station, we knew that the administrative foundation for a healthy unit had been laid. True battle-worthiness would only come from experience, both of conditions in the theatre of war and of working together under those conditions. In the meantime we evolved a full training programme for the voyage ahead, both to keep ourselves physically fit and to improve technical skills wherever possible.

CHAPTER 16

THE EXPEDITION
STARTS

The *Empire Windrush* had taken on board a battalion of the Gloucestershire Regiment and our squadron of Royal Engineers at Southampton, and I, who commanded the Engineers, felt a sense of relief to be aboard and on the move at last. All members of the Squadron had put in long hours of work to prepare for this day and, now that it had arrived, a finite corner in all our lives had been turned. For better or for worse, the preliminary training and all the administrative turbulence was over and ahead lay the real test, war in Korea.

Having dumped my kit on the bunk in the small cabin allocated to me, I set out to seek the troop decks where my men would be based for the next six weeks, unconsciously following the time-less rule of army life that a commander should see to the needs of his men first. The troopship was like a floating low-grade hotel. The multitude of battle-dress-clad passengers had most of their normal responsibilities taken away from them, such as cooking, driving or standing guard. Like so many khaki commercial travellers obliged to take a spell away from home, the soldiers ate the sufficient food when they were told to and took it for granted that their normal needs would be catered for by the ship's crew.

It was mid-September 1950. As the long voyage started the narrow gangways echoed to the thump of metal-heeled boots as luggage and some pieces of equipment were moved into place in the new surroundings. Men swore loudly at the awkwardness of the space available to them, and at one corner I had to clamber over a small mountain of files and papers that had been stacked up to await the decisions of the Gloster's orderly room sergeant.

Unsure of the layout of our new home, I was on the lookout for someone I could recognize and who could help to direct me. Most of the men were new to the unit, as indeed I was myself, but by then I knew the senior sergeants by name and some of the more junior ranks by sight. Emerging from a door marked 'Ablutions' came Sergeant Orton, a smile crossing his face as we recognized each other. He was one of the Troop Sergeants and was to prove that he had immense reserves of determination when under fire. He was just the man to help me.

'Do you want to have a dekko at our troopdeck, sir?' he said, correctly divining my intention.

'Yes. What's it like?'

'As a matter of fact, I think it's a bit better than usual. We are pretty tight for space but everything is spotlessly clean.'

Once inside it, the deck looked like a disturbed ant heap. A hundred men were settling in there, moving things about, trying out hammocks or unpacking. The light was poor, not only because of the numerous metal pillars that supported the deck above, but also because the low headroom meant that the electric light bulbs were constantly being screened by bedding, clothes and bodies. In spite of the superficial cleanliness, there was no escape from the distinctive, slightly acrid smell of massed male humanity.

Recognizing one man, a bulldozer driver who had only recently joined us, I soon found from his rough good humour that things were about as good as could be expected. As a reservist, called up for the Korean emergency, this driver was no stranger to troop-ships.

Sergeant Orton was doing his own enquiring. 'Do you know where your boat station is, lad?' he asked one Sapper.

'We've been told it's on C Deck at the stern,' he replied, adding mischievously, 'That's the back isn't it, Sarge?'

'You know damn well it's at the back, but make sure you know how to get there quickly. There will be a trial run any minute now, and if we don't get off the mark smartly they'll make us do it again. Corporal Higgins,' he went on, turning to a fair-haired young NCO who was unpacking nearby, 'send off one of your

130

men straight away to find the quickest way to the stern of C Deck.'

Shortly after I asked Sergeant Orton to explain what he had meant about a practice muster at our boat stations, as I had heard nothing. When would it be?

'One of the crew tipped me off,' he explained. 'They always have a trial muster as soon as they can on a voyage. I think they do it to show who is boss!'

Bertie Beyton-Evans joined us. 'I have been looking at all this piping,' he said, indicating the dozens of various sized grey pipes that covered the ceiling of the troopdeck like an upturned dish of spaghetti, 'and some of it is an air blowing system. I wonder if you could get the crew to turn it on? The atmosphere in here is becoming pretty horrible.'

'Yes, I quite agree,' I replied, 'I'll go and dig out the Ship's Adjutant. I am sure he can arrange it. Is there anything else that needs doing?'

With no more suggestions, I soon left and made my way to the top deck, where past experience told me that the ship's administrative offices would be located. Going up there was like entering a new world. Everything was order and tidiness. Inside a door marked Ship's Adjutant sat a rather short, square-shouldered army captain, writing a letter on an otherwise empty desk.

I introduced myself to this self-controlled man, who stood up politely and said his name was Pat Angier. As he spoke, I felt appreciation for the obvious interest he showed in what I was saying. I explained the advantage of switching on the air circulation system, and Pat agreed to see if it could be done.

The troopship was still on the very earliest stage of its long voyage to the other side of the globe. Reaching the end of Southampton Water, it crept past two large flying boats anchored off Calshot. In September 1950 these relics from the pre-war system of communication between the distant outposts of Empire already looked like prehistoric monsters, now that the whistling jet engine was coming into its own in the skies.

As the ship gathered speed and swung round to the east to pass into the Solent on its way to the open sea, I retraced my steps to my cabin with a definite purpose. In those days, when soldiers were sent abroad they were not entitled to army accommodation for their families left in England. Diana and I had searched frantically in the short time available for a suitable home for her and our children and had finally settled on one on the Isle of Wight, where prices seemed slightly lower. So, as the ship steamed past Cowes, I would have a last fleeting chance to wave goodbye to the little family that meant so much to me. Anticipating this moment, Diana had said she would keep a lookout and would wave to me, although I was not at all sure I would be able to pick her out from so far away. One good thing was that my cabin was on the starboard side and therefore conveniently placed for scanning the shore of the Island.

Just then a hideous bell jangled and over the ship's loudspeaker system came the order 'All ranks proceed to emergency boat stations immediately.'

This routine alert was standard practice on all troopships, and on all civil passenger ships for that matter, and with good reason. This same ship, the *Empire Windrush*, was to sink in the Mediterranean about a year later without any loss of life, because all on board knew exactly where to go and what to do. From my point of view, the trouble with this particular alarm was that my boat station was on the port side of the ship facing, not Cowes, but back up Southampton Water.

Having no option, I found my correct boat station and fretted there whilst precious minutes passed and one of the ship's officers explained slowly what had to be done in an emergency. At last I could restrain myself no longer and quietly slipped away, crossed the now deserted centre of the ship and found a porthole on the starboard side. I was just in time. A great white sheet was hanging out of a bedroom window in my family's house, flapping gently in the light air. Delighted, I waved my handkerchief to and fro across the porthole in a forlorn hope that they would know that I had seen and appreciated their efforts.

Quite suddenly it hit me. I had a clear presentiment that I was heading for death and that I would never again see my family.

This was a startling experience. In five years of war I had been shelled, bombed and shot at by rifles and automatic weapons. I was no stranger to that sudden stab of fear for one's personal safety that makes a man fling himself into a ditch only a fraction of a second after he has heard the first warning whistle of an incoming shell. But the circumstances of this presentiment were

132

entirely different. I felt no fear. It was as though some higher authority had passed me a factual message and I have to add that, although I believed in the existence of a God of some sort, my communications with Him were limited to occasional attendances at church parades. Standing in a large ship within sight of land, I was certainly in no danger of any sort. If anything, my morale was rather higher than usual, since we had just completed a very successful few weeks of hectic training to weld our men together into an effective unit and this had been a rewarding time. The main need had been to develop some comradeship and it had given me quiet pleasure to detect the growth of that fragile plant in the different groupings that go to make up a military unit. Such news as we read in the papers was not too bad about the war. There just seemed to be no logical reason why such a thought should have entered my head.

My musings were interrupted by a quiet voice. 'Hello; are you all right?'

The speaker was Pat. I never did know what he had seen in my expression, but I sensed from his tone that here was a sympathetic personality, prepared to help.

'The Captain is making his rounds,' Pat continued. 'If you are quick you can get to your boat station before he arrives.'

I could hear footsteps approaching, so I thanked Pat hurriedly and as I slipped away I heard him add, 'By the way, I have fixed for those air blowers you asked about to be turned on when this practice is finished.'

Back at the boat station the ship's officer was still droning on about what should and should not be done in various unlikely circumstances. The whole incident had only taken a couple of minutes.

Of course I did not die on some Korean hill, or I would not be writing this now, but when the feeling first hit me, there was an element of absolute inevitability in it. I just knew it was going to happen. I could not explain it; I felt that I should not discuss it with anyone else; I just had to accept it.

Life had to go on, and it was a busy life, but at the back of my mind there was to rest, during the whole time I spent in Korea, a certain knowledge that I would die there. Looking back now, I do not think that it affected my actions in any way, nor do I think that the actions of others who have had a similar experience have been noticeably altered. On a handful of occasions when real danger faced me, the sense of inevitability made me, if anything, slightly carefree: if this was to be the end, then so be it.

In the human being fear is a highly complex emotion. It lurks round every corner in wartime, whether your side or your enemy is winning. Each person controls it as tightly as possible and it is hardly ever readily apparent. Perhaps a wise psychologist can define fear accurately, but this is much too difficult for the ordinary soldier caught up in a war, as there seem to be several different kinds of fear. One kind pumps adrenaline into the blood stream, resulting in greater efficiency and even, if the situation calls for it, bravery. The voices of men in dangerous positions become crisper and sharper. Their senses operate at maximum awareness, seeking information to send to the brain so that the most effective action can be taken. Of the other kinds of fear, perhaps the most insidious is worry. Why has somebody not arrived yet? Supposing he never arrives, what shall I do? On and on the questions buzz through the head, while the answers to them become fewer and fewer. Looking back now, I wonder why I did not worry myself cruelly about my presentiment, but I did not. I was able to push the thought to the back of my mind, never quite forgetting it but not allowing it to alter my actions. Perhaps the Marquess of Montrose summed it up when he wrote:

"He either fears his fate too much,
Or his deserts are small,
That puts it not unto the touch
To win or lose it all."

We soon settled down to the routine of life aboard a troopship. All of us had lived through six years of war, with all that meant in terms of food and clothing rationing, and shortages of practically everything else. The ship's food turned out to be at a definitely higher standard than the usual army fare and, although they might be considered a bit ordinary today, meals were something to look forward to then. Beer, spirits and cigarettes were available at proper duty-free prices, administrative responsibilities were at a minimum, so life was not unagreeable. There was even a minute leavening of the usually all male environment, provided by two lively nursing sisters on their way out to a military hospital in Japan.

All day long we trained hard. We knew what war entailed in the way of physical hardship and speed of reaction, so we tried to keep both our muscles firm and our brains active. We had plenty of live ammunition on board, and one of the most popular training sessions was that of rifle shooting over the stern of the ship. A corporal would take half a dozen of his men to the aft deck, fire his rifle into the sea and then the others would fire at the splash made by his bullet. At first their shots would be spread over a wide area, but as skill developed they would close onto their target. Later the corporal would try to surprise his men by shooting where they were least expecting, but their following shots usually managed to converge in a tight circle round the splash of his.

Apart from co-ordinating the training, I spent much of my time going round the groups as they worked to get to know the men of my squadron. Each one had his problems, and quiet questioning would gradually elicit what these were. Most were concerned with how to better themselves so that in the uncertain future, when they had hopefully survived the campaign ahead, they might get a decent job when they had been demobilized. Nothing much could be done on board to alleviate these anxieties, but it still seemed worthwhile to bring them into the open, in the hope that, if all went well, courses might be arranged to suit individual needs at some later date.

The Bay of Biscay was rough, as we had expected, but after passing Gibraltar and sailing past the harsh stone cliffs of Southern Spain, we enjoyed the warmth and calm of the Mediterranean.

A ten-mile route march was arranged for us at Port Said. Carrying rifles and ammunition and our full marching equipment, we set off early in the morning along a dreary road that became hotter and dustier as time went on. The Glosters were in front of us and I well remember the lean figure of Colonel Fred Carne leading his men back past us after he had reached the half-way mark. We were sweating from every pore by the time we returned to the port, but someone had had the foresight to arrange for us to cool off by swimming in a large open water tank. We stripped off and plunged into this, a thousand naked bodies showing up as blazing white against the all-pervading brown of our surroundings.

Back on board, I warned the men of the dangers they must face when they were given the afternoon off to wander through the port. Venereal disease is a constant worry for soldiers at war, but Port Said had a bad reputation for every form of petty thieving as well.

There was a minor occurrence at dinner at Port Said. I should explain that the officers were all allocated seats at different tables in the dining room and I was at the Captain's table. Here, each evening, a strange ritual took place. The Commanding Officer of the Gloster's, always known as Fred, was one of the most silent individuals I have ever met, before or since. He seldom spoke, even to answer a question, and the only other person in my experience who was in the same class of keeping himself to himself was the Captain of this troopship. Fred sat on the Captain's right and each evening they would come down to the table, nod briefly to each other and to the rest of us, and then become totally immersed in their own thoughts.

In those days troopships always carried a resident officer, called the OC Troops, who, as the only other lieutenant colonel on board, sat on the Captain's left. A splendid officer, large, round and hospitable, he would appear every evening, usually a bit late, and his hospitality would be clear for all to see. Parting company from whoever he had been drinking with, he would carry on the story he had been telling, while his laughter burst across the room.

Having sat down, the icy quiet at his end of the table would gradually have its effect on him. His efforts at conversation became more and more stilted until, towards the end of the meal, he too sat in silence. On this occasion, at Port Said, the OC Troops was even fuller than usual with bonhomie, and as he sat down he slapped the Captain on the back in a friendly way. Not a muscle stirred on the iron man's face. Nothing was said, but this liberty was never taken again.

At the other end of this table sat Pat, the Adjutant, with me on his right and Dennis Harding, the acting second-in-command of the Glosters, on his left. Without intruding on the nightly ritual taking place at the more senior end of the table, we could carry on quiet conversations. It was on one of these evenings that Pat told me that he had a metal plate in his skull as a result of a wound incurred in Italy during the World War.

'Does it hurt?' I asked,

'No, no. Nothing to complain about. I get headaches occasionally, and I mustn't drink too much. The doctor who put it in told me I shouldn't really be alive, so I certainly cannot complain and I take each day to be a special bonus.'

We did not know it then, thank goodness, but not too many of these special bonuses lay ahead for Pat.

That night we slid through the silky desert darkness, raising a little wave on each bank of the Canal as we sailed slowly south.

Next day was bright and hot, and we returned to our now customary training. Shots were ringing out from the stern, as I went down to the sick bay to see a sapper. My Sergeant-Major told me the story. This young man, who was only nineteen, had gone on shore at Port Said with an older member of our Headquarter Troop. Together they had wandered round the bazaar until the older man decided to buy a trinket for his wife from an Arab, whose wares were displayed on a large wooden table.

Inevitably, the Arab gave the sapper short change. An argument developed and the sapper, who was rather hot-tempered, and saw he was getting nowhere, became so annoyed that he upturned the table, tipping all the Arab's goods onto the street.

A roar of rage went up from the Arab and friends of his closed round the two soldiers. Fighting broke out as the younger sapper went in to rescue his friend. Police arrived and set about all and sundry with heavy lathis. Unfortunately one policeman hit the young sapper a severe blow across the small of his back, before a group of the Glosters, seeing what was happening, moved in and rescued our pair.

The older man was bruised but all right, but the younger one was in obvious pain and spent the night in the sick bay. When I visited him next morning he said that he felt a bit better but that whenever he went to urinate blood came out.

There were two doctors on board, the ship's own doctor and the Glosters', and the latter seemed to be in charge. He discussed the case with me fully, explaining that the man's spleen had been ruptured and that he reckoned that an operation would be necessary to remove the spleen.

A strange perversity seemed to ensure that whichever way a troopship travelled through the Red Sea the wind was always astern. This was the third time I had made the trip and the pattern was faithfully followed. Down in the troop deck the blowers were at full power day and night. They succeeded in causing some circulation of air, but it was still dreadfully hot down there.

In the Officers' Dining Room the heat was just the same, but lunch was always more light-hearted than dinner, as the formidable ship's captain never attended. Colonel Carne of the Glosters would take a light snack and leave, so the rest of us could then relax. A couple of days after leaving Port Said, however, Pat was very serious.

'The Captain is furious,' he said. 'One of our men who was shooting over the stern was seen by a member of the crew to shoot a dolphin. He says this is inexcusable and that all shooting must stop at once.'

I remonstrated at this. The shooting was excellent training and was enjoyed by the men.

'No,' said Pat, 'the Skipper is adamant. It seems to be the fact that it was a dolphin that has annoyed him so much. He says that it will mean a death on board. I suppose that there is some nautical tradition to that effect.'

Of course I had to bow to the Captain's authority and I recast the training programme for the rest of the day, and for the following days.

Next day the Glosters doctor came to discuss the forthcoming operation that would have to be performed. He had decided to carry it out in the evening when the sun had gone down and it would be somewhat cooler. Unfortunately, the air-blowing system would have to be turned off, as it would be dangerous for dirty air to be blown onto an open wound.

In due course the time for the operation came round. Everywhere on the ship became too hot for comfort except the open decks. The messenger came to me from the doctor to say that blood donors would be required, so I went down to the small sick bay with three or four others. When we had given the blood it was

138

a relief to get away from the sticky heat of the lower decks.

Sometime the next day the doctor came to see me to report that the unfortunate patient had died. He put the death down to heat exhaustion which, in his weakened state, had proved too much.

Sadly I had to write to his parents to try to explain this need-less tragedy and he was buried at Aden, our next port of call.

Death is always sad, particularly when it seeks out someone so young. This occasion hit me very hard, I felt it was all so point-less. The argument had been about a few shillings and nothing more. Who should take the blame? The Egyptian police certainly over- reacted, but why? Had they suffered under some officious Englishman who threw his petty authority about, leaving a sullen resentment in those under him? Then, seeing an opportunity to reverse the scales, the Egyptians lashed out against a sudden chance target that presented itself. We considered sending an official complaint about the police, but decided not to. Already we were hundreds of miles away and any such action would undoubtedly be futile.

We missed this man sorely. He had been very inexperienced, but he was of the material that permits the human race to move upwards to better things – cheerful, willing, strong and anxious to learn. Raised in simple surroundings in Northern Ireland, he was one of Nature's gentlemen; now he was gone.

The troopship steadily plodded on methodically. The news from Korea became better and better. BBC programmes used to be broadcast over the ship's loudspeaker system and as we approached Aden we heard of that master stroke of a master strategist – General Douglas MacArthur's capture of the port of Inchon, half-way up the west coast of Korea. Overnight the scales were turned, and by the time we had completed a broiling route march through the streets of Colombo we heard that Seoul had been recaptured.

By that time we had really settled down to life on board ship. Even taking a bath in warm sea water was routine, although the slime produced by the salt water soap never made one feel prop-erly clean.

Our last port of call was Singapore which I had last visited in 1948. It made a welcome change to sample Chinese cooking again and I even managed to telephone up to Kluang in Malaya to talk to Colonel Herbie Carrington-Smith who was still commanding the Engineer Training Centre that I had raised and commanded.

We could not know the sad fact that the war in Korea was to be a unique attempt by the United Nations to punish wanton aggression. At the time it felt to be a lucky chance that the Soviets had walked out of the Security Council and hence had not been able to exercise their veto when the rest of the Council decided to go to the assistance of the beleaguered South Koreans. After each of the World Wars in this century, man has made an attempt to outlaw war. The nations have united to try to ensure that they and their people should not have to go through the extreme agony of major war again. Presumably mankind just forgets how unpleasant war is. Certainly the idealism that resulted in the League of Nations in 1920 did not enable that organization to last long enough to stand up to the Fascist dictators in the late 1930s.

The United Nations was potentially far more powerful than its predecessor when it came into being in October 1945. Less than five years later it was faced with a clear example of aggression when on 25 June 1950 the communist regime of North Korea sent its forces, well armed with Soviet tanks, against the South. The Security Council acted at once, asking all member states to give assistance to the South. We know now that the eventual success was still three years ahead from the time we were sailing towards Korea.

Okinawa was low on the horizon when an albatross joined us. Hardly using its tremendous wings except to adjust its angle of glide, this beautiful creature kept watch over us for a couple of days as we traversed the South China Sea.

We heard that MacArthur's advance had reached Pyongyang in North Korea. As we celebrated the successive items of good news in the ship's bar, the opinion gained ground that our journey was a wasted one and that we would be home again soon. None of this altered my conviction that tragedy was in store for us. Of course I did not say anything about this to anybody, not even to Pat, who was a firm friend by now. Such an admission would have smacked of defeatism, which was unforgivable, and would certainly have risked exposure to ridicule.

Finally, on the last day of October, the engines were cut and we inched slowly into Pusan harbour, at the southern tip of the Korean peninsula.

Surprisingly, we were greeted by an American Army band. The gangplank was lowered and Fred Carne descended first, to the salutes of the Port Commander and some of his staff. This seemed a rather light-hearted way to start the serious business of going to war, but we appreciated the gesture and the obvious trouble that had been taken on our behalf.

One by one we all stepped down onto the dry land of a country about which we knew virtually nothing, saying goodbye to the kindly crew who had watched over our needs for six long weeks. The voyage was finished at last and a new chapter in the lives of each one of us was opened.

CHAPTER 17

FIRST IMPRESSIONS
OF KOREA

When we landed the first thing that we heard was that our transport, which had come on a separate ship from England, had already arrived. We were told that our drivers must take this up to the city of Suwon which is a few miles south of the capital of South Korea, Seoul. I decided to travel up with this transport because the rest of the squadron would be going by rail and I believed that I would get a much better feel for the country by taking the road trip up.

We were driven first to a transit camp in the northern outskirts of Pusan. Here we were fed and obtained some maps for the route north. Transit camps are dreary places and this was no exception to the rule. We were pleased to be on the move later in the day, taking the only good road which left Pusan by the western suburbs and followed up through Taegu towards Suwon.

Warfare in the middle of this century involved countless hours spent driving convoys of vehicles from one area to another. On the whole this was a boring occupation, as speeds were kept down to about twenty miles per hour, presumably for safety reasons. However, this result of mobile warfare was certainly preferable to the equally boring but much more dangerous vocation of living in a trench, as required by the static warfare earlier in the century. The officer commanding the convoy had to keep himself fairly alert if only to ensure that the correct route was followed. Even in England all signposts had been removed for the duration of the

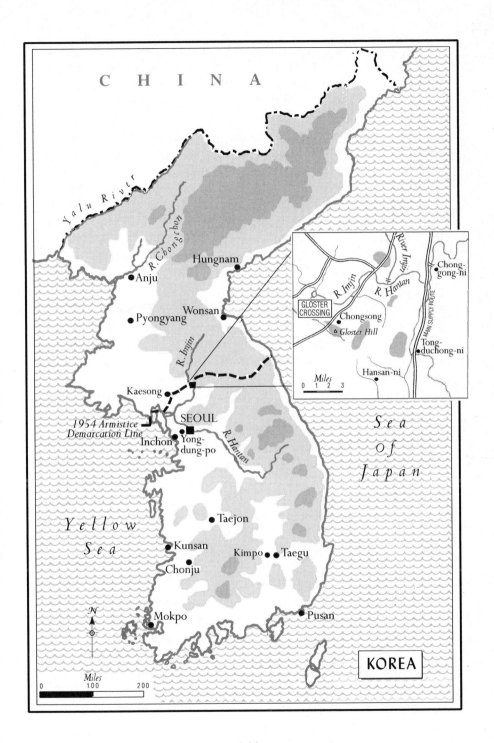

CHINA

Yalu River

R. Chongchon

Anju

Hungnam

Pyongyang

Wonsan

R. Imjin

Kaesong

*1954 Armistice
Demarcation Line*

Inchon

SEOUL

Yong-
dung-po

R. Hantan

*Yellow
Sea*

Taejon

Kunsan

Kimpo

Taegu

Chonju

N

Mokpo

Pusan

*Sea
of
Japan*

Miles
0   100   200

KOREA

River Imjin

R. Imjin

R. Hantan

Chong-
gong-ni

GLOSTER
CROSSING

Chongsong

△ *Gloster Hill*

Tong-
duchong-ni

MAIN SUPPLY ROUTE

Hansan-ni

Miles
0   1   2   3

143

war, whilst in Korea, if there had been any, we couldn't have understood them. Additionally, in an operational theatre such as Korea wear and tear of the road network, sometimes due to deliberate demolitions by either side in the struggle, often meant alterations to the route one expected from pure map reading. We were all very accustomed to this pastime and took it in our stride, hoping always that nothing would go wrong to lengthen a trip that would be quite long enough as it was.

There was not much to look at on this trip. The country consisted of hills and more hills, covered by low scrub and small stunted trees. Everything was a dull brown colour. The villages had often been damaged but some repairs had been made. Houses all had thatched roofs and the thatch was amazingly thick, up to one metre in many cases. On the northern side of the houses, the thatch often went right down to the ground so that there were no doors or windows on that side and all activity took place on the warmer, southern side. Such people as we saw were going about their business, usually using primitive tools such as shovels or brooms. There was no civilian transport of any sort, in fact the only traffic we saw were occasional groups of United States Army supply vehicles moving south, presumably to be refilled before they took their next load up to the fighting forces. Our total journey was about four hundred miles so, for hour after hour, we travelled along the dusty roads with only the usual residue of war, burnt-out vehicles and tanks, occasionally catching our interest. However, this was what I had expected to see. After all, few countries in the northern hemisphere are particularly interesting in early November; Korea was no exception.

The dress of the Korean peasant showed a remarkable uniformity throughout the land, extending, as we were to discover later, to the North as well. The men wore white jackets and baggy white trousers, heavily padded as a protection against the cold. Their socks also appeared to be well padded. Their shoes were simple affairs made of either string or grass, plaited to cover their feet. Gloves did not seem to exist, but sleeves were long enough for the hands to be concealed inside when necessary.

The older men's headgear was most unusual and consisted of a small round tophat-shaped creation made of horsehair, which was perched on top of the head. Underneath this was worn a dark

144

skull-cap of cloth. When it was really cold, a more practical fur hat, that could be pulled down over the ears, was worn.

The women wore voluminous skirts, sometimes fastened under the armpit and sometimes under the breasts. Over their shoulders they wore a padded jacket which extended down to breast level. They wore white cloth headgear, except in summer, as we were to see, when they often wore wide conical hats made of bamboo, similar to those seen in most of east Asia, when they were at work in the fields.

Children, like those in poor countries all over the world, were often in rags, and usually filthy rags.

We stopped for the night beside the road and a hot meal was cooked. A slight diversion occurred when our guard arrived with an American officer who requested permission to spend the night with us. He explained that there were remnants of the North Korean armies still in the hills in these parts and he therefore wanted to spend the night with a unit that would provide a guard. What was particularly surprising was that he had with him a young Japanese girl. He explained that he had been posted from Japan and that he had brought with him his servant. This seemed a most odd way of going to war and I often wondered what happened to him, and his servant, when the fighting really became unpleasant later on. However, he was a cheerful and likeable character. Not only did he keep us amused during the evening but when he left he gave me a camping kettle. This was designed to take fire up the middle and proved to be an absolutely invaluable piece of equipment, producing boiling water quickly throughout the winter, however unpleasant the circumstances. Next day we said goodbye to our American guest and our long convoy of vehicles completed the journey to Suwon.

I left all the vehicles outside the town and drove in to find where we had to go. Suwon is dominated by a huge wall which surrounds the old city. This wall had been built, so we were told, on the orders of Genghis Khan. It still remains as a spectacular boundary to this ancient city.

I soon found our signs and located the area that had been allotted to us. This proved to be a school building and some huts surrounding a flat gravel patch, rather like a barrack square. I returned and guided the vehicles to their new location which had been efficiently marked out by our Advance Party Officer, Desmond Holmes.

During this trip northwards there had only been a slight wind which was coming from the south. Once we arrived at our destination the reality of winter in Korea was suddenly brought home to us. The wind changed and came from the north and the temperature dropped many degrees. We had been told that it would be cold in winter and all our soldiers had been allocated one extra blanket to meet this eventuality.

The coldest place in the northern hemisphere occurs in Siberia some way north of Manchuria. In meteorological language this is termed the Siberian High. Temperatures there can reach minus 100 degrees Fahrenheit and we were in for a bad winter. This temperature is so much colder than anything experienced in Europe that it cannot easily be comprehended. So when the wind comes from the north it starts in this exceptional cold and warms up gradually as it crosses Manchuria and Korea. It can still be at minus 30 degrees Fahrenheit on the 38th parallel, which is the sort of cold that can have been experienced only in winter in western Europe by a handful of Alpine mountaineers and by Lapps far to the north of the Arctic Circle.

Our school building appeared to be made of matchwood, with internal walls made out of paper. There was clearly no question of lighting a fire inside the building and indeed even one outside had to be well away from it. After the first night of north wind, the whole unit was at a virtual standstill. The oils in both vehicles and weapons had turned into a kind of glue so that they could not be operated, but above all every man felt chilled to the bone. It was just as well that no operational tasks had been given to us yet. All that anyone could think about was how to get warm. Mercifully, after about thirty-six hours of this, the wind changed to the south, bringing a mild breeze from the Sea of Japan and utter relief to the raw newcomers to Korea.

But we had been warned. One day that wind would come again, doubtless even colder as the nights shortened.

Our second-in-command, Little Keith, who was responsible for administration, wasted no time in finding out what Brigade Headquarters could do. Already they had cabled to England asking for duffel coats for each man, but these would take some

146

time to arrive. In fact the War Office sent them by sea, which took five months, by which time the winter had ended, and anyway, some joker sent Women's Royal Army Corps coats which were waist- length cream-coloured creations of no use to us. These never left the port of Pusan, where, so we heard, they proved useful to procure the services of local girls. This was not the fault of Brigade Headquarters, but it did mean that we were left to our own resources.

By this time the war in Korea was going very well for the United Nations forces. American troops were up to the very north of North Korea near the Yalu River. We heard that the Chinese Army might intervene, but we did not really believe that this would prove to be any problem.

The tasks of Engineers in the sort of mobile warfare that was being fought are all concerned with keeping communications open. As a result of the experiences I had already had in war in Europe I was well aware of the problems that would face us. I was also well aware of my own lack of knowledge of the country of Korea. Therefore I managed to arrange a trip to North Korea to discover what conditions were really like there. I took Desmond with me, since he had much more knowledge of the country than any of us and also since he had already achieved a wonderful reputation with some of the American units.

So, a few days after arriving at Suwon, I hitched a ride with Desmond on a U.S. transport plane from the airfield at Kimpo up to Pyongyang, the northern capital.

In those early days we were very ignorant of the real conditions in Korea. Fighting was going on far to the north, near the border with China, but what was it like up there? Presumably it was colder, as it was two to three hundred miles further north, but were the hills steeper, were the roads any better or worse than those around us, was stone and gravel available for work on roads and tracks, how wooded was it, how wide were the rivers, what were the bridges like, etc., etc.? Nobody in our brigade could answer these engineer questions, so the only thing to do was to take a look and find out for myself, since the answers would change our preparations for the war that lay ahead.

I arranged to visit our sister British Brigade, located well to the north and involved in operations up there. This was 27 Brigade, consisting of the Middlesex Regiment, the Argyll and Sutherland Highlanders and an Australian battalion, all commanded by Brigadier Aubrey Coad, whose tactical good sense had already made him a name to be reckoned with.

The British units in 27 Brigade had come to Korea from Hong Kong. Whilst our Brigade had required troop ships to be assembled and then a six week long voyage, 27 Brigade had been moved very soon after Prime Minister Attlee's government had decided to assist the Americans by sending troops. They had fought gallantly in the Pusan perimeter in the days when it seemed that North Korea might finish the war by occupying the whole peninsula. Then, after General MacArthur's masterly landing at Inchon which cut the supply lines from the north and precipitated a headlong withdrawal by the North Koreans, 27 Brigade had advanced quickly northwards with the other troops from the perimeter.

So when 27 Brigade had landed in Korea the situation had looked really bad for the United Nations force, whereas when we landed, a couple of months later, the situation was reversed and all appeared to be going well.

Desmond came with me, largely because two pairs of eyes are better than one on a reconnaissance of this sort, but also because he was the only person in our Squadron who knew anything at all about Korea, having flown out as the advance party officer whilst we came by sea. Desmond was a Canadian, who had volunteered to join the Sappers after doing well at his military academy at Kingston, Ontario. He was an open-hearted man who fitted in well in any company, particularly, of course, with Americans. Together we were driven to Kimpo airfield and hitched a ride on a cargo plane to Pyongyang, an efficient, if cold method of travel.

The northern capital was desperately damaged when we reached it, obviously from bombing. However, I felt little remorse for the people who lived there, since they had elected to start this war. Somehow we borrowed a jeep with a Korean driver and set off to the north along roads jammed with American administrative transport. It was a slow journey and we had plenty of time to view the countryside, which was perceptibly bleaker than it had been in South Korea. There, great stretches of mountainside would be covered in dwarf oaks and firs, but in the North it seemed that such trees that grew at all were only near the valley floors. Like South Korea, the North seemed to consist of an endless succession of mountain ridges. They were appreciably higher than those we had encountered in the South, but otherwise much the same, apart from the lack of vegetation.

After stopping for the night with a friendly American outfit, next day we reached the River Chonghon and crossed by a military floating bridge near the ruined town of Anju. In the foothills just north of the river we met the first tactical sign pointing the way to the headquarters of 27 Brigade and by lunchtime we had reached our destination.

After reporting in to the Brigade Major, I climbed a nearby hill to see what the countryside looked like. There was little difference in the view compared with South Korea. The endless snow-covered hills stretched north towards the Manchurian border. The only breaks in the whiteness were patches of brown where snow had been blown away, uncovering the barren earth. Unlike South Korea, where every lowlying flat area showed signs of cultivation, here there were no such signs. Probably there were some simple villages tucked down in sheltered valleys, but I could see none. It all looked peaceful, but inhospitable. Obviously this was tough country to live in. The hills were often steep at their lower slopes, but most were rounded on top, not too much unlike parts of the Lowlands of Scotland, but higher and on a larger scale.

The only signs of life were on neighbouring hills where occasional khaki-clad figures went about their business. 27 Brigade was tactically distributed round a perimeter of hills so that battalions could support each other in the event of an attack, with the headquarters centrally placed below them. Their whole set-up looked sensible and professional.

It was not readily obvious from our local maps that 27 Brigade was blocking much of the route from China that the Mongols had taken in the early 13th century and the Manchus in the 17th century. They little knew that their professionalism would be most severely tested by yet another Chinese mass invasion very soon.

Having seen what conditions were like, Desmond and I drove off to see the American First Cavalry Division, with whom

149

Desmond had won his spurs previously. It was bitterly cold and we travelled in an open jeep driven by our cheerful Korean, who had very little grasp of English. We had not gone far when it became obvious that something was seriously wrong with the jeep. The driver looked under the bonnet and then announced, 'We frozen.' However, this had happened to him before, and with our help he set about collecting bits of wood from a damaged house. He then lit a fire under the front of the bonnet of the jeep. I fully expected the whole vehicle to go up in flames, but after about a quarter of an hour he suddenly announced, 'OK now,' and started the engine. Sure enough, all seemed to be well and we continued our journey without further incident.

We were met with the greatest friendliness by Desmond's acquaintances in First Cav. One of them was a lieutenant colonel, who said how cold we looked. We certainly were very cold indeed, as our British Army uniform was totally inadequate for the temperature, which was below zero Fahrenheit. However, he said he would do something about it and he was as good as his word in presenting us each with two most valuable pieces of clothing, an American Army hat, a proper winter garment with padded ear flaps that could be laced together under the chin, and a pile liner. The latter was a long-sleeved khaki jacket lined with nylon fur. The moment I put mine on, I felt a retentive warmth stealing over me. Today, over forty years later, I still possess this magnificent piece of kit, which has warmed me on countless occasions. It looks scruffy now, so I only use if for winter gardening, but I believe I would class it as the most useful gift I have ever received.

Another item we noticed that the Americans all had were their sleeping bags. These were well-padded inner liners that fitted inside a waterproof canvas outside bag. They were the sort of proper winter equipment that we should have brought with us and I was most envious of them. However, we spent that night in a tent in which an object referred to as a space heater, a metal burner fuelled from a jerrican of petrol, kept us warm.

Before we left next morning we were invited to try on American winter boots, and were then presented with the pairs that fitted. These were robust calf-length rubberized boots with inner soles that were a good half-inch thick. They were far warmer than the good old leather British Army boots that we had worn up till then.

What marvellous hospitality, and what generosity! I thanked our hosts from the bottom of my heart, but they only replied that it was nothing compared with what Desmond had done to help them. He really must have impressed them.

In war the Sapper has many tasks but the main one can be summed up as keeping open adequate routes for the transport required by other Arms. This applies particularly in an advance, when bridges have to be built, and a corollary is that in a withdrawal he must damage the road system as much as possible so as to delay his enemy. When neither advance nor withdrawal is taking place, the Sapper can still be severely tested as his Army's transport subjects the local road network to a beating for which it was never designed.

I had expected that this last alternative would be what the American Army engineers were having to put up with in North Korea. What I had not realized was how low the temperature would be up there. Earth roads, that would have needed constant attention in Europe, were now frozen like concrete and were capable of taking almost unlimited traffic. Presumably a thaw would set in, in March or April, and then the work that would be required on the roads did not bear thinking about, but our trip had been worthwhile if only because I then realized just what happened in Korea in winter. It was still only November and the temperatures of minus thirty Fahrenheit and even minus forty Fahrenheit that we would encounter were still ahead of us.

Back in Pyongyang we made ourselves as comfortable as possible in the unheated cargo aircraft, greatly helped by our pile liners, and endured the slow flight back to Kimpo.

Altogether our reconnaissance trip had proved most instructive, as well as most rewarding from the hospitality of our American hosts.

CHAPTER 18

PREPARING FOR REAL WAR

Life for us in Korea for the first fortnight of November 1950 was rather akin to the 'phoney war' period in 1939–40, before the Germans launched their attack that culminated, for us, in the Dunkirk evacuation. We were not shot at, as only our own aircraft crossed the skies above us and no enemy interfered with our activities. It was valuable to have a settling-in period, short though it proved to be.

Among all my varied war experience I had hardly ever spoken to an American soldier. I was, of course, under General Eisenhower in Europe, but as a commander of a squadron of armoured engineers I was much too far down the ladder of command ever to meet him. The same was true for most of our Brigade when we landed in Korea.

A Brigade is normally under the command of a Division in a military force, and a Division under a Corps. Here in Korea we were classified as an Independent Brigade Group and so came directly under one of the American Corps Headquarters. Initially, and so it turned out for most of the time we were out there, we came under First (US) Corps – always known as I (eye) Corps.

55 Independent Squadron, Royal Engineers, which I commanded, had three working Troops, a Park Troop, which held heavy equipment, such as bulldozers, for use by the working Troops as they required, and a Headquarters Troop. If we were to be called upon to carry out a major task, such as to bridge a

wide river, to demolish major bridges or to build an airstrip, the necessary stores and equipment would have to be allocated to us by the Engineer Branch of I Corps. I therefore had, in effect, two commanders, first the Brigadier commanding 29 Brigade, Tom Brodie by name, whose needs were my prime operational concern, and, secondly the Commanding Engineer of I Corps, without whose help those needs could never be met.

The moment I returned from the far north I set out to make my number with the Engineer Branch of I Corps. They turned out to be both helpful and friendly, but above all, the commanding engineer, Colonel Itschener, was a most experienced and sensible officer. I took to him from the very first meeting I had with him.

We had not been long in Suwon when I received a call from Colonel Itschener who asked if we could build a floating bridge over the Han River just upstream from Seoul, the capital city. I accepted this with alacrity, as taking on a major task like that would help us to settle in to our new environment better than anything.

I did a reconnaissance, ordered up all the necessary equipment for a floating bridge over a river about the size of the Thames at London, and soon the Squadron were hard at work. The equipment was, of course, American and therefore new to us. However, we were provided with some American Engineer manuals and, since most of the men in 55 Squadron were reasonably experienced, we found the construction straightforward.

The job took us about four days, as far as I can remember, including the building of approach roads on both banks. It was not until the third day that I realized that one or other of the staff officers from the Engineer Branch of I Corps was at the site, watching all the time. The penny dropped! Of course Colonel Itschener, being an experienced commander, was putting us through our paces just to see how we made out. Luckily for us, we completed the bridge and opened it for traffic in just under the planning time for a task of this size that was recorded in the American manual. From then on Colonel Itschener accepted us as equals to his own engineer units. We were soon to learn that in fact we were not equal to the Americans in the essential task of improvised bridging. In this their experience far exceeded ours. However, in demolition tasks we had the edge

153

over them; perhaps we had been involved in more retreating than they had!

Whilst we were working on our bridge the news filtered through that the Chinese had launched a massive attack against our forces on the western side of North Korea. 27 Brigade had held their positions brilliantly, but other troops had been driven off theirs and our whole army was in full retreat. Our Brigade was ordered to send a force up to Pyongyang to act as a rearguard, through which all the troops who had been attacked would pass. With the bridge completed, I sent Bertie with his Troop to accompany this rearguard and carry out any demolitions that might delay the Chinese advance.

It was then December and, after a brief pause on Christmas Day, we moved up with the rest of the Brigade to an area just north of Seoul where we prepared a defensive position against a possible Chinese onslaught.

All too soon Bertie was back, having carried out several minor demolitions. Bertie was not a man to miss a chance and on his way south he spotted a slightly damaged D8 bulldozer, abandoned by its American owners. Our bulldozers were classified as D4s, and were tiny things compared with this D8. Knowing the potential value of a D8, Bertie succeeded in hoisting it onto a low-loader and then delivered it to our Park Troop, who soon had it in running order. We somehow forgot to report this find to Colonel Itschener, who might have told us to return it to its original owners. It was an excellent machine and served us valiantly for the rest of my time in Korea. It was capable of doing about five times as much work as our little D4s, and as we became more and more over-stretched by the tremendous amount of work required of us in the spring, it is difficult to imagine how we could have coped without it.

Passing through Seoul on Boxing Day, 1950, I had an unpleasant experience. The streets were quite crowded with pedestrians and some bicyclists, but little other than military traffic drove along the streets. On one wide avenue we overtook a surprising procession of about fifty people. They were in a long file, three deep, and the first half of the group had their heads concealed in straw coverings, similar to those in which champagne bottles used to be packed. As we approached, I

CHRISTMAS, 1950

Just what are we doing here?
Ice cold on a ridge in a foreign land,
Chilled by winds from the ends of the earth,
Far, very far from the homes we love,
Just what are we doing here?

The Korean peasant, gentle but strong,
Is swept up in a desperate fight;
His livelihood smashed by land engines of war,
Whilst death seeks him out from the skies.
Just what are we doing here?

Refugees trudge southwards below us,
With faltering, shuffling steps.
Do they know we are here to protect them,
That we hope they've the strength to survive?
Just what are we doing here?

In a Moscovite palace a tired tyrant sits,
Whose words mean these people must die.
A few hours more and their breath will be stilled,
But he'll never know, never care.
Just what are we doing here?

Someone, someday, must face up to his power
And say 'no' to that tyrant's greed,.
Then peasant and wife can enjoy their old age;
Those of us who survive can go home.
That's what we are doing here!

A.E. Younger,
Major, Royal Engineers.

noticed that they all had their hands tied together with electric cable, and that there were guards with rifles scattered round them. About the first dozen files were men and the last four or five were women, several of whom were obviously in great distress and were being roughly treated with rifle butts by the guards.

I asked my driver, Sapper Fenton, what on earth was going on. He had heard that the Korean authorities were only allowed to execute prisoners in one particular valley, which was to the north of the city. What we were looking at was a group of condemned people going to their execution.

It was a sobering sight, particularly as we had heard that summary courts were in continuous session and that it only required a simple, uncorroborated accusation that a person was a communist for that person to be condemned to death. We further heard that people who were owed money would find themselves arrested and marched in front of these courts, to be sentenced without any further discussion after a trumped-up charge had been made against them by their debtors.

Having moved the squadron to the north of Seoul, where we helped the forward battalions, the Royal Ulster Rifles and the Northumberland Fusiliers, to prepare defensive positions in the frozen soil, I was called into I Corps headquarters and given instructions to prepare three of the four bridges that spanned the River Han for demolition. I knew that these would be major tasks, having experienced sufficient problems when demolishing much smaller bridges in northern France before Dunkirk, and I drove at once to the river to see the targets that had been selected for our attention.

On my way back I noticed a sign pointing just to the east of the road which indicated that the Glosters were there. I called in to see whether they needed any Engineer help and was told a surprising story. It seemed that the reserve company in their battalion defensive layout had been astonished to see a group of about fifty people, all wired together, being marched in the valley just within their position by men with rifles. There was a Korean officer in charge and the Gloster company commander asked him what he thought he was doing. The Korean commander explained that this valley was, by ancient tradition, the execution ground for the city of Seoul and that this group would now be executed. The

Korean officer was brusquely informed that if so much as one person was executed the second person to die would be himself. Since he appeared to be unsure what to do next, he was then ordered to release the prisoners from their bonds and to clear off and tell his superiors that no more groups would be allowed into the valley for execution.

I was more than pleased to hear about this, particularly as there were many more groups following this first one. However, the wretched prisoners were then marched south in the bitter weather, sleeping in the open, without anything more than the clothes they stood up in, and a high proportion cannot have completed their journey.

The value placed on human life is not the same in all parts of the world. How easy it is to say this but how shattering it is to be faced by what it really means.

CHAPTER 19

ONE DAY OF WAR, 4 JANUARY 1951

Part I

War has been described as being made up of 10% terrifying excitement and 90% boredom. Whilst agreeing with the level of excitement, I cannot agree with the 90% boredom. I was kept busy enough during the war in 1944–45 and the huge amount of engineer work in Korea meant that every single day was full of activity. Of course, widening a track designed for bullock carts to take loaded lorries can certainly not be called exciting, but the people who have to do it do not suffer from boredom. Before the work actually starts reconnaissances have to be carried out, plans made and materials allocated, and even after it is finished checks are necessary to make sure that unexpected faults or damage are corrected.

To give a picture of a day in the life of a sapper at war I am now going to describe what happened on 4 January 1951 in detail. This day was special in that we demolished some huge bridges, which was something we did not do every day, but as far as having a busy time, it was not special. If I may quote from my diary for the next day, Friday 5 January:

"Up early, breakfast filthy, no washing water. Scout car not ready so had to take jeep which had not been winterised and had no wireless. Reported to Brigade HQ at 0800 hrs for reconnaissance of new defensive line through Pyongtek. Very cold day.

Called in at HQ 1 Corps at Chonan to report locations of the 14 bridges we are preparing to demolish. Back to Squadron at Suwon, getting dark. Unit had moved. Found them at Songhwan about 10 p.m. No food, slept badly."

And so life went on, visiting Brigade and Corps HQ, visiting our three infantry battalions to find out what help they required, giving orders to our Troop Commanders, checking their work and everlastingly reconnoitring roads and tasks that we had to do or that we might have to do. Luckily our Troop Commanders were of the highest quality and the work they did was magnificent, but, because of their quality, they would often foresee that extra tasks would have to be undertaken because of previously unforeseen difficulties.

However, to revert to Thursday, 4 January 1951 – this is how it went:

First, I should explain that since the beginning of recorded history rivers have been obstacles to the free movement of armies. A bridge can overcome the obstacle and, since freedom to manoeuvre is fundamental to success in war, a bridge becomes of great value to the side which controls it.

In a retreat, a river takes on tactical and sometimes strategic importance as it forms a natural line where the advance must stop, but only if all the bridges over it have been demolished by the withdrawing troops. The act of demolishing a bridge acquires considerable significance for the overall success or failure of operations. If it is destroyed too soon, withdrawing troops will be cut off on the wrong side of the river to face certain defeat, or at least have to abandon their weapons and their ability to fight as they swim for their lives. If the destruction is left too late, the enemy will seize the bridge and the potential of the river as an obstacle to his movement will largely be lost.

Great responsibility rests with the commander of a bridge demolition, as was illustrated when General Patton's troops reached the River Rhine in 1945 and were able to sweep over it because they seized the Remagen bridge. The German demolition commander who had permitted this to happen was court-martialled and shot.

In Korea many of the rivers were quite shallow but wide and with gravel bottoms and thus could be forded. They were not of great importance as obstacles, particularly in winter when they froze over or dried up completely. There was one dramatic exception, the River Han, which flowed deep and strong past the southern capital city of Seoul, crossed by huge bow-string girder bridges designed to take road and rail traffic and built on high piers to avoid the regular floods. In the initial retreat from the North Korean onslaught in July 1950, it was reported that the South Koreans succeeded in demolishing all these huge structures but one. That failure meant that the Soviet tanks that had been supplied to the North Koreans could maintain their momentum and the bridge demolition commander of the retreating forces was made to pay the same penalty as his predecessor at Remagen.

As I have said before, a considerable strain is placed on a bridge demolition commander as his time of crisis draws near. The technical preparation of a demolition is highly complex and involves intricately detailed work where a seemingly minor error of wiring can cause failure. At the same time the enemy will undoubtedly do anything possible to cut electric cables by artillery fire or kill the team who guard the exploder.

When General MacArthur's master stroke of landing troops at Inchon transformed the military situation, the South Korean and United Nations forces swept north towards the Chinese border and bridges had to be rebuilt over the River Han to support their advance. However, the mass of the Chinese armies soon turned the scale and they started to push south with irresistible pressure. As the Chinese approached the Han, the Engineer commander of the I Corps allocated responsibility for the demolitions over the strategically important river; an American unit was to attack the pontoon floating bridge at the western end of the city, and we, the British engineer unit, would do the rest.

A quick reconnaissance showed that this left us three bridges. One was a roughly made affair of empty oil drums with a timber deck which was in continual use by civilian refugees as they moved south to avoid the war. This was just a footbridge and it presented no great problem technically.

The second bridge carried twin railway lines. It was one of the huge bow-string girder bridges mounted on massive piers that dominated the skyline of the stricken city. We decided to prepare to remove one of the piers with an appropriately massive charge.

This had to be perched high enough to make it difficult to tamper with, but otherwise was also not much of a technical problem.

The third bridge was something different. This was what was known as a decked rail bridge, which meant that both trains and wheeled traffic could cross it. No civilian vehicles used it. It was constructed of sixty-six wooden trestles on which metal girders had been laid. It was called the Shoofly Bridge. All day and all night long a continual stream of transport crossed this bridge, interspersed by freight trains. Clearly it would be a great asset to the advancing North Koreans and Chinese if it should fall into their hands undamaged.

I gave Bertie the task of taking out these three bridges. His job was made much more difficult by an edict issued by the Americans that when bridges constructed with wooden piles were demolished, the piles must always be cut below water level. This made engineering sense because it is comparatively simple to "cap" a pile if it is out of the water and thus re-use it to replace the bridge. The difficulty that arose from the edict was that the river contained numerous ice floes, mostly quite small, but quite sufficient in size to knock off any carelessly tied on explosive charge. Also working in water at freezing point was no joke, particularly when the air temperature was many degrees colder still.

As this immensely complicated task proceeded, Bertie was forever dangling under the Shoofly, checking what had been done and testing that all was secure while the traffic still passed across overhead. Disaster almost occurred in an unforeseen and sudden manner when a spark from a train fell through the decking and landed on some explosive, which caught fire and started burning with a brilliant blue-white flame. Bertie was too far away to do anything, so he shouted to the sappers nearest the fire. Already the quick-witted men were wriggling their way towards the flaring menace, knowing that the burning explosive would detonate when it reached a critical temperature. If this happened there would be no hope for any of them working there, or for the train that was still rumbling across the bridge. A hearty kick and the charge fell hissing into the icy water to disappear in a stream of bubbles.

161

After a few days the preparatory work was completed and defensive positions prepared on both banks to prevent a surprise attack, while day after day the traffic poured across.

Further north the battle moved nearer and tension became obvious in Bertie's behaviour. Normally a cheerful extrovert, he became more and more silent and took to leaving his bed at odd hours of the night to check that the sentries were alert in the arctic conditions on the river bank.

Finally the long-expected day came. Before the first streaks of light lit the sky I left our camp to visit John to the north of the city because he had prepared two other bridges for demolition in order to block the main road from the north before it reached the city limits. Bertie had left already. On my way down to the Shoofly I took a curious message from an American voice on my jeep radio to the effect that the emergency explosive request for the Shoofly would be fulfilled. I passed this message to Bertie as I crossed the bridge and asked him what it meant. He was evasive and I had not much time, so I left him to it.

On the north side of the river the capital of South Korea was silent and utterly deserted. Dawn broke and along street after street, normally teeming with an oriental profusion of men, women, children, bicycles, cars, lorries and the odd cart in from the countryside, there was nothing. Instead of the usual bustle, shouting, gear-changing, horns and bicycles bells, there was silence. Even the flags and bunting that bedecked the main streets had gone, as had the washing from the side streets. No light was visible in or on any building. To start with it was like a deserted film set, but this was one of the major cities of the world, with a population well into seven figures in peacetime, and the cumulative effect of driving on and on through deserted avenues and passing huge empty buildings was most eerie. My normally relaxed driver, Titch, started to drive faster and faster until I had to tell him to slow down. I could see the strain he was feeling in his expression; he wanted to finish this trip as quickly as possible. I certainly sympathized with him, but the situation was so fluid that I could not be quite sure who we might meet along one of these streets, friend or foe.

I chatted with him to make him answer questions and take his mind off the unusual circumstances we were in. Some days later

162

he was to thank me for doing this and to admit frankly that he had been verging on panic before I had started talking. He realized at the time that I was doing it to steady him down and it had just that effect. I admitted to him that I had shared his worries. Fear is an odd emotion. When it grips a person it dominates all other feelings, driving out such things as hunger or thirst, love or hate, but it is remarkable how it can be soothed or sublimated by some simple words or appropriate action by another, particularly if he is sharing the same experience.

We approached our first port of call, the headquarters of the 27th Commonwealth Brigade, who would form the rearguard over the Shoofly. A solitary, lean, khaki-clad figure was standing in the street, the first person we had seen since leaving the river. He was the Commanding Officer of the Argyll and Sutherland Highlanders and he calmly and efficiently explained the timings and order in which his men would cross. This was what I wanted to know, so I thanked him, had a word with the Brigade Major who would stay by the bridge till the last man was safely over, and then I moved on.

In the cold clear early morning the first air strikes were going in. Four jets whistled down onto targets just to the east of us and slightly behind us. The enemy must be moving up.

Titch and I continued towards the northern outskirts of the city. We passed the huge prison complex. The dull grey buildings were deserted and the gates hung open. Leaving the prison behind, we drove on north up the main exit from the city. Now we met one or two small groups of British troops trudging south, obviously exhausted. Their positions had been attacked by overwhelming numbers during the night. They had acquitted themselves well and inflicted enormous casualties, but they had been asked to hold too wide a front and their determined enemy had infiltrated deeply between the units. The same darkness that had permitted the Chinese to achieve this then gave some protection to our men as they were forced to withdraw.

It was a confused and confusing situation. Our artillery gave covering fire for as long as they could until they too had to move south. In the very cold temperatures their shells made a crackling sound as they passed overhead, almost as though they were forcing their way through ice crystals, and quite different to the

163

usual whistle. As the guns fell silent, the infantry knew they were on their own and must reach safety behind the demolition line as quickly as possible.

A mile or so north of the city limits we parked the jeep below a rock and I walked forward to find John, whose men had prepared the two demolitions to block this vital road. He was with his namesake of the Royal Ulster Rifles, John Shaw. It was a delight to meet these two. Their characters were rather similar, both observant, critical, professional and thoughtful. The strain of the previous twenty-four hours showed clearly on the Ulster John's face. He was waiting for his final platoon to come through before he would give our John permission to complete his demolition. The men were expected any minute and they duly arrived carrying two wounded and, after a short pause, pressed on southwards.

The Royal Ulster Rifles were now accounted for, but we had no exact knowledge of other elements that might still be approaching the bridge from the north. Brigade Headquarters had moved south and was far out of range of our radios, so we would receive no advice from that quarter. There were no signs of imminent attack by the leading Chinese troops, although we knew from the Rifles that they could not be far away.

It was just after half past six and we decided to wait another half-hour, while keeping a sharp lookout. It was just as well we did because soon a truck appeared from the north carrying the Adjutant of the Glosters, Tony Farrar-Hockley. This was excellent because he was able to confirm that no other vehicle from his Battalion was left on the wrong side of the bridge.

Then John spotted some tanks moving fast towards us. These could not be British as we knew that all ours that had been involved in the fighting had become casualties, but we had heard nothing of our enemy having tanks. It was with some feelings of relief that we found out that they were indeed American. We accepted the evidence of their commander when he said categorically that his were the last troops travelling down that road. His understandable anxiety was noticeably reduced when he heard that the bridge would be blown.

Although no formed body of United Nations troops were left now to the north of us, quite a number of men were unaccounted

164

for, but these would be casualties, prisoners of war or lost in the difficult country they had tried so hard to defend.

Electric connections were quickly completed and, with a final nod from the Ulster John, the exploder was pressed down. We took cover from the rain of small and not so small rocks after the crash of the explosion. Then we looked up. Perfect. What had been a small bridge had disappeared completely and now the cliff on our right fell away into the ravine on the left. This would not stop determined infantry for long, as they could clamber across the resulting boulders, but it would certainly stop any wheeled vehicle until a repair could be effected.

Part II

John had another bridge to blow, but I did not wait to see it go. It was still only ten minutes past seven in the morning and there was much to be done. Also I felt complete confidence in his ability to do his job properly, as indeed he duly did.

Driving back, we watched another American air strike going in in front of us and over to our left. Four jets dropped ungainly projectiles containing napalm. These burst without much noise but with a sheet of flame, followed by a black smoke cloud that drifted slowly into the cold sky. Then the aircraft wheeled round and came in again one after another and, as they approached the hillside which was their target, a stream of tracer sped from the nose of each. First there was no sound other than the whistle of jet engines throttled back to slow speed, but this would suddenly be overtaken by the crashing roar of the multiple cannon fire as the sound caught up with us. Twice and three times they returned, working over the smoke-covered area. The pilots could not possibly have seen any troops through the pall of dust and smoke, but I did not envy anyone who was unfortunate enough to be at the receiving end.

Back at the Shoofly I had a word with the Argyll platoon commander on the north bank. All was quiet and vehicles had been crossing at their planned times. He was very much on the alert and seemed to be well in control of his task.

On the south bank of the river, where the piles in the water ended and there was an earth abutment, there now stood a pile of boxes on each side of the track. I saw these were American explosive containers. This must have been what the strange radio signal I had received earlier had been about. It was obvious what had happened. Bertie, inevitably uncertain whether his difficult plan would prove successful in the event, had taken the precaution of a last-chance charge to crater the abutment if all else failed.

This was a waste of good explosive as, although there were hundreds of pounds of it stacked there, it would not have much effect on ground which was frozen like concrete. But it was too late to do anything much about that and it would have only added to the tension to have countermanded Bertie's orders.

Colonel Ike was the senior American engineer in overall charge of the demolition plan. I had taken a great liking to this experienced, friendly man. The British administrative supply line stretched half across the globe and it took months for stores or equipment to arrive. Colonel Ike made sure that whatever we needed was made available to us from American depots with an equal priority to his own engineer units. I now ran him to earth in an office truck and obtained his authority to demolish the two least important bridges.

The foot bridge was, as anticipated, no problem. The guards from the north bank were withdrawn and they fixed a barbed wire obstacle on the bridge as they left, to stop any refugee trying to make a final dash for it. Then the exploder was pressed and, after the bang, nothing but a debris of wood and metal covered the ice floes on both sides. The river was already frozen at this point and soon the ice would be strong enough to take a marching soldier, so this was not of too much importance.

Next we moved to the huge railway bridge. Here we had a problem. The last train to cross over from the north was still standing about a hundred yards from the bridge and it was literally covered with Korean civilians, both men and women. There was nobody in the engine and it looked to me as though the wood fire there was very low. I found someone who could speak English and explained that we were going to blow the bridge and that those on the roofs of the carriages must descend and take cover to avoid the mass of lethal debris that would be hurled through the air by the explosion. Nobody moved. My interpreter explained that no one would ever give up a hard-won place on the roof of this train; after all I must be the best person to realize that no other train would be going south after this one. A high probability of death waited for those who missed this last train, so they were quite prepared to take the chance of being hit to keep their places on or in it. With a heavy heart, I told Bertie to go down to his firing point and press the exploder.

With a deafening thud the single bulk charge of three thousand pounds of high explosive went up, to be followed a few seconds later by a whole series of thumps as bits of the stone pier landed among us. On the train there was utter silence.

Then a carriage door opened, followed by another and another. Streams of people emerged and came towards me. For an awful second I thought they were going to tear me apart for being instrumental in smashing such a valuable national asset, then I realized they wanted to shake my hand. Happiness and relief radiated in their faces and I shook hands with dozens of them. All the time I was moving down the train looking at the people on the roof, who waved cheerfully. Amazingly, not a single person had been hit by that terrible rain of stones and masonry.

Looking across the river from the south bank, one pier of the enormous railway bridge had disappeared as completely as when a child knocks a wooden support from a toy bridge. Two bow-string spans, each containing hundreds of tons of high quality steel, had dropped into the river, while a great yellow dust cloud drifted slowly to the east in the light air.

So far so good. I was breathing more freely when I rejoined Titch and he drove us once more to the Shoofly. It was still only just after eleven in the morning. There was a lot of dust about from bursting artillery shells, from air strikes and from the movement of traffic on the dry flood plain of the River Han. But Titch knew the way well and he wasted no time.

As we approached the Shoofly a drawn-out convoy of British vehicles was crossing it towards us. This was not the usual nose-to-tail mass of administrative military traffic that constantly battered the surface of the poor Korean road network. These were experienced operational troops on the move, well spread out and alert, ready for anything. As we passed we exchanged nods as busy people do to indicate that all is well.

Bertie had established a firing point about a hundred and fifty yards from the river bank. This was a slit trench with some sandbags round the top to give extra protection. It was about five feet deep so that the surrounding area could be observed comfortably when we stood up, and we could crouch down quickly for protection when necessary. An electric cable leading from the charges on the bridge terminated at the trench. It had not yet been connected to the terminals on the exploder box, as a safety precaution to avoid premature firing.

Once at the firing point I sent Titch back half a mile to a safe distance and then jumped into the sandbagged trench. Sergeant Ball, smiling and calm, thrust a mug of hot, strong tea in my hand and I had a brief chat with him. This tough and reliable man was the perfect foil to Bertie's mercurial temperament. He had a strong face which broke into a ready smile whoever he spoke to, old or young, rich or poor, senior or junior: a man of great potential.

Colonel Ike arrived, interested in everything as always. His steel helmet contrasted with the blue berets that the rest of us wore. American regulations strictly enforced the wearing of this awkward headgear, but for British troops the decision was left to each commander. We always opted for the more comfortable alternative for as long as possible. Stuart, the Brigade Major of 27 Brigade, was methodically checking the sub-units of the troops that were still crossing the bridge.

'That's it,' he said, 'let her go now. Good luck.'

He climbed out and into his jeep and, with a cheery wave, moved off.

Sergeant Ball fired a Very pistol. The round burst and a green ball of light hung in the sky. This was the pre-arranged signal to recall the infantry from the far side. They wasted no time. Before the burning light had hit the ground men appeared from their weapon slits. Two groups marched back at a smart pace, looking remarkably fresh after their long and uneventful vigil. When they were safely over, the final group came, not quite at a run, but obviously keen to leave their exposed positions as quickly as possible. Although they had had no trouble, they knew that the advancing Chinese could not be far away.

'Are you the last?' Bertie questioned the young subaltern with the last group.

168

'Yes, all complete now. Good bye,' he replied without slackening his pace.

In silence we waited as the infantry moved out of the possible danger area for flying fragments. The moment of truth was approaching fast. Bertie made no effort to conceal the tension that showed on his face. He was smoking a cigarette, inhaling deeply, and his eyes were never still as they searched the far bank, then the near side and then back again over the bridge.

He looked at me, raising an eyebrow in an unspoken question mark. I looked similarly at Colonel Ike, the senior man there. Already he had signed the brief order required by our regulations before blowing the charges.

'OK,' was all he said to me.

'All right Bertie,' I said

Sergeant Ball, at the exploder, had connected up the cable. He took Bertie's nod and pressed the handle.

The result was quite unexpected. There was more than two tons of explosive distributed around this bridge and instinctively we expected a colossal bang, the blast from which would punch us in the face. Instead there was more of a rumble; nothing too loud at any time but spread over a couple of seconds or so.

A look of sheer horror came over Bertie's face. 'Jesus,' he said.

'I think it's all right,' I told him as we clambered up onto the parapet.

There in front of us was the wide sweep of the River Han. The Shoofly had disappeared in a huge smoke cloud, leaving innumerable bits and pieces on the ice floes. Where there had been sixty-six trestles, each of four or five wooden piles, all capped by the decking of the bridge, there now remained two solitary piles sticking out of the middle of the river. Clearly the hundreds of underwater charges, all connected together by miles of cable and detonating fuse, had produced the strangely unnatural rumble of an explosion that we had heard.

The only failure in this massively successful effort was in the last- minute backup arrangements. One of the boxes of explosive that had been stacked on the home bank had been ripped open, scattering the others, which, for some unaccountable reason, possibly connected with the extreme cold, had not detonated. The remaining explosive was almost certainly in a most sensitive condition, so we left it severely alone as we stepped up to the bank to survey the scene.

'Well,' said Ike in his warm drawl, 'that is the best demolition I ever did see. You British sure should be proud of yourselves.'

Thinking about the Shoofly demolition later, I realized that it must have ranked among the biggest ever attempted by our Corps. We cannot have been asked to demolish many bridges with more than sixty-six spans, if any, and very few would have spanned a river as wide as the Han at Seoul.

I looked at my watch: it was twenty minutes to one. One half of one day of the war in Korea had passed.

Part III

Half of Thursday, 4 January 1951, still lay ahead. All that it held for us was a very long and very dreary drive. We had thirty miles to cover through a frozen and almost featureless landscape. The occasional cluster of brown mud huts had been deserted and open doors indicated that strangers had already been through them to search for food or temporary shelter. The hills to the east were under a mantle of snow and looked uninviting. The journey took seven hours and was an occasion that would never qualify for mention in any conventional account of operations of war.

Yet driving was a major activity in warfare in the mid-twentieth century. All units had great masses of transport and when armies were on the move each vehicle had to find space on a road that would carry it to its next destination. The surface of all minor roads quickly disintegrated and there was only one road in the western half of South Korea that would have qualified as a major road by European standards and that was the trunk road connecting Seoul, through Taejon and Taegu, to the main port, Pusan. This meant that in dry weather there was a permanent dust cloud coming off road surfaces, while in wet weather the roads became slushy and the numberless potholes would fill with water as drivers evaded them, only to be emptied later as someone splashed through them. A third alternative occurred when the roads were frozen and the traveller could come upon the awesome sight of a 40-ton tank sliding sideways across the road and into a paddy field. The thaw which followed such a deep frost led to the complete collapse of many stretches of road.

The responsibility for maintaining the roads in a divisional area was allocated to the various engineer units in each division. Outside the few large towns of Korea, the only industry was farming and the normal vehicle for moving heavy loads was a long, low cart hauled by oxen. The villagers had no tractors and certainly no private cars. If they needed to travel any distance they would walk to the nearest railway or just walk to their destination. Consequently, the main roads were only of sufficient width for two carts to pass, except for the less important ones which were only one cart's width. There were ruts, usually several inches deep where cart wheels had bitten into the surface, and often a smooth dust path at the side sufficed for pedestrians.

Civilians quickly learned to keep off the main supply routes (MSRs) used by the United Nations forces, but along other roads life still had to go on. Men and women, swathed in padded cotton clothing against the cold, criss-crossed the inhabited area carrying loads of all sorts. More often than not they would be bent double under the ubiquitous A-frame, made of bamboo poles, which enabled them to carry on their backs a hundredweight or so of branches, their principal fuel. The Japanese had issued an edict when they formally annexed the country in 1910, ordering that no trees should be cut down for firewood, they could only be pruned. This was to preserve the scanty topsoil against erosion and the villagers faithfully obeyed this law still.

Another common method of transport was a long bamboo pole with a heavy wooden bucket at each end. When properly balanced across a man's back he could jog along in a seemingly effortless manner, synchronizing the natural oscillation of the buckets with the rise and fall of his own shoulders. The popular guess about what these buckets might contain was confirmed one day when a driver in an open jeep went too close and hit a bucket. The bucket was knocked forwards, so that its mate, pivoting round the neck of the carrier, came from behind to deposit a full load of night soil down the unwary driver's back.

The open country between the few modern roads was interlaced by numerous tracks and paths between paddy fields with often a complete disregard of the shortest distance between two points. Then a track would perhaps come to a rocky outcrop, where the paddy ended, drop down to ford a river and climb round the hill on the other side up to some more paddy fields.

For centuries these tracks had been sufficient for the commerce of a simple peasantry. They must have changed little since the Tartar hordes of the Great Khan used them. Then suddenly in 1950 the United Nations unleashed across these same country roads all the paraphernalia of an industrial society at war. It was too much. All over the combat area roads disintegrated under the constant pounding of wheel and track.

The engineers had, somehow, to overcome this hopelessly inadequate road system in order to enable the army to move. Like cleaning the Augean Stable, this was a never-ending task. Sometimes our squadron alone dumped five hundred tons of broken rock onto the roads for which it was responsible in two days, and the effort to keep on top of the continuous deterioration was maintained day after day, month after month.

Working in a combination of dust and cold may have been the main cause for the number of cases of pneumonia we suffered, but also throughout the winter frostbite was a serious hazard. All through the winter months working conditions on the roads were terrible, but for some reason many developed a perverse amusement from the situation. I remember seeing one man getting into his blankets for the night. As there might be an alarm and since boots froze like concrete if left in the open, he had all his clothes on including his boots. We had empty sandbags available that could be put on each foot to keep the bedding clean, and each of his feet looked enormous and ridiculous, bound in the coarse hemp of a sandbag.

'If my old woman could see me now,' he said as he struggled into bed, and we all laughed because we knew that we looked equally absurd, but that in reality all was well.

To return to the awful, interminable drive south on this day, there was one habit I had picked up from Colonel Ike whilst driving. Every so often something would block the road, slowing every driver down as he negotiated the obstacle. Usually this would have fallen off a truck, say an empty jerry can or a heavy box. These were invariably useless things, as anything that might conceivably come in handy would be annexed quickly. Sometimes it might be the side of a wooden house that some careless driver had knocked into, or a piece of fencing or a bridge parapet. Hundreds and hundreds of vehicles would have to crawl over or round these obstacles, delaying the whole convoy behind them, but doing nothing about the obstacle itself. This infuriated the Colonel, who would invariable stop and either clear the road himself by pitching the offending item into the ditch, or else, if it was too much for him to handle alone, he would order out the nearest group of soldiers from their transport to help him..

It was truly amazing how nobody ever seemed to take this action except for a small group of engineers. Of course it was cold outside, and once a driver was successfully past the bottleneck, why stop? Let someone else worry. Yet the removal of each obstacle would reduce the travel time for hundreds of vehicles and lessen the not inconsiderable risk of accidents.

On this day, probably since there was a very cold wind blowing in the evening, there seemed to be an exceptionally large number of pieces of junk on the road. Whenever I jumped out of the jeep to remove an obstacles, the trucks behind would start up a cacophony of hooting, which just made me walk more slowly and scowl at the drivers.

We drove past the shell of the offices of the local Water Authority, which John's troop had occupied before Christmas. In the process of cooking turkeys on petrol burners a fire had started and the building had to be evacuated in a hurry. Bertie and Desmond enlivened their journey when they found a Churchill tank that had been abandoned behind the wall of this block. It was obviously wrong to leave a modern tank for the Chinese, so they put some surplus explosive in it and destroyed it, together with what remained of the Water Authority's property.

Soon after the iron grey evening slid into the darkness of night I caught up with the rest of the squadron at the bare patch of ground we had been allocated. These were still early days and we had not developed the art of moving the whole unit to a new location smoothly and without unnecessary discomfort.

We made ourselves as comfortable as we could and crept into our sleeping bags, dusty and dirty as we were, after a cold supper of biscuits and bully beef, to sleep fitfully in arctic conditions. At that stage we had not learned to go to sleep with an open mesh cloth, like a dishcloth, over our faces. By the time we had been on the move for a few weeks and learned the tricks of the trade, an inventory of our personal possessions would have surprised our loving friends back at home, with our dishcloths and sandbags and the pieces of broken mirror that the lucky few had for shaving. But priorities change with circumstances and we thought it neither odd nor funny that we should be carrying such items around.

Sleep is a bountiful treat after a very tiring day, but I found I was restless and I tossed and turned all night. I thought that I was perhaps overtired and I certainly felt like that when the sentry came over to tell me that it was 6 a.m. As I dragged myself reluctantly out of my bedding I saw the cause of my restlessness. Fearing that he was about to be crushed by the hulking lout that had given him such a bad, albeit warm night, a small grey field mouse stepped purposefully out of my sleeping bag, looked me straight in the eye with an expression that said clearly, 'I have had quite enough of this, thank you,' turned and walked away.

CHAPTER 20

WINTER IN KOREA

It was soon after we blew up the bridges over the Han River at Seoul that winter really set in. By chance, I had written to a Scottish cousin about the wickedness of the Siberian wind when it swept down the peninsula. It happened that he ran a whisky distillery and I received a reply from him to say that he was sending a case out to me. What a gift! Nothing could have been more appropriate or useful. Furthermore, this excellent man showed his understanding of the conditions we lived in, because he had arranged for it to be taken by hand from Hong Kong to Tokyo by a member of the firm of Jardine Matheson, whose commercial links spanned the Far East.

The details were all complete – the man's name, where he would be and when. I wasted no time in summoning Desmond. We concocted as likely a story as we could that he should proceed to Japan to purchase on the open market a special bolt for one of our bulldozers. Desmond had a marked gift of quick thinking and was capable of producing as smooth a story as most, backed by plentiful twinkles from his blue eyes and tugs at his military moustache. If he could not talk his way back with his precious cargo nobody could. There were plenty of aircraft flying daily between Seoul and Japan, but we had no right to be on them. All the same I knew that the busy staffs at the airports had little chance against Desmond when he really wanted something.

Early next morning it was bitterly cold as Desmond left. I drove to the American 1st Corps Headquarters and on the way we passed the area that had been taken over by the newly arrived

Turkish Brigade. These troops were to give formidable evidence of their martial nature later on, but on this day we saw a different side of them. The entrance to their compound was on a steep hill and there was ice on the road. As we approached, with no desire to visit them, only to drive on past to 1 Corps, a sentry unslung his rifle and stepped towards the middle of the road.

"Christ! That idiot is going to stop us. We'll never get started again on this hill," said my driver.

"Try to steer round him," I said, as I waved at the man to move out of our way. This only seemed to make him more determined to stop us and when he cocked his rifle there was nothing for it and we slithered to a halt. For a moment I thought we would slide back down the hill, but the tyres held.

The thick-set Turk, with his black moustache and black eyes, went round to the driver and said something in his own language. My driver let him have it.

"You utter bloody idiot, how do you think I am going to start now?"

Warming to this theme, he continued, "Don't you have anything better to do than stand there stopping people who have work to do? Any bloody fool could see that this road . . ."

The Turk interrupted him, "You say bloody fool? You English?

"Of course I'm f-ing English. Do I look like a Chinaman?"

A slow smile spread over the Turk's fierce features. "Ok, Ok. You good man; Turks, English, number one," he said, giving a thumbs up sign. "Other buggers all no good," he continued, giving a thumbs down.

We had to laugh. "Ok, you number one Turk," said the driver, stepping out of the jeep, "now how about plenty more number one Turks and plenty pushing," and he indicated his meaning by putting his shoulder to the rear of the jeep. Already half a dozen other members of the guard had gathered, attracted no doubt by the commotion. I got out to help and while the Turks were sorting themselves out round the jeep, I asked the sentry where he had learned to speak English.

"Me sailor," he said proudly. "Me dock in Liverpool three times. You know Liverpool?"

I had to admit that I did not.

"Liverpool bloody fine place," he said.

The driver climbed back into his seat and we went with a will to the task of shoving. Our new friends laughed and jabbered away as they slipped and slid on the treacherous surface. Gradually the tyres gripped. I jumped back in and, with cheerful waves and a couple of toots on the horn, we drew away from them.

"Did you notice their clothing?" said my driver. "It was all the latest American winter kit. I wish I had a fleece-lined coat like that and one of those caps. How is it that they can get them and we can't?"

I tried to explain that the British government was responsible for our administration, but I could see he was not impressed.

This particular trip to Corps Headquarters turned out to be different to the countless others I made in yet another way. After our brush with our Turkish allies, when I met up with Colonel Itschener, he expressed a desire to take a look at a couple of the bridges that we were preparing for demolition. This was quite normal; he would often stop to have a look at a job that we were doing. What made this unusual was the fact that his car was being serviced and so was not available. He asked me if I could take him. Of course I agreed, putting my driver in the back of my jeep and the Colonel in my seat.

As I drove we discussed different points, until he suddenly said, "Say, Tony, are you going to volunteer for this?"

I had no idea what he was talking about, but I saw that he was holding an Army Council Instruction (ACI). I always had trouble keeping up with all the paper I had to read and this happened to be the top document on the pile that I had been ploughing through on my way to his Headquarters when I was not map-reading or getting mixed up with Turks.

ACIs reached us regularly from London, but I hardly glanced at them as they contained little of interest to someone serving in Korea. I had taken a quick look at the one he was holding, but I felt it to be of no importance, so I had just initialled it as 'seen', and to be returned to Keith Bean's filing system when I got back.

I asked the Colonel what the ACI was about and he said that it was calling for volunteers to the American Army Staff College at Fort Leavenworth, Kansas. I told him that I had completed our own Staff Course some years before and that I did not particularly want to do another one. However, he went on to say that he thought I should volunteer because, as he put it, "I think you would really enjoy the course and also your experience would make you a very worthwhile member of it."

His visit to our tasks went off smoothly and I drove him back. When he reached his destination he thanked me for driving him and his last words were, "Tony, you will volunteer for that course, won't you?"

I agreed, knowing full well that my chances of being the one to be selected, out of all the hundreds of officers in my age group, were remote. However, back at our office, I read the ACI more thoroughly and sent off my name. This little incident passed out of my mind completely almost immediately.

Two days later, before we were even expecting him, Desmond was back, laconically explaining that he had had no problems. The man from Jardine's had been there, together with his own bottle which he had generously shared with Desmond before taking him out to dinner and showing him something of night life in Tokyo. Above all, Desmond had the case, wrapped in heavy brown paper and clearly marked as 'Map Glue'.

"After all," he explained, "you can hardly expect to be believed if you say you are carrying bulldozer parts and their container goes 'glug' whenever it is moved."

Good thinking, Desmond.

Our Quartermaster had found out that an American truck driver would arrange for his truck to be filled with anything we wanted in exchange for a bottle of whisky. It seemed that a combat soldier in their Army could ask for anything, without the usual official forms in quadruplicate that we had to submit. As whisky was a luxury that was unobtainable to the Americans, they would be only too pleased to carry out an exchange. I heard about this and arranged with our Quartermaster to see what he could get for one of my bottles. Later one evening, a couple of days later, he came to see me.

"I've got a present for you," he said, as one of his storemen came in with a puffy bundle that was obviously a sleeping bag.

"Marvellous," I said, "how many have you got?"

"Three hundred and sixty," came the reply, "one for each member of the Squadron."

What would we have done without this little transaction? Of course, it was top secret at the time. We knew that the American driver would be in grave trouble if he was ever found out. Worse still, he would never be able to help us again.

The bags themselves were all we had ever expected, and more. I still have mine after more than a quarter of a century of war and make-believe war, and of occasional bouts of family camping – and all for one three hundred and sixtieth part of a bottle of Scotch whisky.

Successive bottles were to result in tentage and petrol-burning heaters for tents, in fleece-lined coats which made all the difference in the world to sentries and guards during the long winter nights and in the marvellous so-called 'pile liners' with their nylon fur on the inside. Also the Quartermaster collected a good number of caps with fur ear flaps, which could only be worn at night for fear that the Brigadier would see them and blow up, and rubberized boots with beautiful thick insoles.

Those all lay ahead, but for that night we broached another of those wonderful bottles and we all drank deeply and sincerely to our generous benefactor, Uncle Sam.

General Ridgway took over command in Korea, after his predecessor had been killed in a road accident. He showed a realistic determination to overcome the difficulties faced by the forces in Korea.

Our infantry patrols probed deeper and deeper and found no enemy. The air forces were having an effect on the supply lines from China, although the reports we had received earlier of thousands of enemy troops being caught on the roads and machine-gunned had ceased. Farther to the east of us, in the hills, our forces edged forward.

We had brushes with the enemy, perhaps the most spectacular one being an attack put in by the Glosters on a very steep hill. I watched this from the tank of George Butler, who commanded a squadron in the 8th Hussars and who was giving supporting fire. We watched groups of Glosters climbing the hill, frequently having to face hand grenades being tossed down against them. Finally, a khaki-clad figure emerged at the top; it was unmistakably Colonel Carne, the Commanding Officer. Obviously he was a man who led from the front. The attack had been successful, but at the cost of some casualties.

Having witnessed this, I had to take a long circuit back to look at a possible route for our Brigade. I took Bertie Bayton-Evans with me as his Troop would have to work on this. I made notes as I went along of all that would need to be done, and it was a great deal of work. Evening came and darkness fell, so I decided to stop in a fortified village for the night rather than attempt to return to our Squadron harbour, which was too far away. I located the police station, where they were most friendly, offering us food and a warm room to sleep in. Bertie and I unrolled our sleeping bags and settled down with our drivers.

I was just dozing off when Bertie said that he had something he must tell me. I was wide awake at once, and what he said was that he had had a premonition that he would die in Korea. He hadn't told anybody, but he felt he must tell me. This was a most vivid reminder of my own premonition, but I felt that I could not tell Bertie about this. Looking back now, I am sorry that I did not tell him. I would have liked to discuss the whole business with someone and this was my only chance. However, I still felt that it would be wrong of me to tell a subordinate of my premonition, so I said nothing. All I did say to him was that he must not let it worry him, as nobody could foretell the future – my father's reply to his brother before the latter was killed on the Somme in 1917.

Watching Bertie's behaviour during the months that lay ahead, I often remembered this remark of his, but I could not detect that it made any difference to the actions he took. He was a most competent and professional officer. I later put him up for a bar to his Military Cross, which was duly awarded.

Similarly, as I have said before, this reminder did not make me change my own activities in any way.

We heard that our sister formation, 27th Commonwealth Brigade, had met a massive attack head on and had broken it, yielding not one inch of ground. Quite close to us the Turkish Brigade was attacked at night, held and then counter-attacked with the bayonet. It was reported that their terse signal to Divisional Headquarters, "Chinese attack; two hundred and sixty-two killed with bayonet; four Turks dead," was disbelieved. In a rage the Turkish Brigadier demanded that the staff officer concerned should visit him at once, and when he did, forced him to count the Chinese dead. The poor man was sick before he reached three figures. Certainly there were four neat graves beside the road with Turkish helmets on them and each with a little red star and crescent flag.

One day the Brigadier called me in to discuss the roads in front of us. A plan was being hatched for us to move forward but, knowing as he did that the maps were untrustworthy, the Brigadier needed more information before he could make a work-manlike plan. Nobody had been up there, but such was the confidence we felt that I said I would take a look.

Next day I went off in one of our scout cars. These were lightly armoured vehicles, but quite strong enough to withstand the odd rifle shot, which was the most that was to be expected. We travelled slowly and I kept a very wary eye open for mines in the road. Odd bits of stick and other debris seemed to indicate that this road had not been used for some time. Our own forces had not been on it for three weeks at the least, but neither, it seemed, had anyone else.

We came to the junction I was looking for and turned east. This was in a small hamlet that once held half a dozen houses, all of which were now derelict. We passed between the broken-down walls and the road turned slightly north into open paddy fields.

The most awful sight then met our eyes. The road itself was comparatively clear but half in and half out of the ditches on both sides were the bodies of hundreds and hundreds of refugees. Obviously they had been caught on the road and dived for cover in the ditches. Either aircraft had swept over with multiple machine guns or cannon fire or they had been caught by ground fire. Neither of us spoke as my driver drove carefully round a woman on the road. I could not tear my eyes away from this dreadful spectacle. As we proceeded the detail was worse than the general view had been. My eye was caught, as a man's always would be, by one woman whose breasts had become uncovered in her fall. The pale skin showed off her youthful form, but, in contrast to her paleness, the head, which was all that could be seen, of the baby on her back was blue-black. What mortal wound had the baby suffered to cause this to happen, or was it the blood of the mother? I shall never know.

181

'How much further must we go, sir?' my driver asked.

'Right to the end, I'm afraid. We have about two miles still to go.'

We crawled forward. Twice I had to jump out and push bodies away so that we could proceed. It was like moving statues, and all the time we were flanked by scores more bodies. There were hardly any men and there was hardly any blood to be seen, but each body was different and all were horrifying. I dragged my eyes away to the low hills to the north. All was quiet; there was no sign of life of any kind.

Eventually this nightmare ended. We reached another road junction, turned south and soon drove into the American unit that had been warned to expect us. I called on the commander and told him of our gruesome find. It turned out that he had already received a report from one of his patrols about the dead refugees. Through binoculars they had been able to look down on the eastern end of the road and my evidence confirmed and extended his information. He said he would ask for permission to launch a special operation to bury the corpses.

Two days later we went that way again. All the bodies had gone. It was difficult to realize that they had even been there, but we saw two large mounds of freshly turned earth and we knew what these meant.

Since that day, and it is now a far-off day, I have occasionally heard the opinion that soldiers become callous with too much exposure to sudden death. My mind always goes back to that drive. I have seen death all too frequently in other circumstances, but only at Belsen in numbers similar to that occasion in Korea. Sudden death concentrates the mind when it occurs in ones or twos, but when it happens in thousands it drives out all other thought. In my personal opinion, and I know that it may be different for others, the effect of too much exposure to sudden death is just the opposite of increasing callousness. It is those who may have been in close proximity to it on one or two occasions who adopt a casual and apparently callous air. This is perhaps a kind of defence mechanism by which they want to pretend to themselves that they have seen it all. Those who have really seen it a thousand times are a thousand times more disgusted by it.

As for the refugees themselves, some presumably survived as

some always do when tragedy strikes, but their total death toll was enormous. I had seen great columns of refugees before, in 1940 during the campaign that culminated for us at Dunkirk. They, too, were hit by the up-to-date weapons of that time, bombs from Stuka aircraft, and suffered their own tragedies, but nothing to match the scale of the blows that were delivered at Korean civilians.

For centuries the wretched civilians of a country being overrun by an aggressor have abandoned their homes and fled, preferring the hazards of the open road to the attentions of an invading army. Two lessons emerge from these events in this century and the first is that the weapons of modern war have increased in their lethality so much that the penalties of being exposed to them are most severe. It may have been worthwhile trying to escape from the massacre and rape handed out by the hordes of Attila by taking to the road, but the dangers of being caught in the open under hostile air or ground attack today are too great. It would seem to be more sensible to lie low and hope for the best in a future war, especially so if it should be atomic.

The second lesson must be that a government that so neglects its defences as to fail to deter a neighbour from carrying out aggression against it commits the greatest crime of all. Nothing can hurt a civilian population one hundredth as severely as when it has to abandon its homes and take to the roads as refugees. To turn a blind eye to the awful implications of this is an act of frightening callousness.

CHAPTER 21

MUDDY PADDY

As winter changed to spring, the rains came to Korea. Day after day the heavens opened and all that we possessed gradually became soaked, except for our bedding rolls which had to be kept dry at all costs. We developed the art of setting up and striking camp at a peak of speed and efficiency. To do this everything had to be in its correct place so that it would be in the right order when it was wanted, but always the last things to come out of the farthest, driest corner of a truck and the first things to go back in were the bedding rolls.

The main problem caused by the rain was in getting off the roads. We were moving all the time, edging our way northwards, and each night we would be allocated an area in which to halt. Sometimes this area would include a village, in which we could park our trucks on hard ground, but often the only level areas off the roads were paddy fields, which became a sort of black soup after rain. It was not too hard to find dry spots for sleeping, in places unsuitable for rice growing because they were too steep or contained outcrops of rock. The difficulty lay with our vehicles which would quickly sink up to their axles when their drivers tried to move them off in the morning. Of course we did what we could, bulldozing rubble into the paddy and breaking down the little bunds at the sides of each field so that the water would flow off. Every occasion produced its own special problems, but each night spent in a paddy field involved an exhausting effort of improvisation for everyone and a tremendous struggle to move off again on time.

Goaded by this difficulty, our Brigadier had an idea. He would give a week's leave in Japan to any member of the Brigade who produced a worthwhile solution to the problem. The Engineers would judge suggestions which should be sent to them and marked MUDDY PADDY to differentiate them from other mail and messages.

The carrot of breaking away from the muck of Korea for a week was enough to stimulate much ingenuity. Bits of paper of all shapes and sizes poured in. Unfortunately each suggestion was more impractical than the previous one.

'MUDDY PADDY. Each vehicle in the Brigade should have a spade- shaped extension made for its exhaust pipe. It would then back into a paddy field, drying up the field as it went. Signed . . .'

I gave the job of sorting out all these efforts to Big Keith. Although young, he was a good engineer, and he had the right combination of reliability and humour to deal with this sort of exercise.

'MUDDY PADDY. A maypole should be erected in the middle of the paddy field to be dried out and a bucket fixed to the end of each rope. Members of the engineer squadron should then run round the maypole dipping the buckets in the water and emptying them when they come to the end of the field. It would be an advantage if this could be done to music and perhaps the Sapper band could be flown out to provide this. We realize that this might be too expensive and suggest that a male voice choir would possibly be an adequate substitute. As the engineers continued this process the ropes would wind round the pole ensuring that they moved in ever decreasing circles until the whole field had been covered and the engineers disappeared up their own coat tails. Signed, Three Members of the Gloucestershire Regiment.

'PS When we have won this competition, as we are sure you will agree we should, we intend to take our leave at a hotel in Tokyo called The Friendly Geisha. We will spare a thought for you whilst we are there and we may produce an even better idea to enhance the skill of our excellent engineers.'

When this suggestion arrived Big Keith's roar of laughter could be heard right across the paddy field we happened to be in. Keith had won the heavyweight division in Boxing at Sandhurst and he had that combination of great strength and gentleness that sometimes seem to go together. During the previous winter his robust physique made him the envy of us all as he seemed to be immune from the coughs and colds that the rest of us suffered.

Through March and early April we crept northwards and the weather steadily improved. After the frosty nights the morning sun would warm and invigorate us. On 10 April we carried out a major assault crossing of two rivers, the Hantan and the Imjin. This was a tremendous task for us engineers as the rivers were wide and fast- flowing after all the rains. The American bridging equipment we used was good and by the end of the day a battalion was safely lodged on the north bank on a rugged hill mass called Kumgulsan. This was a good position to hold as it gave us observation far to the north, but it was also very exposed. If the Chinese intended a major attack, and there were rumours that they were massing for just this, they would have to eliminate this battalion first.

In mid-April the Belgian Battalion was attached to us and took over responsibility for Kumgulsan. We had worked with the Belgians several times before and got on well with them. They were a robust and likeable bunch and I lost no time in visiting their command post to explain our procedures for maintaining the floating bridges over the two rivers behind them. These bridges were vital to their survival; without them the Belgians could not easily withdraw or be reinforced in case of trouble. We were constantly on the alert to carry out adjustments as both rivers were subject to rapid changes in depth, due to heavy rainfall. Luckily it was after we had ceased to care for these bridges that the Imjin rose twelve feet in one night, but the sudden changes of two or three feet that we experienced presented problems that required immediate attention, if the bridges were to remain open for use.

At 10.30 pm on the night of Sunday 22 April Big Keith took a message that the Belgians were being attacked and that they wanted protection for their bridges. I was just zipping myself into my sleeping bag when he came over to tell me this. I pulled myself out of my little bivouac tent, put on a coat and joined him in the stale air of the carefully blacked-out office truck. The Royal Ulster Rifles were acting as reserve battalion, so a plan was made that they would despatch half a company immediately to secure the

186

bridges. Keith volunteered to go with them, both to act as a guide and to ensure that the efforts of our own guards of half a dozen men on each bridge were co-ordinated with those of the riflemen.

Keith was cheerful and smiling, as always, when he left, and I told him not to become more involved than was essential because the whole front was becoming alive with artillery and rifle fire and it was obvious that we would be severely stretched during the next few days. Buckling on his belt, he nodded sagely and left.

Next day we heard what happened. The party crossed both bridges, collecting the Sapper bridge guards as they went, but became heavily engaged by a large group of enemy who were infiltrating behind the Belgian positions. The bitterness of the fight that developed can be judged from the cold statistics of the action. Fifty riflemen and about a dozen sappers were involved and of these only twenty-seven finally returned to the home bank, and ten of these were wounded. But they did what they had set out to do. The Belgians were able to withdraw successfully next morning under cover of artillery fire and air attacks.

Keith survived all this. In the early hours of the morning he was returning to the home bank over the Hantan bridge under heavy rifle fire. The aim of the Chinese infantry was wild in the darkness, but a rifleman in front of Keith was hit, fell into the river and immediately swirled downstream in the fast current. Keith dived in and with a few powerful strokes reached him and was seen to be holding the man's head out of the water as they were swept out of sight in the darkness.

So much we learned next morning and it was several days later that a remarkable story was sent to me. This was in the form of a written report from a hospital in Japan by an officer of the Royal Ulster Rifles. He recorded that he had been taken prisoner in this fierce little action and had been marched at bayonet point into the hills immediately overlooking the south bank of the Imjin River. As dawn came he arrived at the top of the hill to join a group of other prisoners, some riflemen, some Belgians, and Keith. As the most recent arrival, he was put at the end of the line of dispirited men and he noted that Keith was at the other end.

When the sun had risen a bit higher, there came a noise of aircraft approaching and soon an attack was made on the area, first dropping napalm, which was close enough for them to feel the heat, and then following with cannon fire. As the aircraft came in the officer in charge of the sentries guarding the prisoners started shouting what sounded like obscenities. Then he cocked the automatic rifle he carried and, to the horror of the author of this story, pulled the trigger and fired a long burst into the prisoners.

This vicious action started at Keith's end of the line, so the narrator had a few seconds in which to make up his mind. All attention was directed, as might be expected, at the activities of the man with the gun, so he took a chance and literally bounded down the hill. This was sufficiently unexpected to enable him to avoid the fate that had so nearly claimed him. The hill was very steep indeed and covered in fir trees, and with the energy of desperation he put sufficient distance between himself and his erstwhile captors so that he was too difficult to hit by the time they could train their weapons on him. He saw enemy soldiers in his headlong flight, but the air attacks were still coming in and the Chinese were too busy concealing themselves to worry about him.

Somehow this quick-witted man made his way through the enemy forces and back to the safety of our own lines. Mother Luck must have been really working for him that day, as the odds against him were enormous. We read his fantastic story, not quite knowing how much to believe, but there seemed no reason to doubt the entries concerning Keith. In particular he had given a grid reference of the hill on which this unforgivable crime had been committed and I made a note of it for future reference.

At that time we were in full retreat and on our way back to the River Han again. But the line held north of Seoul and as April turned to May we edged forward until by the end of the month we were back near our old positions, just south of the Imjin River.

At the first opportunity I collected a small party and, with Desmond, set out to find the hill on which the prisoners were alleged to have been slaughtered. Prepared for the worst, and carrying picks and shovels, we mapread our way from the nearest track, through to the bank of the Imjin and then up the hill. It really was very steep and we had to hold onto trees to help ourselves up as stones bounced down and out of sight, dislodged by our boots.

It was very hot and we were sweating profusely when we finally reached the summit. The report had been correct. An awful sight of unrecognizable remains met our eyes. We had come to find and bury Big Keith, not the others. Their units could and would deal with them.

Desmond and I looked for clues as to which was Keith. We thought one suit of battledress uniform looked bigger than the others, but I knew we must do more than guess; we must be certain. Gingerly Desmond put his hand into a pocket of the stained clothing on the ground.

"Yes, there's something here," he said, and drew out two or three filthy sheets of paper. I took them from him and turned them over. Clear, in block capitals across the top of one sheet, I read MUDDY PADDY.

We hacked a grave for him from the rocky hill top. It was back-breaking work but it was finished in the end. The pathetic remains of what had been one of the finest of men were laid to rest at last. We were not men of the Church, but before we left we took off our hats and stood humbly round the simple grave for a final prayer.

189

CHAPTER 22

GLOSTER CROSSING

When we moved up to the Imjin River in April 1951, where Big Keith was to lose his life, the Sappers' tasks widened out from the eternal road maintenance, or road-bashing as it was called, to embrace the more glamorous responsibilities of bridging and ferrying. Apart from the bridges we built, first to supply the Royal Ulster Rifles and then the Belgian Battalion, we conscientiously searched for fording places. The river was at least a hundred yards wide and its bottom was sand and shingle, so, as the wet weather had eased up, there might well have been places where either side could wade or perhaps drive across.

One place to the west of the hills held by the Royal Northumberland Fusiliers looked promising because on the map a track led down to the river. I tried to cross there, but the water became imperceptibly deeper with each step until about two-thirds of the way across it was up to my waist. The pressure of the current became too great and I was bowled over and had to swim back, rejoining the south bank a couple of hundred yards downstream. It was a cold experience, but at least I had satisfied myself that no Chinaman would be coming that way on his feet, unless the river level dropped considerably.

But in all the dozen miles of the river for which we were responsible there was one place which was different to all the rest. Since this was just to the north of the Gloucestershire Regiment's position, it became known as the Gloster Crossing. A road to it came down to the river from each side. On our side there was a vertical sandstone cliff, about thirty feet high, broken only at one place where a steep ramp had been cut running down to the river's edge. The unsurfaced road ran down this ramp at a slope of one in three, so drivers had to exercise great care in using it.

After a narrow shingle beach, the river was only two to three feet deep under normal conditions, although it carried so much silt that the bottom was not visible. The shallowest route across started in a straight line towards the northern bank, but involved a half turn to the right in the middle, which we marked with stakes to assist drivers.

On the north side there was no cliff, but the road disappeared into enemy territory past a ruined house, perhaps occupied by a ferryman in better days. Rumour had it that historically this was the classic invasion route from the north.

We had to find out whether the enemy were in strength on the other side, so early in the morning of 12 April this crossing was tested by a strong force of two companies of the Glosters supported by tanks, artillery and engineers. The infantry crowded onto the tanks, laughing and jostling so as to keep their feet dry, and the great beasts crawled down the ramp and into the water. All went well and they soon emerged on the far side none the worse, and proceeded further north. The country was pleasant and obviously more fertile than the rocky hills on our side of the river. We followed a wide valley northwards, with low tree-covered hills on each side. There was a succession of derelict farm houses, each surrounded by trees to give shelter.

Spring was in the air and the clean greenness of bursting leaf buds made a welcome change from the drab browns we had become so used to through the winter. A sapper party scouted for mines and found a few loosely covered with earth in the road. These were wooden boxes, undetectable by our metal mine detectors, and containing about fifteen pounds of explosive; quite sufficient to shatter the track of the largest tank or remove the wheel of a scout car or heavy truck. Bertie was up at the front with his men and he provided the only excitement of the day when he suddenly dropped onto one knee and fired five rapid rounds from his American carbine. He had seen a figure running off in the unmistakable olive green uniform of the enemy. He did not succeed in hitting his fleeting target.

191

At midday we ate sandwiches and relaxed for half an hour in the warm sun, confident that our spotter aircraft overhead and our sentries would report anything unusual. We had penetrated some four miles into territory that we had never seen before and had encountered no opposition. After the midday halt we turned round and retraced our steps back to Gloster Crossing. The country was suitable for ambushes, so we took no chances, moving in carefully co-ordinated bounds.

We carried out similar probes with different units on Tuesday, 17, and Friday, 20 April, still finding no sign of the Chinese, and then in preparation for yet another I made an air reconnaissance.

A young American artillery observer pilot took me up and chatted languidly about this and that as we flew north over the river. I looked at the road we were planning to use. There was nothing on it and so it was difficult to judge its true width. However, it was not the first time I had been faced with this problem and my eye sought for some object that would give me a clue. Suddenly I saw it; a cart such as was used all over Korea. It was damaged and half in a ditch, but it gave me the vital lead. To my surprise I realized that the thing that was marked as a decent road on the map was scarcely wide enough to take the narrow cart and would certainly not carry our tracked vehicles and trucks.

To confirm this assessment I asked the pilot to circle the cart. He was chewing gum and nodded his understanding as he put the plane into a steep bank. I was just studying what appeared to be a fallen tree for further evidence when we were fired on from the ground. The popping sound should not have been too frightening as it was not particularly loud, but it succeeded in worrying me as my imagination pictured our petrol tank exploding in flames.

"God damn those yellow bastards," announced the pilot, accelerating the aircraft. He was going round again, so I told him that I had seen quite enough. He took no notice and then I heard him relaying a message back, with a request for artillery fire.

The popping multiplied and became more menacing, but to my great relief at last we headed back south and duly landed safely. My feeling of relief was further strengthened when inspection showed a dozen or so bullet holes in the fuselage.

One feels cheerful and even elated after emerging scot free from a potentially dangerous situation, so as I drove back to the tent we called home, I looked forward to having a laugh with the others over this little escapade. To my surprise and pleasure, Pat Angier happened to be there enjoying a quiet drink. He became serious on hearing my story. By then he had been promoted to command a company in his battalion and his position was more or less opposite where I had been flying.

"I am sure there was nobody there yesterday," he said. "We sent a patrol deep into that area. They must have moved up last night and have been lying quiet all day."

I tried to press him to another drink, but he refused. Showing obvious gratitude for the little chance he had had to relax with us, he excused himself. But that ready smile had left his lips.

"I really must go," he said, "I just have a funny feeling about tonight. I think we may have some problems ahead of us."

Gloster Crossing was an obvious danger point. If the Chinese were planning a major attack they could bring boats and ferries down to the river at dozens of places, but at Gloster Crossing they could dispense with such extra equipment and just walk through the water. Because of this danger, at dusk the Commanding Officer of the Glosters arranged for a strong patrol to go down to the Crossing. As the cold night air crept over them, the men from English shires lay still, listening. At 10.30 pm they thought they could hear splashing and they called for a mortar flare to light up the crossing.

The sight that met their eyes was as unexpected as it was startling. Hundreds and hundreds of Chinese soldiers were approaching the crossing and others were halfway across. The patrol did not know it at the time, but this was the 187th Chinese Division, nine thousand strong.

While his men opened fire, the patrol commander called for artillery support and made sure that the mortar flares continued to give light so that his men could shoot. This is the kind of situation that really tests a leader. With such odds against him, he could easily have gathered his men and made a bolt for the comparative safety of their company position back in the hills, but the Glosters were of sterner stuff. They had carried extra ammunition with them and they exacted full toll from their attackers as they fired into the masses below them. Bodies started to float downstream, but the remainder, showing undoubted courage, came on.

At such a high rate of fire their ammunition could not last long, but by the time the patrol were forced to pull out, their actions had alerted the whole front, as well as inflicting a significant number of casualties on the enemy.

Attacks soon started on the main battalion position. A Company caught it first and one of its platoons was overwhelmed by great numbers of Chinese infantry. The stalwart Pat Angier organized a counter-attack to redress the situation, at the cost of his life. And so it went on. Inexorably, the attacks on this gallant battalion continued for three long nights and days. The defenders had some respite during daylight hours when heavy artillery support and air strikes enabled the Glosters to attend to their wounded and regroup, but even then every move drew bursts of fire from their foes.

Withdrawing into an ever tighter perimeter, the survivors showed a determination that deserves the highest admiration. After the first night they succeeded in transporting forty wounded men by road and by helicopter to the hospitals further south, but two more Chinese Divisions were over the river and completed the encirclement of the battalion, which was then irretrievably cut off from the rest of us. By the morning of the third day the seven hundred men were down to four hundred, with another hundred wounded, and with hardly any ammunition, food or water left and no wireless batteries with which to talk to the remote world outside. Two strong task forces tried without success to rescue them, so with a final convulsive effort the unwounded men broke out from their positions and attempted to rejoin the rest of the Brigade to the south. But it was hopeless. Those not killed in this attempt were taken prisoner, save for one small party that success-fully escaped.

Even then their trial was not ended. Thirty more were to die in captivity and the rest were to spend more than two years in prison camps.

Taken in isolation these statistics represent a horror story. There can be no other way to describe such an overwhelming event. Seven hundred men are gathered together in the country of their birth, transported half across the globe where there is a conflict that is none of their making, are exposed to murderous attacks by equally brave people with whom they have no personal quarrel, and succumb. And yet if you ask the survivors about their experience they say they are glad they were there. Of course they know that those who never returned cannot answer the question; they do not need to be reminded of that. But the fact is that the depth of man's goodness comes out under stress, and the greater the stress the greater the depth is seen to be. People who have stood firm in the face of a threatening disaster instinctively forge links with each other which cannot be removed or broken. It is not the casual boasting of a sadist when a soldier who has been through a desperate engagement says that it was the most rewarding period of his life. It is just that he has been privileged to see the human qualities of determination, endurance, fellow-ship and unselfishness taken to their inspiring extremes.

The survivors of the Glosters had a last look at Gloster Crossing when they waded the river there under the eyes of Chinese sentries on the start of their seven-week march north to a prison camp near the Yalu River. Their Adjutant, Tony Farrar-Hockley, made the first of his many escape attempts on the way over by ducking down in the water and then swimming downstream.

At the time, while we all recognized the great gallantry of the Glosters, the loss of almost the whole of the fighting element of the battalion seemed an unmitigated defeat. However, there was another side to the coin. The 187th Chinese Division had been one of three such formations in the Chinese 63rd Route Army. The cutting edge of this force had been blunted by its encounter with the British units. The Chinese attack was finally stopped in the hills north of Seoul by American troops in well-prepared positions behind an extensive anti-personnel minefield, but long before this happened, the 63rd Army had been withdrawn from the battle after suffering an estimated 11,000 casualties. The survivors were sent back to China and that Army never again took part in the Korean War.

After the bitter fighting during the last days of April, when the Chinese had succeeded in advancing to the outskirts of Seoul, a succession of limited attacks forced them to give up most of the ground they had gained. By the time a month had passed we stood once more overlooking Gloster Crossing. The extent of the disaster suffered by the Chinese was all too obvious. They had laid their dead in the deep drainage ditches beside the roads, head to toe for mile after mile. Doubtless they had covered the bodies with earth, but heavy rain had washed away what must have only been a light covering. The whole area was permeated with the rich, sickly stench of death.

Gloster Crossing itself was battered by the results of shell fire. A lot of work would be necessary before vehicles could use it once more as a route for crossing the river. Bertie had found three wooden anti-tank mines in the great ramp down the cliff on the south side and we strongly suspected that there would be more in the dogleg route taken by the natural ford across the river. At mid-morning, when we returned to the Crossing, the weather was hot and the river now looked blue and inviting, so we decided to waste no time. We cut ourselves some long sticks to mark any mines we found and then Bertie and I, together with Sergeant Ball and two of Bertie's sappers, carefully edged our way into the water.

Sure enough, there were mines for us all. I soon found one, lightly covered in sand, so I stuck my marker in near it and exposed the top of it with my hand. Working round the square sides of the box, I scooped out sand and gravel to feel the bottom. Soon I could feel all round it, so I slowly lifted the mine out, took it back to the bank and removed its detonator.

My driver shouted down from the top of the cliff that I was wanted on the wireless. This turned out to be a call for help from the Canadians who had just moved into our area so I explained to Bertie that I must leave and then drove off.

That evening I was working in our office truck when Bertie came in.

'"Do you know what that is?" he said, laying a tarnished thin metal tube about four inches long on my desk.

I inspected this object, which had a plunger at one end. There were no visible markings on it to give a clue.

"I have certainly never seen one before," I said. "Is it some form of release mechanism?"

"That is exactly what it is," said Bertie. "It has to be a Chinese release switch which they use to boobytrap anti-tank mines, because I unscrewed it from a mine. Guess where we found it."

"Tell me."

"It was sticking out of a second anti-tank mine underneath that mine you took out this morning. You are a lucky man, you know."

How stupid, how very, very stupid. I knew I had been a bit casual in just feeling round the bottom edges of that mine and not scooping out a larger hole in order to test the whole bottom surface. If the mechanism had gone off as planned both the mines would have detonated, probably killing us all. Certainly I would have been reduced to very small pieces.

How could I have been so inexcusably careless? Perhaps some of the answer at least lay in the cumulative strain of the previous months. It would hardly have been human to have passed through all that without losing the keen edge of alertness, and mine had obviously been blunted. At the time I felt a sense of relief at my good fortune at coming unscathed from this close brush with death, and also I felt disgusted with myself at putting others at risk unnecessarily.

The door of the office truck opened again, allowing a blue twist of cigarette smoke to escape. Two clean-looking American officers, complete with the inevitable steel helmets, stood there. They explained that they came from an Engineer Intelligence Team that was collecting items of Chinese equipment. Without a word I handed one of them the release switch.

"Good Lord, incredible! This is at the head of our list. It is our prime objective to find one. How could you have known?"

"Don't worry yourself about that," I replied. "Come and have a drink. I think we all need one."

197

CHAPTER 23

KANAK SAN

During the night of 22 April 1951, whilst the Glosters were defending their hill above Gloster Crossing with such determination, the rest of our Brigade also came under attack. The forward Troops of the sapper Squadron happened to be located between the Northumberland Fusiliers and the Ulsters, so they were forced to defend the hill overlooking the camp side, thus filling a gap in the defensive line formed by the two battalions. We used our weapons to good effect to stop an enemy attack on our hill.

Next morning I called in to Brigade Headquarters to see what plans were being made and was told to move the Squadron back to the southern end of Kanak San, handing over our hill, now known as Sapper Hill, to the Northumberland Fusiliers.

There was a great deal of shooting going on so, having reconnoitred a suitably defensive position for us in our new area, I returned to my Squadron Headquarters. It was obvious that we were in for a major defensive battle, so I ordered our headquarters and all our administrative staff and vehicles back to our Plant Troop location at Yong-dung-po, just south of the Han River at Seoul, where they should be safe.

I then went to the HQ of the Royal Northumberland Fusiliers to finalize the handover of Sapper Hill. I spoke to the Commanding Officer, Lieutenant Colonel Kingsley Foster, who I had grown to like during the previous months. I noticed that he was not his usual cheerful self, but I knew that his battalion had had a hard night and that they knew there were more exacting times ahead. He knew all about the handover of our hill and had made arrangements for it to be done. His HQ was located on the top of a ridge and already slit trenches had been dug there so that they could defend themselves.

As I prepared to leave, he asked me to follow him. He led me along the ridge and then said he must tell me something that he did not want any of his officers or men to hear.

'Tony,' he said, 'I have had a premonition that I am going to die on this hill. I feel that I must tell somebody, but not any of my own people.'

He looked utterly depressed and miserable as I gave him my, by now standard, reply that he should relax as nobody could foretell what the future had in store. A difficulty that I experienced was that I felt that my own presentiment was an entirely private matter, not one for discussion with anybody else, not even my own wife. I felt that the whole subject was taboo. If I had not felt this way, I could at least have asked him if there was anything I could do for him if the presentiment turned out to be correct. However, at the time I did not believe that there was anything constructive that I could do, as I felt certain that it would be correct, just as I also felt certain that my own one would prove to be correct.

I had to leave the understandably dejected Kingsley, make my way down his hill and return to our new location to lay out our defences there. My jeep was waiting for me and as we drove southwards along the valley I could see occasional movement on the great ridge called Kanak San to the west. Clearly the attacking Chinese forces were already up there, probably in considerable strength.

Kanak San was a big feature, about five miles long from north to south, with rolling country on top but with very steep sides. The enemy forces already up there could doubtless find routes to clamber down the steep sides, but they would need to capture the road, which we held, for the movement of vehicles or artillery.

Back at our new location, I allocated defensive areas for each Troop. Then, after a meal, it was time for sleep, although, as the author of the 8th Hussars history put it, 'It is to be doubted if even the eldest soldier slept with much tranquility.'

The last day of the Imjin River battle, 25 April 1951, was to be long and full of incident. I dozed fitfully as the noise of rifle fire became louder, until I felt that it was becoming too close for comfort. At midnight I got up and ordered a fifty per cent stand-to of the Squadron. There was a lot of firing, but none seemed to be directed at the hill we were defending, although it was getting closer. I should explain that our hill was only a couple of hundred yards in front of Brigade Headquarters, so that the all-round defence we had established there for our own protection also served to prevent the enemy from occupying a feature that would have enabled him to dominate the Headquarters and also the only road out.

On returning from a tour round our positions, I checked with our wireless operator to find that he had received a message calling me to attend at Brigade HQ for orders, together with all the other unit commanders in the Brigade. I had time for a quick shave and then walked down the hill and over to the Headquarters. I was one of the first to arrive and was able to have a few words with the others as they came in.

As far as I remember, the time given for the start of this orders group was 4 am. Henry Huth arrived just before the start time. He was the commander of C Squadron, 8th Hussars, and had been on leave in Japan when he heard that our Brigade was under severe attack. At once he cancelled the rest of his leave and flew back to his Squadron. I sat next to him and explained the up-to-date locations of our infantry. An American colonel also arrived, the commander of 65th Regimental Combat Team, that had been ordered to attempt to extricate the Glosters. His group contained a tank battalion and two infantry battalions, which were due to carry out an attack along the only track leading to the Glosters. I did not see 65 RCT go into action, but I heard afterwards that his leading tanks were quickly knocked out, completely blocking the track, thus ending the last hope for the Glosters who had fought so very gallantly against such tremendous odds.

4 am passed and there was no sign of our commander. At about 4.15 a young-looking officer from the 8th Hussars came in and spoke to Henry Huth and myself. It turned out that he was standing in for our excellent Brigade Major, Ken Trevor, who happened to be away on leave. He explained that he was in a real

difficulty as he could not wake up the Brigadier, who had taken some sleeping pills. I told him that this was a most critical meeting and that he really must wake up Tom Brodie, even if it meant pouring a bucket of water over him. I realized what a difficult position he was in, but he went off saying he would do what he could.

We all waited for about another quarter of an hour, but this time was not all wasted, because Henry Huth was really getting down to the best way to help our two infantry battalions who were still at the head of the valley to the north of us. I had met Henry often enough before, but I had not realized what a most sensible, and indeed dedicated, soldier he was. He knew that our two battalions would never be able to run the gauntlet of all the Chinese troops that were moving in behind them, unless he could support them with fire from his tanks. Luckily, both he and I knew the layout of the valley well by then. There was a cross ridge of low hills about half-way up and Henry felt he could reach there quickly. Then, if some infantry could hold that ridge, he would move his tanks farther north and fight a rearguard action moving slowly back to the south and covering the withdrawal of the infantry. There was no reserve of infantry to hold the critical cross ridge for him, so, realizing the sense of his plan, I agreed to provide sappers to do the job.

We arranged a meeting point and Henry said that our sappers could be carried up to the hill on his tanks, where he would drop them off before he went farther north.

Just after we decided on this Tom Brodie appeared. I looked to see if his hair was wet from a bucket of water, but it did not seem to be. He was in rather a dazed state and talked about the Brigade withdrawing to new positions south of the Han River. I know only too well how much strain we were all under during this intense battle. I was finding it impossible to sleep at night, with a host of thoughts running through my mind – should I do this? – should I do that? This was the strain of battle, when one knows that the lives of the men one commands are at stake, and from which all commanders suffer. Tom Brodie, whose responsibilities greatly outweighed those that the rest of us carried, would have been under proportionally greater strain. Also he was a good deal older than his subordinate commanders. It is not surprising that he succumbed to the very human response of taking sleeping pills to try to get some much-needed rest.

However, Henry Huth was not put out by this in any way. He had decided what needed to be done to attempt to save the two exposed battalions and he knew that the sooner he started the better.

I returned to our hill and summoned my own order group. We had received a request from the Corps Engineer, Colonel Itschener, to prepare two bridges for demolition. The first of these was on the northern outskirts of Seoul and was a bridge that had been rebuilt by American Engineers to replace one blown by John Page's Troop in January. The second was the so-called Shoofly road and rail bridge over the Han River at Seoul, which had, again, been rebuilt by Americans to replace its predecessor, which had been blown by Bertie Bayton-Evans' Troop in January. So the tasks for each Troop fell into place, John and Bertie had to prepare the same bridges that they had previously blown, leaving Desmond Holmes to take his Troop to give infantry support to Henry.

Brian Swinbanks, our Plant Troop commander, was also there. I had already arranged for all our heavy plant, such as bulldozers and cranes, to be evacuated to the factory building that we held as a stores dump in Yong-dung-po. So there was nothing much for Brian to do and, since Desmond's Troop officer happened to be away, entirely on his own initiative Brian volunteered to stand in for him and go with Desmond. I agreed to this, as I could well imagine that it would be valuable for Desmond to have another officer with him.

I received a request from Colonel Itschener to call in and see him, so, having checked the departure of the Troops on their various missions, with Desmond resolutely leading his men to the meeting point with Henry's tanks, I took off in my jeep to Corps HQ.

I could see that Brigade HQ was already on the move as I walked down our hill to meet up with my jeep driver. The road was crammed with vehicles and we made rather slow progress to Corps. Once there, it turned out that Colonel Itschener wanted confirmation that we would be able to complete our bridge demolition preparations within the next seventy-two hours. The problem here was the Shoofly Bridge, particularly as he insisted on a technical point that each pile must be cut below water level. This was to make it more difficult for the enemy to rebuild the bridge by re-capping the old piles. As there were over sixty spans, each of five or six piles, and as the recent rains had made the Han River fast-flowing, this was not a simple request and he knew it. However, anticipating this, Bertie and I had already talked about it and Bertie thought it would be possible to fill lengths of rubber hose with explosive and nail one onto each pile below the water level. The first thing he would do when he reached the bridge would be to find an unused pile and carry out an experimental explosion on it. Itschener was pleased with this proposal. He also told me that a massive anti-personnel mine-field was being laid in the foothills north of Seoul, where another attempt would be made to stop the Chinese if they broke through our Brigade positions. Already the three-day delay imposed by our infantry had given time for this defensive measure to be completed.

I knew that Bertie and John were well able to complete the tasks I had given them, although Bertie's would probably take him at least forty-eight hours. I paid a quick visit to each of them and was happy to see that Bertie's test explosion had been completely successful. I then left these two Troops to complete their work and drove back up to our old hill position, as that was were the main problem lay.

It was late afternoon before I passed the hill where we had spent the night and turned north up the valley track to make for the central ridge that Desmond should be defending. There was a great deal of shooting going on and I realized that it might be unwise to continue northwards in a vehicle as vulnerable as a jeep. We drove slowly to the top of a slight rise where I dismounted to see what was going on.

A truly amazing sight met my eyes. I could see far up the valley, particularly on the western side, where the mountain Kanak San lay. Dotted all over the hillsides were hundreds of small groups of soldiers. The groups were twenty to thirty strong, well spaced out and were moving steadily southwards towards us. Not far ahead I could see some of Henry's tanks, spread in a line across the valley. Beyond them were some more tanks moving slowly southwards and continually firing at groups of the enemy that were closest to them.

I saw that there were soldiers riding on most of the tanks and realized that they were probably our sappers, who had been collected from their hill defence and were being transported back. I saw the unmistakable figure of Desmond Holmes, standing in the turret of one of the tanks with a rifle. He was calmly taking aim, firing, reloading and taking aim again. The enemy groups were all round. I saw one such group hit by machine-gun fire from one of the tanks, which knocked them all down, but another, and then another group followed the first one, only to be hit in their turn. The discipline of the Chinese troops in this environment was remarkable, although their commanders could be seen at the backs of the groups and they would no doubt have dealt summarily with anyone who wavered.

Henry's moving tanks halted soon after they had passed through the stationary line and took up new firing positions. I realized that he was leap-frogging his tanks back, delaying the enemy at each position. Quite close to me on my right, a line of our soldiers appeared, moving slowly southwards. They must have been the Northumberland Fusiliers. They were moving so slowly that I felt like shouting at them to get a move on, but I realized that they had already endured three days and nights of continuous battle, and they were exhausted.

Henry's control of the battle was nothing short of masterly. I could see him, standing in the turret of his tank and talking almost continually on his wireless net. However, having seen all this, I realized that this was far too dangerous a place for a spectator to hang about. Bullets whistled round us as we moved fast back down the track to where Brigade Headquarters had been. Desmond's transport was there, and the Belgian battalion that was temporarily attached to our Brigade were in defensive positions. The light was fading as we left to drive to safety in Yong-dung-po.

Desmond arrived there much later, with the sad news that Sappers Judd and Wylie had been killed and four others were missing and probably wounded. Also he reported that Brian Swinbanks, who had so gallantly volunteered to go with him, had been badly wounded by a bullet in the head. He had been evacuated by helicopter to a hospital in Pusan and next morning we were to hear that he had died in the night. Desmond said that Brian had shown great courage in remaining cheerful during his trip back. He was lifted onto Desmond's tank, conscious but not able to move. Desmond tied him onto the tank with the sling from his rifle and he remained, uncomplaining and smiling, until he was loaded into the helicopter. Desmond feared the worst and this turned out to be correct.

Our Brigade suffered 1091 casualties during this three-day battle, out of a total strength of about 4,000. High as it was, if it had not been for Henry's magnificent control on the last day, this figure would have been much higher. There was tragic news from the Northumberland Fusiliers that their commander, Kingsley Foster, had been killed. On the first day of the battle he had told me of the presentiment he had had and this proved all too correct.

Henry was awarded the Distinguished Service Order after the battle and Desmond the Military Cross. Desmond's Troop Sergeant, Orton, was awarded the Distinguished Conduct Medal after he had taken command of one of the tanks, when the original commander was killed. He fought it back under Henry's orders, and at one stage had to jump onto the ground to extinguish a fire started on the front of the tank by a Molotov cocktail. Chinese troops were all round him and one ordered him, in English, to surrender. Orton knocked this man out cold with his fist and then climbed through a hail of bullets back into the tank. He set a truly magnificent example.

It is a matter of some debate to decide who really won the Battle of the Imjin, as it came to be called. We were driven from the battlefield, which is the usual indication of the losing side. However, undoubtedly the Chinese expected to swamp all opposition and retake Seoul and this was a major effort by them to win the war. They suffered so many casualties (about eleven thousand) in attempting to overrun 29 Brigade, and their march was so delayed, that the defensive line put up by the Americans behind us, north of Seoul, proved completely effective. So, on balance, whilst the battle was a severe setback for us, it was disastrous for the Chinese.

Our preparations to demolish the bridges were soon dismantled. These had been sensible precautions to take in case the Chinese attack was successful, but the boot was soon on the other foot as we gradually drove our enemy north of the Imjin River again.

CHAPTER 24

A BRUSH WITH DESTINY

There was no time to relax after the traumatic events of April 1951. After a whole series of attacks, we moved back to the Kanak San area. Our lives were not made any easier by the huge number of Chinese dead lying in the ditches alongside the tracks that we had to use.

All our units were much more thorough in their defensive preparations than before, so the engineer tasks were legion. We had to move up great quantities of barbed wire, sandbags and mines, and assist with installing these. We made an airstrip for light aircraft and built bridges and roads to the forward battalion positions.

Remains of the battle were everywhere, not only in the form of the countless Chinese casualties, but burnt-out tanks, damaged artillery guns and a blanket of the litter of warfare, such as rifles, equipment and clothing.

It was mid-May before I could climb the hill on which Big Keith's body had been left, an unforgettably sad excursion.

Once we had cleared all enemy forces from south of the Imjin River there was a noticeable easing of tension all round. The amount of work that was demanded from us did not decrease, but some of the urgency for its completion went. This meant that we could make sensible schedules and plan each day's work more efficiently. Units started to send out invitations to evening drink parties, which were always most enjoyable occasions since we knew each other well by then.

Another element of change was that it was decided to create a

Commonwealth Division. This would consist of Brigadier Coad's 27 Brigade, which already included an Australian battalion, our 29 Brigade and a newly arrived Canadian Brigade. This new organization probably affected us Sappers more than any other arm, as, instead of our Squadron being the only one in Korea, another British squadron would be sent out for 27 Brigade, plus a Park Squadron with heavy equipment and a headquarters. I would cease to be the senior British Sapper in Korea and soon my boss to be, Lieutenant Colonel Peter Moore, arrived.

I must say that I could not have asked for a better commander. Making a preliminary visit to reconnoitre what his life would be like, he travelled round with me for about a week. He was most complimentary on everything that we were doing and when he finished his visit I knew that we had a really first-class future commander.

The arrival of the Canadian Brigade in an area close to ours also made a change in our lives. We visited their Sappers at the earliest opportunity and soon found that we could help each other. For example, we saved overheads by using the same quarry for obtaining stone for road work and used each other's water points when this would save time. Also, particularly in the Canadians' early days, we could help them with our greater knowledge of Korea and of where things were available.

Another foretaste of better things to come was the arrival of the officer who would command the new Commonwealth Division, also, like Peter Moore, on a fact-finding reconnaissance. This was Major General Cassels and he had the endearing habit of stopping his car to talk to whoever he happened to run across when he was being driven around. He spoke to several of our Sappers working on different roads and bridges, and each one said that he was most friendly. He would take a cup of tea off them, if they happened to have a brew going, and would then question them about life in Korea. This disarming good will was much appreciated.

It was in May or early June that I began to sense a difference developing in the characters of two of my officers, Desmond and Bertie. They were both drinking more in the evenings and were less cheerful in the face of difficulties than they had been. The business of battle fatigue was something I had not experienced previously, but I sensed that this was what was affecting them. It is difficult to notice a change in one's own personality, but I realize now that I may have been similarly affected. I certainly was unable to sleep at nights unless I had taken a sleeping pill or plenty of alcohol, or both.

Anyway, the work went on, day after day without a break. Gloster Crossing became important, as it was the only place where the Imjin could be crossed by vehicles or by wading. We had no troops stationed on the north side of the Imjin, but our enemy kept back from the Crossing, knowing full well the weight of artillery that could be brought to bear if they were ever observed near the river. They sometimes opened up with machine guns and rifles and I certainly remember one occasion when John Page and his men received quite a lot of attention as they withdrew over the Crossing.

Most of the sapper work at the Crossing, however, was done by Bertie and his Troop. Day after day I dropped in to see how he was getting on, improving access to the Crossing, removing mines (see Chapter 22) and so on.

I used to leave my jeep reasonably far back, so that it would be in no danger if trouble erupted. One day, 16 June to be precise, I saw my driver waving frantically from the top of the cliff overlooking the river. I realized that there must be an urgent message of some sort, so I clambered up and he told me that my second-in-command, Keith Bean, wanted me. Over the radio, Keith asked me to return at once. Back inside our office truck, Keith first handed me a strong Scotch, saying, "You are going to need all of this."

My heart sank, as I assumed that some extra heavy responsibility was being thrust upon us. When I had downed the whisky, he slid a message over to me. This had come from the War Office in London and said that Major Younger was to return at once in order to attend the next course at the US Army Command and General Staff College, Fort Leavenworth, Kansas.

I had completely forgotten about the incident which had occurred back in February when Colonel Itschner had travelled in my jeep and seen the copy of the relevant ACI and had told me to volunteer for this course. As I re-read the signal it all flashed through my mind and I could not get over what an amazing coincidence this was. If he had been in my jeep on any other day, this would never have happened. Indeed, if my papers had been stacked in a different order, it would not have happened.

I was still not absolutely sure that all would be well, as my presentiment had been so definite. Perhaps something would happen during the last few days in Korea, perhaps the aircraft flying back would crash. I could not be sure.

However, I went ahead and arranged a goodbye party for as many friends as we could cope with. I wondered whether I should tell Bertie about my presentiment, to show that sometimes these things may prove to be wrong, but I was still not at home and it could still prove to be correct, so I said nothing.

I handed over command of the Squadron to Desmond, the senior Troop Commander, but I was determined to make my first task on my return to arrange for him and Bertie to be posted away from Korea. They had both had enough.

A week later, on 23 June, I took a Scandinavian Air Line flight out of Tokyo bound for Zurich. We stopped at Hong Kong, Bangkok, Calcutta, Karachi and Lydda, being looked after by beautiful air hostesses who were most kind to us. I was travelling in my battledress as I had no other clothes. It was pretty filthy but at least I had had a bath in Tokyo. Most of the passengers were civilian, but also on board were two others in khaki, an army chaplain and a corporal.

At Lydda, outside Tel Aviv, we were advised to leave the plane for breakfast in the airport lounge. Walking from the aircraft in the cool morning sunlight amid the other passengers, the three of us in British Army battledress were all together and I was talking to a Japanese businessman about, of all things, moral values in Britain. I had noticed a group of people, presumably policemen, in a uniform of buff-coloured slacks and open-necked shirts, and armed. These came towards us and their officer drew his pistol and declared loudly, "You three, you are under arrest. Follow me."

We were all astounded at this unexpected turn of events. We had not been out of the aircraft for more than half a minute, so what could we have done? We were rapidly surrounded and had no choice but to do as we were told.

The officer was a young man of about twenty-five, with close-cropped hair and a singularly unpleasant and unsympathetic expression.

"You are wearing the uniform of a foreign power on the sacred soil of a free and independent country," he announced, "This is a serious offence and you will be held in custody until you can be tried."

"We have no other clothes," I explained. "We have just spent the best part of a year fighting in Korea, and you don't wear civilian clothes there."

"I don't care about that," said this humourless man, "You can explain that to the judge. You are still committing a serious offence."

In vain we argued with him, making no impression whatever. He stubbornly refused even to discuss the matter further.

Inside the small police post I sat disconsolately on a hard bench. Was it for this that I had so miraculously been whisked away from Korea, to languish in a foreign jail to satisfy outraged nationalism? It would have been much better not to have come, in which case I would still be doing the job I knew so well among people who would be lifelong friends, John and Little Keith, Larry and Dan, Peter and Bob, sergeants like Orton and Ball, and of course the mercurial Bertie.

I thought of Bertie. He would be down at the Gloster Crossing by now preparing to mine the approaches to it. I could even smell the unique tang of the early morning air in central Korea, before the sun rose high and the dust clouds drifted away from every road and track, spawned by the wheels of numberless army trucks. I would visit him some time in the morning, just as I had visited him and Desmond and John almost every day of every week of every month, to check what he was doing and whether it would take more or less time than we had anticipated. We would discuss any extra tasks that had cropped up, what stores they would require and who should do them, what snippets of information I had gleaned, who had been hurt and how it had happened and all the minor difficulties that had been overcome in the new circumstances, because no two tasks were ever the same. Sergeant Ball would come up with a cup of tea and we would have a cigarette while hearing what he had to say.

211

All this would be serious talk on which decisions would be taken and plans made. There would be laughter too. Bertie had a better eye for the absurd than most, particularly when he had inadvertently done something silly himself, and his ridicule of anything that smacked of pomposity was boundless. Sitting in this inhospitable jail I could hear his infectious laugh and the comment he would have made at our present predicament, "Christ Almighty! Do you mean to say you can't talk yourself out of that?"

Suddenly an idea came to me. "We serve the United Nations. I insist that we be allowed to get in touch with our superior officer in Jerusalem," I told our jailer.

In saying this I devoutly hoped that there was some senior UN official in the Holy City. I seemed to remember that there had been a UN involvement after the Arab-Israeli fighting in 1948. For the first time I could see some doubt in his face. I pressed my point.

"If you do not allow us to speak to our superior office, you will be committing an insulting act against the United Nations."

"It is far too early to call him now. You must wait in the cells," he said.

At least this meant that there was indeed some senior UN man in Jerusalem, or at least that he thought there was one.

"Don't be stupid," I pressed my advantage, "You know very well that someone will be on duty. And I shall need to know your name and rank for my report."

We already knew that we were dealing with a man of more than usual obstinacy, and that he would not give in easily. However, for the first time he was on the defensive. His original decision to arrest us must have been based on some regulation and he was just the type of thick-skinned bureaucrat to abide by the letter of the law regardless of any ameliorating circumstances. Sensing that his rule book would provide no precedent and that we had therefore found a chink in his self-righteousness, my confidence increased. He seemed most reluctant to give us his name, and this provided me with more leverage in the verbal battle. It took several minutes of hard slogging before, with a scowl, he succumbed. "All right," he said, "you may return to your plane. But don't appear here dressed like this again."

We did not reply to this bit of gratuitous advice, because we had seen our aircraft make its way towards the end of the runway to take off. We wasted no time in racing to our home in the sky, waving our arms frantically to be recognized. As we neared the plane the door opened and we saw the unmistakably Nordic stewardess beaming down at us.

"Wait one moment," she shouted.

We had a problem as the bottom of the door was a good ten feet off the ground, but two strong Swedish crew members appeared to grab our wrists and haul us aboard. It was just as well that this was before the days of the huge modern jets, or we would never have been able to jump up high enough.

"Thanks, Bertie," I said to myself as I sank into my seat and accepted a hot cup of coffee from the charming stewardess.

Nothing about this event is intended to be anti-Semitic. No soldier, whatever his country of origin, can do anything but respect the Armed Forces of Israel, and I, who have had the chance to stand on the summit of the Golan Heights to see for myself the difficulties they had to surmount there, have nothing but admiration for their achievements and liking for those individuals I have met. Equally I both like and admire their magnificent neighbours in the Jordanian Army who I have had the privilege of meeting.

No, this encounter with a man over-dressed in a little authority might have happened in any country in the world, and certainly in Britain. If it proves anything about different races, it is that they are all the same under the skin when it comes to producing petty tyrants.

Zurich followed and then Heathrow, where our dust-stained kit bags, that had looked so normal for so long, now appeared shamefully dirty compared with the neat baggage of our fellow travellers. It was late and, after ringing up my family to confirm my safe arrival, I took a taxi to friends who lived in London. The taxi driver had no change when I produced a pound note for the nine shilling fare and I knew I really was home again.

It was marvellous to have a bath and relax in a happy atmosphere, and I enjoyed it to the full, although sleep did not come easily.

Next morning I clocked in at the War Office to report my return. The staff officer I had to see was an old friend and I thought it a bit churlish of him when he hardly even smiled as I came into his office.

"What is Gloster Crossing?" he asked. "Does it mean anything to you?"

Did it mean anything to me? It was a permanent part of my life.

There flashed through my mind an indelible kaleidoscope of action pictures; our very first attempts to mark the route over the river, when we discovered that it was dog-legged; Centurion tanks loaded with laughing Glosters splashing across; Bertie, soaked to the skin, groping for mines hidden in the shallow water; John's raft crossing infinitely slowly under fire from an enemy patrol while the Ulster Rifles poured covering fire over from the home bank; Sergeant Ball laughing with Larry over some private joke while they warmed their hands on tin mugs of strong tea; my own effort to lift a Chinese mine, and so on. I knew I would remember Gloster Crossing to my dying day, and here was this man asking if it meant anything to me.

"Oh yes," I replied, "it is the easiest place to cross the River Imjin."

"I see," he said, sliding a cable over his desk towards me. "You won't have heard about this."

The cable reported that Captain Bayton-Evans, Lieutenant Robinson, Sergeant Ball and Sapper Higgins had been killed at Gloster Crossing on the day after I had left.

In my head I had composed a letter to Bertie about how presentiments could be wrong. I had not dared to write it until my feet were again on English soil. This signal shattered me completely.

CHAPTER 25

PREMONITIONS

Quite the strangest and most inexpicable experiences of my life have been connected with premonitions. When I read, in his last letter to my father, of my uncle's premonition that he was about to be killed in the First World War, I felt that this was an understandable deduction on his part, based on the two solid years that he had already spent in the trenches in France.

Then in the Second World War several of my friends, indeed most of them, were killed, but I was never with them when it happened, so I do not know if they had any prior warning of the fate that was in store for them.

However, in Korea it was different. Pat Angier, of the Glosters, clearly had a sudden presentiment when he happened to call in on us the day before he was killed. Kingsley Foster, a most responsible and experienced lieutenant colonel, took me on one side to tell me of his premonition that he would die on the hill where we stood. Two days later it happened.

Then there were the curious premonitions that Bertie Bayton-Evans and I had, months before anything happened. Bertie was to die the day after I left, from a mine explosion. So the only exception to the certain truth of these feelings was my own.

Somehow, I had amazing luck. First when the mine that I uncovered was later found to have been sitting on a release mechanism connected to a second mine, but which failed to operate; secondly, I knew when I heard of Bertie's death that if I had not flown to England that day I would almost certainly have been down at Gloster Crossing with him, checking on what he was doing.

Of course, the reason that I did fly off that day was an amazing coincidence itself. Only once had Colonel Itschener travelled in my jeep and had a chance to read the mostly useless papers that I had stacked on the floor where he sat. He was not the sort of man who would have thumbed through my papers, but it just so happened that the one that interested him was sitting on the top of the stack. Again, out of all those who volunteered for the American army staff course, why was I chosen? The odds against such a stroke of luck were astronomical. Clearly my luck was in that day.

The other rather unexpected thing about premonitions is that, certainly in my experience, they do not result in the sort of extreme fear that makes people run away from danger. I presume that my uncle could have reported sick or even wounded himself to avoid going over the top, but he didn't. Nor did Pat Angier or Kingsley Foster; both faced up to what they knew was to happen to them.

Bertie and I, with our months of prior warning of what was going to happen to us, could almost certainly have thought up some excuse to leave, but we did not. I just knew that it was to happen to me and that it was inevitable and it was not until I actually set foot on English soil that I felt relief. Looking back now, I feel convinced that, on the day that Colonel Itschener told me to volunteer for the American course he saved my life.

Two other officers of mine, Keith Eastgate and Brian Swinbanks, died while I was in Korea, and young Lieutenant Robinson just after I left. The excellent Sergeant Ball and several Sappers were also killed. Did they all have premonitions, but kept quiet about them as I had done? I shall never know. However, I do not think that Keith had any foreboding of the disaster that was to overtake him. I saw him leave and he was his usual cheerful self. Brian need not have gone forward with Desmond but volunteered to do so. Surely he cannot have had an idea that it would cost him his life.

So why are some people selected to have a premonition, whilst others are left in the dark? I cannot begin to answer this question, but it is one that has troubled me for many, many years.

The other aspect of life in a war when thousands are being killed is that of luck. A group may be hit by a burst of machine-gun fire or a shell or a bomb. The odds on survival are the same for them all; some will die, others will be wounded, but the lucky ones will survive. Of course most, if not all, hope and believe that they will be one of the lucky ones, but only time will show if they really are.

I have had a couple of unlucky breaks in my military life, but mercifully these were not in wartime. I definitely count myself as being very lucky in my Korean experience, and the sense of relaxation and happiness that I felt when I rejoined the little family in England that I had never expected to see again is too deep for me to express.

CHAPTER 26

WHERE ARE WE GOING?

In the preceding pages I have deliberately glossed over the unpleasantness of war most, but not all, of the time. This was done deliberately to avoid writing something that readers would find disagreeable. However, I feel that I must conclude by commenting on the effect that wars have had on me.

At the time that I met something unpleasant, I usually just passed it by because I had a job to do, and jobs in wartime tend to be critically urgent. However, I did not forget these unpleasant sights, they are lodged for ever in my mind. Even when there was no urgency, there was usually nothing that one could do. For example, I remember walking down a railway track with Pat Lythe soon after we crossed into Germany towards the end of the Second World War. Beside the track was a dead German soldier, not a young man, but a fairly elderly man, presumably called up for the last stages of the conflict to help defend his fatherland. We were chatting about something and we continued our conversation, walking past the corpse as though it did not exist. It was an unpleasant sight, and I still remember that the dead man had a moustache like Hitler's, but we both ignored him. Were we callous and unfeeling? I do not think so. I believe that incidents such as this, and there were many of them and most were much more unpleasant, just build up a disgust for war that still remains.

This disgust does not lead me to pacifism. On the contrary, I cannot accept that it is tolerable to surrender meekly to a dictator, particularly one as murderous as Hitler or Saddam Hussein. No, if such a man initiates a war he must be opposed, and opposed as effectively as possible to end the results of his terror quickly.

It is easy to say this, but not always easy to accomplish it. There is a great deal of common sense in Theodore Roosevelt's comment that one should speak softly but carry a big stick. The big stick must not be used aggressively, but it must be seen by all, and the will to use it against aggression must be made clear.

When I was running the Royal United Services Institute after I had retired, I attended a discussion at which survivors of the Battle of the Somme in 1916 discussed their experiences and memories. This was in 1978, so most of them must have been in their eighties, but they were still most articulate. Surprisingly, they quickly split into two camps. One group stressed the horror of it all, the merciless slaughter of young lives and the thunder of the guns. The other group stressed the amazing comradeship that developed among the survivors, which meant that, looking back, they would not have missed the experience for anything.

There was no meeting of the minds between these two groups, which I found to be strange, because I well knew from my own war experience that both were right. War is awful, the most awful activity that man undertakes, but, equally, the way in which those who have to go through it together form a limitless comradeship is most rewarding and memorable. Keith Eastgate threw himself into the very cold Imjin River to rescue a man who had been wounded. It cost him his life, but I know that if I had been in his shoes I would have done the same. Equally, if Keith had been the one to be hit, I know someone would have gone in to help him. But if Keith had thrown himself in to save me, and if we had survived, the link of friendship that would have been formed would have been of immense strength.

So relationships that are born of war are most rewarding. This does not imply that war itself is good; it is evil in the extreme. Only a month before Keith's tragic death, driving north from our front line into an area believed, correctly, to have been evacuated by our enemy, I had come across countless dead women and children, certainly there were hundreds of them, probably more than a thousand (See Chapter 20). Goodness knows why they had been slaughtered, but this is the worst aspect of war, the killing of quite innocent people. Their unnecessary deaths were the responsibility of Kim Il Sung, who launched his troops to conquer South Korea. If he had not started the war, this would never have happened. Others must share some of the responsibility – those who did the killing, his subordinates who willingly led his armies, and Stalin who equipped his forces with modern arms and probably encouraged him to attack, but his is the main guilt.

Clearly, the need to control aggressive dictators is essential, but it is also not easy. They must be halted before they have committed their great crimes, not after they have started. A world authority must exist to do this, and the United Nations was set up for this very purpose. Looking back at all the wars that have been fought during the half-century of its existence, it has not been very successful, which only shows how formidable the problems are.

The countries of the world really must learn to live together without fighting. If an unpleasant problem rears its head, probably due to some high-handed action in the past, the countries concerned must submit their cases to a higher authority, such as the United Nations, where a sensible solution can be worked out by impartial statesmen. This higher authority must allow its own organization to evolve as it develops experience in the handling of each crisis, in order to make itself more and more capable and more respected. The League of Nations, set up after the First World War, was unsuccessful. The United Nations, set up after the Second World War, has not been tremendously successful, but it does seem to be improving and, in any case, it is all we have. It would be wrong to believe that its present organization is the best that could be devised. For a start, it would be strengthened if it had a small agency in every capital city, tasked with reporting any potential crisis, or any sudden crisis, such as an assassination, and with giving the political background in each case.

Another aspect of the problem of keeping the peace is that it tends to be dictators who start wars, not democracies. The latter must, therefore, remain strong and must be prepared to go to war with aggressors, until such time as no threat from a dictator is conceivable, which is probably a long time ahead. Alternatively, the democracies could club together to provide sufficient force for the United Nations to become an effective world policeman and able to deal with any aggressor.

Regrettably, all this will cost a great deal of money, both in keeping up effective forces and in research and development to ensure that the peace-keepers do not slip behind in the eternal contest of producing better weaponry. But these costs are an insurance policy and they must be met if the goal of a better world for our descendants is ever to be achieved.

The problems that have caused wars in past centuries still exist, as do the all too human sins of greed and aggrandisement. The effects of wars on communities have been bad enough, but they are becoming worse. It is a ridiculous absurdity that women and children should die, as they have so often in the past, for reasons they barely comprehend, or sometimes do not even understand at all. Man now has the capability of wiping out a whole nation, to say nothing of the unfortunate wild life that lives within its boundaries. The penalties of failure to control aggression are too great. It simply must be contained.

INDEX